PALGRAVE *GREAT*

PALGRAVE GREAT **DEBATES IN LAW**

Series editor
Jonathan Herring
Professor of Law
University of Oxford

Company Law
Lorraine Talbot

Contract Law
Jonathan Morgan

Criminal Law
Jonathan Herring

Employment Law
Simon Honeyball

Equity and Trusts
Alastair Hudson

Family Law
Jonathan Herring, Rebecca Probert & Stephen Gilmore

Jurisprudence
Nicholas J McBride & Sandy Steel

Medical Law and Ethics
Imogen Goold & Jonathan Herring

Property Law
David Cowan, Lorna Fox O'Mahony & Neil Cobb

If you would like to comment on this book, or on any other law text published by Palgrave, please write to lawfeedback@palgrave.com.

*PALGRAVE GREAT **DEBATES IN LAW***

GREAT DEBATES IN
COMPANY LAW

LORRAINE TALBOT

Professor of Law

York Law School, University of York

 macmillan education palgrave

First published 2014 by PALGRAVE

Palgrave in the UK is an imprint of Macmillan Publishers Limited, registered in England, company number 785998, of 4 Crinan Street, London N1 9XW.

Palgrave Macmillan in the US is a division of St Martin's Press LLC, 175 Fifth Avenue, New York, NY 10010.

Palgrave is a global imprint of the above companies and is represented throughout the world.

Palgrave® and Macmillan® are registered trademarks in the United States, the United Kingdom, Europe and other countries.

ISBN: 978–0–230–30445–1 paperback

This book is printed on paper suitable for recycling and made from fully managed and sustained forest sources. Logging, pulping and manufacturing processes are expected to conform to the environmental regulations of the country of origin.

A catalogue record for this book is available from the British Library.

Typeset by Cambrian Typesetters, Camberley, Surrey

Printed and bound in Great Britain by
The Lavenham Press Ltd, Suffolk

MIX
Paper from
responsible sources
FSC
www.fsc.org
FSC® C010693

CONTENTS

PREFACE

THE GREAT DEBATE IN COMPANY LAW AND GOVERNANCE 'WHAT IS THE COMPANY?'

Writing about great debates in company law and corporate governance is some-thing of a gift. Company law and governance is an exciting and controversial subject where arguments are vigorously pursued. Except, that is, here in the UK where until quite recently company law scholarship had (largely) striven to make it as dull and technical a subject as was humanly possible! By way of contrast, the US has always viewed the company as a political 'hot potato' and company law and governance as a locus of fierce debate. But things are changing in the UK. New scholars are enthusiastically drawing out the politics from the driest areas of company law and debating vigorously over the purpose of corporate governance, particularly in the wake of the financial crisis. Students of company law enjoy and expect more from their company law studies than technical proficiency. And so they should.

Company law and corporate governance is also a gift in this series because it has its own inbuilt great debate, that of 'what is the company?' This debate raises other debates over what then is the purpose of the company and whose interests are paramount? Or, where the company is managed by a non-owning professional management, in whose interest should they be managing and why?

All of these contested questions are decided to some degree by the law; however, judgments over the years have shown that the law too changes its posi-tion. Often, the question of the purpose of the company depends on the viabil-ity of that particularly company as well as on broader contextual issues such as the prevailing political hegemony, the state of industrial relations and, more recently, global issues like the financial crisis. The debate over 'what is the company' is highly political. It is a debate about who should be the winners and losers in society, what we produce as a society and for whose benefit we produce. It is a debate about the shape of global development. It impacts on the environ-ment, on social cohesion and on human rights. All these issues come back to the same debates: what is the company and what is its purpose? They are debates about the meaning of life from a non-spiritual perspective and they do not have simple answers.

The most famous journal debate around these issues is the one between Adolf A. Berle and Merrick Dodd in the *Harvard Law Review* in the early 1930s. Berle unintentionally commenced the debate with his article, 'Corporate Powers as Powers in Trust',[1] in which he argued that the rise in share dispersal meant there was a greater need for managerial accountability. And, as shareholders no longer had the power to prevail on directors to act in their interests, the law should take the lead. He argued that in the absence of effective mechanisms to control corporate managers, the law of directors' fiduciaries duties should be strongly reasserted so that managers would have to act in the interest of stock holders rather than for their own self- interest. In response, Dodd argued that the 'traditional' view that directors owed a duty to stockholders was based on assumptions that were no longer true.[2] The first assumption was that the corporation was a form of private property. This was wrong.[3] The corporation was indivisible from the productive capacity of society. It was social production and as such 'society may properly demand that it be carried on in such a way as to safeguard the interests of those who deal with it either as employees or consumers even if the proprietary rights of its owners are thereby curtailed'.[4] The second assumption, that stockholders were the beneficiaries to whom managers as trustees were bound to represent, was also wrong. Directors owed a fiduciary duty to act in the interests of the entity, not the interests of individual stockholders. Furthermore, what the law construed as the entity depended on historical and social context. At the time he was writing, Dodd claimed that the courts were as likely to see the entity as the interests of employees and consumers as they were to see it as the interests of stockholders.

Thus having set out his radical social position on the question of what is the company, Dodd addressed implementation. And it is here that his position became really problematic for Berle. Dodd argued that the social corporation could and should be operationalised by an unrestricted management. Society should trust to the discretion of managers rather than bind them with legal rules. He believed that the guiding principles for modern directors were 'the interests of employees, consumers, and the general public, as well as stockholders'.[5] The enlightened management practices of General Electric (which he cited) were a model for the future.

Responding to Dodd's argument in the final article of the debate, Berle argued that the managers of large corporations should not be left to their own devices.[6] And, because there was no strong administrative body capable of responsibly negotiating the differing claims against a corporation, the only existing bulwark against managerial abuse was the assertion of fiduciary duties. If neither a strong government nor fiduciary duties were in place, the result would be that 'management and

---

[1] A.A. Berle, 'Corporate Powers as Powers in Trust' (1931) 44 *Harvard Law Review* 1049.

[2] E.M. Dodd, 'For Whom are Managers Trustees' (1932) 45 *Harvard Law Review* 1145, 1162.

[3] Dodd reviews a number of legislative controls that have prevailed over business organisation and the substantial degree of social planning in respect of public utilities.

[4] Dodd (n. 2), p. 1162.

[5] Ibid, p. 1156.

[6] A.A. Berle, 'For Whom Corporate Managers Are Trustees' (1932) 45 *Harvard Law Review* 1365, 1367.

"control" become for all practical purposes absolute'.[7] There would be nothing to ensure that the investments of the millions of ordinary people who had bought shares in the 1920s would be protected. To replace a director's fiduciary duty to stockholders with one which gave directors more discretion was to 'simply hand over, weakly, to the present administrators with a pious wish that something nice will come of it all'.[8] Giving powerful people more power could not be the route to a more equal society. Having mechanisms to ensure that powerful people acted in the interests of society as a whole may be the route, and that was ultimately Berle's aim.

But that is just my take on the debate. The generally held view about the debate is that Berle supported shareholder primacy and that Dodd supported a more inclusive approach which promoted corporate social responsibility. As a result Berle is often placed in the shareholder primacy camp, while Dodd presides over the court of corporate social responsibility and stakeholding. Both placings are, I believe, incorrect. It is clear from all Berle's subsequent writing that he was the more socialist of the two. Far from promoting the shareholder primacy status quo, he was indicating that wider changes were needed to make the company socially responsible. And he did not trust management. Thus, there are debates, and there are debates about debates.

The debates which I examine and promote in this book emanate from Berle and Dodd's first great debate. For example, the debate about the company as a private property interest or a social interest is addressed in Chapter 2 where I examine the question of whether shareholders are the owners of the company. I look at the issue from a legal perspective, arguing that the law is very specific about what shareholders own and what they do not own. What they own, says the law, is a right to dividend if dividend is declared, a right to vote at general meeting and a right to any residual surplus upon liquidation. What they do not own is the company. What the law is also clear about (at least before the introduction of section 172[9]) is that shareholders' interests are not necessarily synonymous with the company's. Leading cases on the duties of directors show that they owe a duty to the company and that exercising that duty often means decision making which is contrary to the interests of shareholders. The shareholders lack of claim to the company as a whole has obvious political implications. Do they in fact have no special claim on the company's activities or can a special claim be imputed from their bundle of legal rights? This is a political decision. The heated political nature of this debate is illustrated by a recent debate in Norway, set out in brief in this chapter.

The debate over shareholders' control over the company and the problem of unaccountable management is discussed in Chapter 3. This chapter assesses the debate around shareholder governance, mainly expressed through the idea of shareholder stewardship. Chapter 3 takes issue with the view that shareholders

---

[7] Ibid.
[8] Ibid, p. 1368.
[9] Companies Act 2006.

should be involved in the governance of the company and critiques initiatives that aim to achieve that.

Chapter 4 ruminates on the nature of managers, or the board of directors. Dodd saw them as progressive and trustworthy while Berle feared their self-serving tendency. This chapter assesses the socio-economic make-up of board members and whether that affects their decision making. It focuses on two particular socio-economic groups present in the board of directors, Jewish bankers in Germany c. 1870–1930 and women in contemporary society. In respect of both groups the chapter speculates that the socio-economic character of these groups may be as determinate in their decision making and tendency to be self-serving (or socially responsible) as their actual power within the company. This adds another layer to the debate between Dodd and Berle on the nature of management and highlights some issues for company law reform and its implementation.

Chapters 5 and 6 assess the possibility of the company being a social company and the obstacles it faces in becoming social. For Dodd, the socially responsible company was already a reality accepted by the law and management alike. For Berle, only the law and substantial social change could make companies socially responsible. In the context of developing countries it seems clear that the company will not be socially responsible without strong controls to make it so – Berle's point. Indeed, companies have failed even to reach the modest goal of not breaching human rights. Chapter 5 discusses the initiatives largely emanating from the United Nations to make or encourage companies to observe basic human rights when engaging in business. It shows how business imperatives and the disparity of power between countries make this a difficult goal to achieve. Furthermore, it contends that current human rights initiatives in fact institute a form of legal imperialism.

Chapter 6 further discusses the barriers to achieving corporate socially responsibility, asking the question of whether the company can be moral. It looks at the imperative of profit maximisation and the many claimants upon that profit and how this acts as a barrier to the company being socially responsible.

In reflecting Berle and Dodd's concern that the corporation should represent the interests of all those affected by the company, Chapter 7 considers two reform models. The first reflects Berle's particular concern with labour, the second Dodd's more inclusive, stakeholding approach. In order to assist the reader with some of the ideas discussed, Chapter 1 sets out a number of different perspectives on the question of 'what is the company', including economic, business, political and legal perspectives.

In setting out these debates in detail, I make no pretence at impartiality. The book critiques much of what would be considered mainstream thinking, such as initiatives to enhance shareholders' engagement in corporate governance, and does not attempt to find virtue in that position. Thus, from a student's perspective, this book provides a lively supplement to the core text of a company law course and one which I hope will help show some of the excitement of this subject.

In preparing this book I am grateful to Richard Percival for his feedback in general and to Warwick colleague James Harrison for his specific feedback on Chapter 5. I am also grateful to fellow company lawyers, Simon Deakin, Janet Dine, Andrew Keay, Andrew Johnston, Beate Sjåfjell and Charlotte Villers who are engaged in the project of making company law interesting and who have supported this particular project with their thoughts and advice.

CASES

STATUTES

1

WHAT IS THE COMPANY AND IS COMPANY LAW IMPORTANT?

INTRODUCTION: CONCEPTIONS OF THE COMPANY AS REFLECTING POLITICAL ORIENTATIONS

One of the central divisions in the debate over 'what is the company' is between those that say the company is a hierarchical organisation headed by a managerial team (the board of directors) and those that argue that it is an alternative expression of a market of investors. Within the latter group there are various conceptions of the 'entityless-ness' of the company. Some view the company as being some form of investor-orientated organisation while others deny that it exists as any entity at all. The latter theorists are largely drawn from financial economics and construct various economic models of the company (or firm, as they prefer to refer to all business forms). In constructing a model of the company on these lines, they are able to retain the notion of the contracting and bargaining individual. This ideal, rational, self-maximising contractor is lost as a possible actor in the hierarchical entity model, where actors perform according to their role and are subject to the authority of management.

The theorists who emphasise hierarchy and 'entity-ness' as characteristics of the company are often legal scholars who understand the company within a legal model where its rights and powers are set out in the law. The overall effect of the legal framework is the construction of a hierarchical organisation in which a central managing body ensures that the various claims against the company, and in the company, are met. This central managing body must also ensure its own attendance to the legal rules pertaining to its own activities. The idea of a hierarchical organisation is also evident to organisational theorists. This may be presented as a positive model for successful production and profit maximisation. Alternatively, it may be a political model of the company which sees exploitation of human and natural resources as being the primary *raison d'être* of the company.

In this chapter I examine a number of different scholarly perspectives on the question of what is the company, which range from scholarship that dismisses the company as a fiction, to those that see it as an organisation. Within the latter category there are those that view the organisation as providing positive efficiencies

1

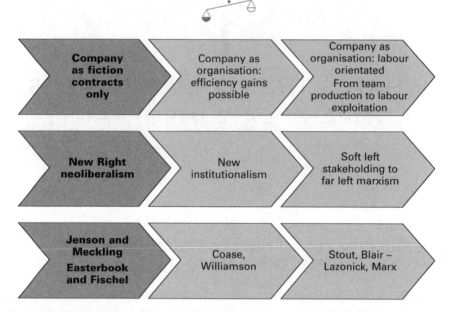

Company as fiction contracts only	Company as organisation: efficiency gains possible	Company as organisation: labour orientated From team production to labour exploitation
New Right neoliberalism	New institutionalism	Soft left stakeholding to far left marxism
Jenson and Meckling Easterbook and Fischel	Coase, Williamson	Stout, Blair – Lazonick, Marx

Figure 1.1 Conceptions of the company as reflecting political orientations

which can be superior to the market, those that want to reorganise the power relations within the organisation and those that view the company as an organisation
which facilitates the exploitation of its employees. The spectrum of opinion also
expresses a political orientation so that the former categories are informed by
right-wing neoliberalism while the final category represents far-left radical
thought. This is represented diagrammatically above.

In the final section of this chapter I assess aspects of the debate over how significant company law really is in creating the modern company. The material examined in this chapter is by no means exhaustive and many key perspectives, such as
stakeholding, are merely alluded to. It is a starting point for the inquisitive student
and one which he or she may wish to develop.

1. ECONOMIC (MARKET) MODELS

Ronald Coase: what is the company?

**The company is an organisational alternative to the market which lowers the
cost of market transactions**

In 1937 economist Ronald Coase theorised that the business firm[1] (the company)
exists because it became more efficient to engage in the exchange of information

---

[1] A term used by economists to designate all business organisations although to the lawyer designates a
partnership only.

and services within an organisation than it would be to contract for those services in the free market. This is because, he explained, of the high costs of market transacting. Were it not for this particular market failure, the price mechanism would be the most effective way to organise capitalist production. As the costs of transacting (transaction costs) are so high, firms or organisations enable a central authority, or entrepreneur, to allocate resources and enable efficient outputs. Coase's model therefore was hierarchical, where managerial decisions were made by those in possession of superior knowledge.

Inherent in Coase's theory was an underlying belief in the superiority of the market in allocating resources and indeed of the unquestionable, historical existence of the market. His economic actors conformed to the neoclassical form in that they would tend to the mechanisms which best achieved self-maximisation. Therefore, if the costs of using the command model of the firm rose, perhaps because of an information deficit, then the organisation would begin to devolve its operations to the market. Equally, where transaction costs in the market were high (because, for instance, the costs of monitoring contracts were high), it might be more efficient to organise in-house and expand into many different products or services. In this scenario the size of a firm would increase. Alternatively, improvements in managerial technique would tend to increase the size of firms by improving the entrepreneurs' ability to accumulate good information.

Unlike the institutional economists, Coase did not see large economic organisations as displacing market transacting, rather they offered a way to engage in market activity with reduced transaction costs. Market forces continue to operate on the organisation so that the firm could contract (reduce in size) or even disappear if ordinary market transactions once again proved more efficient. In accordance with this theory, an organisation is large when and because it is more efficient to be so.

However, large corporations did moderate competitive forces to a degree so that whilst price mechanisms directed resource allocation in the market, within the firm 'market transactions are eliminated'[2] and replaced by 'the entrepreneurial co-ordinator, who directs production'.[3] Whether the entrepreneur continued in this role partly depended on transaction costs in the market. If they could be reduced, so too would the entrepreneur's role in the firm be reduced. However, the continuation of high transaction costs has meant that the company has emerged as the most successful vehicle for the centralisation of wealth and production. It is worth mentioning that although Coase is feted by neoliberal theorists on the firm, his theory may be equally comfortably read as a theory of labour exploitation. Within the firm, the entrepreneur allocating resources is exercising authority over labour and ensuring that labour works as hard as possible. This is a more effective mechanism of extracting value from labour than transacting on the market for individual tasks and services performed by labour.

---

[2] R. Coase, 'The Nature of the Firm' (1937), p. 24. Reproduced in O. Williamson and S. Winter, *The Nature of the Firm: Origins Evolution and Development* (Oxford University Press, 1993).
[3] Ibid.

Alchian and Demsetz: what is the company?

The company is a team of producers who establish mechanisms inter se to ensure fair allocation of tasks

From the 1970s, scholars further developed the market model of the firm. Alchian and Demsetz[4] described the firm as a team of contractors within which some of the members' purpose was to monitor the 'team production process'. Those members acted as such because in a team-based activity there will inevitably be a 'metering problem'. This problem occurs because of the difficulty in ensuring that all team members are performing to their full capacity, as team activity can hide the 'shirking' of some members. There is the likelihood of some team members 'free-riding' on the hard work of others. In a team there will be difficulty in identifying who is performing well and rewarding them accordingly and there will be difficulties in identifying who is shirking and censoring them appropriately. By establishing monitors in the team, they can reward success and censor shirking. In this way the lack of productiveness arising from the shirking of some team members can be addressed so that there will be residual (surplus) produced over and above that which was previously achieved. This residual will be of sufficient quantity to provide reward for the monitors and indeed will usually be the incentive for the monitor to be effective. By monitoring they produce their own rewards.

This analysis makes more sense in the kind of 'firm' which lawyers would identify as something like a partnership; the partners are the monitors as they have the claim over this extra amount. Partners have a direct incentive to enhance the residual with effective monitoring. However, in a company, where managers will be monitoring 'the team production' process to reduce shirking and reward success, they are not the principal residual owners (although they will have some shares). In a company the residual owners are the shareholders, so in Alchian and Demsetz's model of the firm, shareholders are the ultimate monitors, monitoring the monitor-managers.

Thus like many of the economists' models of the firm, they do not reflect the institutional reality of the company and so do not work as effectively in the context of companies. In a partnership, actively involved partners clearly have the incentive and capacity to monitor the team production process. Partners in law have a prima facie right to manage the business and an entitlement to the profits of the business.[5] However, in companies, shareholders are unlikely to have the capacity or the inclination to engage in monitoring the monitor, and in practice the monitor (management) will not be monitored by those that have the incentive to do so, the so-called residual owners. In large companies the monitors will most likely be monitored by non-executive directors and by the corporate governance

---

[4] A.A. Alchian and H. Demsetz (1972) 'Production, Information Costs, and Economic Organisation', *American Economic Review* 777.
[5] Partnership Act 1890.

structures required by the listing rules. Whether the residual owners themselves will monitor is itself another debate, which is discussed in Chapter 3.

In pursuing the market model of the company, it is crucial that the 'team' (in Alchian and Demsetz's model) is composed of a group of market players who must necessarily be volunteers and equals, who are free to pursue their own self-interest without coercion and with sufficient knowledge and capacity to effectively self-maximise. The existence of the manager is not evidence of a hierarchical organisation but that different team members make different inputs and receive different rewards. In Coase's firm, the structure was hierarchical and the 'entrepreneur' had authority over those working in the team (thus enabling a labour exploitation interpretation of his theory). In Alchian and Demsetz's model the team see their self-interest as being promoted by voluntarily electing a member to act as monitor because this ensures the overall efficiency of the group. Thus in this model, there is no authority, no 'fiat' and no centre of power. Monitors ensure optimum commitment from the 'resource owners'[6] (employees) when they are engaged in cooperative activity and ensure optimum efficiency because the team requires this outcome. Breaking away from the hierarchical and disciplinary model of the business organisation is essential for the logic of the neoliberal model of the company promoted by Alchian and Demsetz.

Michael Jenson and William Meckling: what is the company?

The company is a legal fiction which describes a nexus of contracts

For Jenson and Meckling the 'firm' is a legal fiction, an administrative convenience that describes a nexus of contracting individuals.[7] The company does not exist as an entity and it is not a hierarchical organisation. It is the market in an alternative form. For Jenson and Meckling, 'it makes little or no sense to try to distinguish those things that are "inside" the firm (or any other organisation) from those things that are outside of it'.[8]

In this model, shareholders are considered to be residual risk takers who make a bargain with managers that the latter will protect shareholder interests. It is a contract. But it is a contract which is not actually bargained for by shareholders because *actual* bargaining would be inefficient. Company law acts as a standard form contract, and in so doing reduces transaction costs. As Easterbrook and Fischel put it, company law supplies 'terms most venturers would have negotiated, were the costs of negotiating at arm's length for every contingency sufficiently low'.[9]

---

[6] Alchian and Demsetz (n. 4).
[7] M. Jensen and W. Meckling, 'Theory of the Firm: Managerial Behavior, Agency Costs and Ownership Structure' (1976) 3 *Journal of Financial Economics* 305.
[8] Ibid.
[9] F. Easterbrook and D. Fischel, *The Economic Structure of Corporate Law* (Harvard University Press, 1996), 15.

Other issues that were not included in the 'standard form contract' may also be addressed by fiduciary duties.[10] 'In this way fiduciary duties are reconceptualised. No longer a duty to the company (because the company does not exist) their existence is explained as a mechanism to enhance contractual relations and to reduce transaction costs. The additional protections for shareholders are also justified on the basis that shareholders are unable to protect themselves contractually in the same way that other creditors are able to.'[11]

In this contractual model the key governance issue is that of agency costs. These costs arise because managers (the agents) may frequently find themselves in a position where their contractual duty to their principal (the shareholders) comes into conflict with their own self-interest. The cost of making the agent and principal relationship functional involves management inducements such as performance-related pay (bonding costs) and disciplining measures such as those provided by the market for corporate control.[12] This particular part of their theory has had massive implications for management pay. Corporate governance has promoted performance-related pay as a mechanism to reduce agency costs, and management pay has, as a direct result of this approach, increased exponentially over the last 30 years. Far from enhancing corporate governance, it has been widely blamed for bad governance and short-term decision making designed to enhance share value (and thus performance-related pay) at the expense of long-term growth.

2. ORGANISATIONAL MODELS

Alfred Chandler: what is the company?

The company is a rational organisation which enables management to steer production and development to optimum efficiency

Chandler's contribution to this perspective is essentially to demonstrate that the large firm is not a by-product of the market, emerging because of high transaction costs, but that it is a conscious organisation of production that frequently does not follow market rules and indeed is more effective for not doing so. This form of organisation involves trained management organising around hierarchical structures, able to respond to the productive capacity of the company. He sums up this approach in the pithy phrase, the 'visible hand'. Rather than the invisible hand of the market providing efficient production, the conscious and visible hand of management has, in his view, given the American company in particular, the competitive edge. American companies embraced the idea of a professionally

---

[10] Ibid.

[11] L.E. Talbot, *Progressive Corporate Governance for the 21st Century* (Routledge, 2012), 124.

[12] A theory which originated with Henry Manne's piece in 1965. H. Manne, 'Mergers and the Market for Corporate Control' (1965) 73 *J. Pol. Econ.* 110.

trained management operating outside of shareholder control early in the 20th century, and therefore American companies were able to make rational decisions about production.

In contrast, Chandler shows that in Britain during the same period, boards of directors continued to be dominated by controlling or substantial shareholders, usually family shareholders and usually linked to the founding members. Chandler argues that the failure to move away from the 'personal capitalism' of family-run companies meant that British companies did not develop into the sophisticated management organisations which were key to meeting the challenges of rapid technological development and global competition. Indeed, in British companies, decisions were made that benefitted family shareholders in the short term. Chandler estimates that before the First World War, an astonishing 80–90% of earnings were distributed as dividends.[13]

The myopic, short-termism of shareholder management meant that in the areas of production which would come to dominate world trade – chemicals, electronics, metal – family owners of British companies failed to make what Chandler calls the 'three pronged investment in production, distribution and management essential to exploit economies of scale and scope'.[14]

Britain had the technical skills and scientific expertise, but it lacked managerial expertise in its companies to exploit them commercially. Furthermore, although investors were keen to invest in projects, management's priority was to protect their proportion of the equity which they did not want to dilute.[15] The owner-controlled companies in Britain thus quickly fell behind their German and American competitors who happily utilised outside investment.[16] This meant that by the time of World War I, Britain was so far behind its competitors that two-thirds of electrical equipment manufacture was made by the subsidiaries of GE, Westinghouse (prior to it returning to British ownership in 1917) and Siemens.[17] Chandler noted that where British industries could easily succeed without sophisticated managerial expertise, it did so. Thus in those companies that focused on consumer goods, such as Cadbury and Rowntree, business did well within a family-owned structure.[18] Britain had proximity to the world's richest and most concentrated consumer market, and the production and distribution of consumer goods required less costly facilities and less complex managerial and technical skills than other capital-intensive industries.[19]

---

[13] A.D. Chandler Jr, *Scale and Scope. The Dynamics of Industrial Capitalism* (Belknap Harvard University Press, 1990), 390–1.

[14] Ibid, 286.

[15] R. Michie, 'Options, Concessions, Syndicates, and Other Provisions of Venture Capital, 1880–1913' (1981) 23 *Business History* 147.

[16] Chandler (n. 13), 276.

[17] Ibid. The loss in advantage to Germany in chemical and electrical engineering was regained in World War I through the straightforward expropriation of successful German subsidiaries such as Siemens.

[18] Ibid, 262.

[19] Ibid, 268.

Chandler concludes that 'the development of British organisational capabilities was held back not only by less vigorous competition between firms but also by the desire of the founders and their families to retain control'.[20]

Oliver Williamson: what is the company?

The company is an organisational mechanism designed to transcend the problems of market behaviour such as bounded rationality and opportunism

In *The Economic Institutions of Capitalism*, Williamson argues that given bounded rationality, opportunism and uncertainty, organising within an economic institution was more efficient than organising through the market. Williamson sees opportunism as a calculated non- or partial disclosure of information by one party, in order to distort a transaction and to wrong-foot the other party when making a calculation as to the value of a transaction; 'the incomplete or distorted disclosure of information, especially to calculated efforts to mislead, distort, disguise, obfuscate, or otherwise confuse. It is responsible for real or contrived conditions of information asymmetry, which vastly complicate problems of economic organization.'[21] This opportunist inclination will only be effective when there is inadequate knowledge or capacity by one party and therefore it must accompany what other economists have termed 'bounded rationality'. Bounded rationality is where actors who want to self-maximise in a rational way cannot do so because they have insufficient information or ability to effectively utilise existing information. The existence of these two factors increases transaction costs. The effects of both become particularly problematic when there is uncertainty and change. This will enhance bounded rationality as actors struggle to come to grips with how to operate in an uncertain situation. When encompassed within an institution, mechanisms can be put in place to reduce their deleterious effects.

For Williamson, economic institutions were better able to reduce the transactions costs arising from economic activity. In his analysis the market *would* be the most efficient mechanism for organising production were it not for human frailty. The behavioural economics from which Williamson's work emanates emphasises the imperfect market conditions which prevail in real, as opposed to perfect, market conditions. Williamson identifies bounded rationality, opportunism and uncertainty as elements which operationalise transaction costs. Thus, by identifying the particular causes of transaction costs, it becomes possible to more effectively organise around reducing them. In this respect, Williamson differs from Coase in that he locates transactions within the economic institution as well as in the market, but argues that they may be effectively managed by good governance within the organisation. He also differs from the contractarians because not only does he acknowledge the existence of organisation and hierarchy in firms, he

---

[20] Ibid, 335.
[21] O. Williamson, *The Economic Institutions of Capitalism* (The Free Press, 1985) at pp. 47–8.

maintains that they are more efficient than the market. However, like Coase, he retains some commitment to the idea that the ideal market (which does not and perhaps cannot actually exist) is the most efficient forum for economic activity. Unlike Coase he provides explanation drawn from behavioural economics to explain why humans cannot be ideal market actors and necessarily increase transaction costs.

Institutional economics: what is the company?

Institutional economics originated with Thorstein Veblen. It analyses the firm from outside the assumptions and methodology of classical and neo-classical economics. It broadly maintains that the company is no longer driven by the classical model of efficient production and profit and that market forces no longer control the structure of the organisation or management decision making. Instead, managements were relatively free to pursue self-interest such as power, prestige and job security but were also likely to pursue socially valuable goals. All participants in the company were constrained by the institutional framework of the company which was traditionally skewed in favour of capital.

Adolf A. Berle

The company is an organisational form whose size enables it to dictate the shape of the market and renders it a quasi-public institution despite its legal conception as a private institution[22]

For Berle, 19th century entrepreneurial capitalism involved companies that both represented the entrepreneur's interests and which were managed by the entrepreneur. Ownership and control were possessed by the same persons. For those companies that wished to be much larger and to draw on public investment, they could be accommodated by the charter system, where states granted a charter to create a corporation with separate legal personality. However, because the charter was a concession from the state and in many respects was monitored by the granting state, such companies as quasi-public institutions were obliged to conform with prevailing political objectives. For example, those charter companies that created a monopoly through holding other companies and then exploited their monopoly position by charging excessive prices could find their charter revoked. A number of gas companies in Chicago formed a trust under a holding company which was formed by a charter. The trust proceeded to raise the price of gas by 25 per cent and the residents complained to their state authorities. As a result, the attorney general successfully brought *quo warranto* proceedings against the company on the basis that it had exceeded the power granted to it under the charter.[23]

---

[22] Particularly in A.A. Berle and G.C. Means, *The Modern Corporation and Private Property* (Harcourt, Brace & World, Inc., 1968, first published 1932).
[23] For more examples see Talbot (n. 11).

When New Jersey passed a series of general incorporation Acts which allowed companies the legal facility to do all they wanted, including having holding companies, companies were able to separate themselves from state control. They became private institutions. The legal freedoms in New Jersey company law rapidly spread in other jurisdictions. Companies grew in size and shareholding became increasingly dispersed into the wider public. From Berle's perspective, there was now a disjuncture between companies' legal conceptualisation as private and their practical function as holders of public money, employers of the public and creators of products for the public on a grand scale. Furthermore, companies had grown to such a large size that it was they, not the market, which dictated what was produced, when and how. Additionally, they were no longer controlled by their state of incorporation or by the shareholders who were too dispersed to exercise any control function. Instead, companies were controlled by a team of professional managers. Berle promoted the idea of a company, now freed from shareholder and market demands, as being a public institution whose remit was to operate in the interests of the community.

John R. Commons[24]

The company is an institution in which transactions are undertaken by participants in accordance to its organisational framework which defines inequalities but limits exploitation

Like other institutional economists, Commons saw companies as one of many institutions which composed modern society. However, he dismissed both the classical economist's notion of an economy composed of individuals (or of institutions representing the will of individuals), as well as the determinist notion of people as mere products of social institutions. For Commons, individuals exist in various institutions from the moment of birth, but he introduced into that premise the notion that individuals will transact with the institutions in which they find themselves. As individuals they negotiate within those institutions and their personal development is formed through their transactions with and within those institutional frameworks and norms. Conversely, those institutions themselves are not fixed and immutable but will change through the actions of individuals transacting within the institutional structure.

Transactions within institutions are between individuals who are necessarily in conflict with each other as all pursue their preferred outcome. However, most transactions are not between equal individuals, though transactions differ in how that inequality is exercised. Unequal transactions, he argues, are either managerial or rationing. In the former, one party has more power over another, the terms of which are generally described in common law. He uses the example of the bargaining

---

[24] J.R. Commons, *Institutional Economics: Its Place in Political Economy* (Transaction Publishers, 2009, first published 1934).

power between a master and servant or an owner and slave. Rationing transactions, in contrast, involve power exercised through an institutional framework which both empowers and restrains. Rationing transacting occurs within a company because managerial power is exercised through a framework of rules, norms, precedent and custom. As such, a company, though a legal person, should not be treated as an individual but as agreements between many individuals to participate in the goals of the institution in accordance with its organisational (and unequal) rules. Common law decision making in respect of companies and business practice mediates and controls the exploitative potential of companies, but does not create equality. Indeed, he argues, private property and the laws relating to property secure inequalities.[25] They represent, in large part, political decisions on how wealth will be distributed in society. In particular he noted the ability of business property in the form of patents, monopoly and goodwill to generate rents, while labour, in contrast, could only sell their time, suffering low wages and unemployment. Furthermore, he argues, the property that individuals possessed was itself an institution. The institution of private property designated ownership and set out the relationships in respect of the thing, expressed in large part through the law. As private property is a relationship and not a thing, it can develop as any other relationship. Thus it can become a relationship in respect of all manner of arrangements such as debt or future earnings as well as over tangible property. In the context of a company, relationships are negotiated through rationing transactions, and unequal bargaining power is mediated through a framework of norms and rules which privileges capital over labour. Thus, it could be argued that the property forms that emerge from the company, such as shares, debenture options and so on, represent expressions of capital's institutional power over labour. As such, Common's analysis takes him much closer to Marxist conceptions of the company discussed below.

3. LEGAL MODELS

Stephen Bainbridge: what is the company?

The company is an organisation whose effectiveness is derived from the superior decision-making power of the board of directors

Bainbridge contends that the economist's notion that individual actions are based on rational, self-maximising choices, and that this is the most effective mechanism for enhancing wealth, is entirely inaccurate in the context of corporations.[26] Corporations are organised on a hierarchical model made up of teams, and at the

---

[25] Following a line of thought from Marx to Veblen.
[26] S. Bainbridge (2002) 'Why a Board? Group Decision-making in Corporate Governance', 5 *Vand. L. Rev.* 1.

top of this is yet another team, the board of directors. Bainbridge maintains that the team production in corporations, particularly the decision-making process in the board of directors, is more effective and efficient than individual decision making. He is an advocate of director primacy rather than shareholder primacy.

Andrew Keay: what is the company?

The company is an entity whose purpose is to self-protect and maximise its value as an entity

Andrew Keay argues that the company is best conceptualised as an entity which should be enabled to maximise but whose assets should be protected and sustained. He calls this the entity maximization and sustainability model (EMS).[27] This distinctive model is not shareholder primacy orientated, where the corporate governance goal is to deliver shareholder value. Neither is it stakeholder orientated, where the corporate governance goal is to represent the interests of all stakeholders in the company. Instead the aim is to maintain the company as a financially viable entity with a long-term financial future. The emphasis is on maintaining the company as a going concern and avoiding risk and possible insolvency.

Keay's model proceeds from a presentation of the many ways in which the law conceives of the company as an entity. From the legal doctrine of separate corporate personality, to the derivative action, to the requirement for group accounts, it is almost impossible to conceive of the company without simultaneously envisaging an entity. He then proceeds to theorise that the purpose of this entity is to self-protect and to self-maximise. This necessarily entails a long-term approach rather than the often parasitical approach of shareholder primacy, particularly in respect of gains from takeover activity.

In maximising the value of the entity, he argues, many different social goals *may* be achieved but that is not the primary aim of EMS. For example, he argues, Nike was obliged to abandon child labour because of the reputational damage done to the entity. Indeed, better standards for labour *may* proceed from an entity maximisation approach either for reputational reasons, legal reasons or simply to retain good employees. Similarly, in maximising the entity, shareholder value *may* be achieved. The result of this *may* be that transactions and the costs of transactions are reduced. However, under the EMS model these are not goals in themselves. The goal is entity maximisation from which other benefits to those affected by the company may arise. In his words:

> 'Entity maximisation involves the fostering of entity wealth, which will entail directors endeavouring to increase the overall long-run market value of the company as a whole, taking into account the investment made by various people and groups. In other words, directors should do that which value maximises the corporate entity,

---

[27] A. Keay, 'Ascertaining the Corporate Objective: An Entity Maximisation and Sustainability Model' (2008) 71(5) *MLR* 663–98.

12

so that the net present value to the company as a whole is enhanced, and so is its strategic importance. In doing this directors should have concern for "the community of interest." This means that the common interest of all who have invested in the company is to be fostered, but it does not mean that at some point one group will not benefit at the expense of another.

Maximisation may, in concrete terms, lead inter alia to improved dividends for shareholders, timely repayment of, and reduction of risk for, creditors, improved working conditions, greater job security and bonuses for employees and a contribution to a stable living environment in which the company operates, and so on. But, rather than the focus being on the investors and their interests, as stakeholder theory requires, the focus is on the entity and what will enhance its position. Any benefits for investors flow from that very object. The entity's interests are to be maximised for the long term – this might entail making less profit one year compared with a previous one, but still maximising the entity for the future.'[28]

Within company law, Keay finds ample space for directors to operate within this model. Section 172 of the Companies Act 2006 gives directors sufficient discretion to act on behalf of the entity. There is similarly no legal imperative for directors to make high distributions to shareholders. Under EMS, profits should be distributed with a view to maintaining the financial stability of the company. Thus Keay's model utilises the existing legal structure of the company to emphasise the entity-preserving aspects of company law and the financial and human logic in following this direction in corporate decision making.

Margaret Blair and Lynne Stout: what is the company?

The company is team production

Blair and Stout conceptualise the modern public corporation as a team production in which rewards are allocated and shirking and free-riding are addressed.[29] In public corporations, members of the team, which includes employees, shareholders and creditors, cede authority to another group (managers) so that they can ensure fairness in productive contributions. The model of team production explains, they argue, company law's restriction of shareholder control over directors as well as norms in the public corporation such as an independent board. For Blair and Stout the public corporation is designed to encourage the firm-specific investment essential to certain forms of team production. In other words, boards exist not to protect shareholders per se, but to protect the *enterprise-specific investments* of all the members of the 'corporate team'. The nature of the company and its social purpose can be discovered through an analysis of the legal rules relating to companies. So, they argue, in respect of company laws in the United States, the tendency for all states to have extensive powers for the board of directors and the CEO in particular, while at the same time giving limited powers to shareholders,

---

[28] Ibid, p. 685.
[29] L. Stout and M. Blair, 'Team Production Theory of Corporate Law', 85 *Va. L. Rev.* 247 (1999).

indicates an intention that the board is empowered to protect the interest of the company as a whole, not just shareholders. Because Blair and Stout identify the nature of the company so closely with the legal rules that are applicable to companies, they are placed under the 'legal models' heading. However, because they identify labour as a key part of the team productive process that is the company, they could also fall under the next heading.

4. ORGANISATIONAL MODELS OF THE COMPANY WITH A LABOUR ORIENTATION

Margaret Blair and Lynne Stout: what is the company?

The company is team production where investments are made to firm-specific human capital

The team production model also encapsulates the idea that the modern corporation is built on investment in specialised and firm-specific labour (human capital). When employees are engaged by the company, they enter into contracts which cannot fully encompass the forthcoming relationship and therefore the contract can be said to be incomplete. The notion of an incomplete contract was one mooted by those promoting the economic model of the company, such as Easterbrook and Fischel, but in respect to shareholders. In this version, the fact of incompleteness justifies the claim that directors should focus their decision making on that which will produce the best outcome for shareholders. However, in Blair and Stout's version of the incomplete contract, employees too must have a claim to managerial attention, because they too have committed to a contract which cannot encompass all eventualities. Accordingly, employee interests should also be reflected in corporate governance. Furthermore, they argue, as employees develop their skills and knowledge in the course of their employment, their personal investment becomes very firm-specific. In so doing they bear a significant risk that their investment may diminish in value should they lose their employment with that firm. Indeed, unlike shareholders whose liquidity is sacrosanct in company law and increasingly enabled through ultra-fast electronic trading, employees cannot easily 'reinvest' in other firms. Some employees may be able to reinvest at a 'profit' as changing employer may involve a promotion. However, forced removal from a firm through, for example, redundancy will most likely result in a less skilled and less remunerated contract of employment.

All of these issues in respect of employees justify employees' claims in corporate governance as near equal to those of shareholders. Employees and shareholders are interdependent: neither can engage in productive activity without the other's investment and both bear a risk in their relationship with the company. However, what it particular about Blair and Stout's analysis in respect of human capital is that it only seems to apply to skilled labour; unskilled labour is not part of the productive team. As Johnston points out, when capitalism involved companies that invested shareholders' capital into complicated machinery and expert management and where labour was divided into a series of unskilled activities, 'the providers of finance were basically viewed as taking all the risk, and therefore were the residual claimants'.[30] However, as capitalism develops, the capacity of companies to create wealth is based on the expertise of their employees and the ability of management to effectively utilise that expertise.[31] Thus the company must ensure that it retains its skilled labour force because 'the value of these investments depends on continued access'.[32]

Though promoting a labour orientation of the firm, Blair and Stout's position is problematic in that it only encompasses labour as part of the team productive unit when labour is skilled. I will critique this from two different perspectives on the question of what is the company: first, labour process theory through Braverman's conception of the company; and, secondly, Marxist theory on the nature of the company. Both can be considered organisational models of the company but where the organisation is viewed as a site for the effective exploitation of employees.

Harry Braverman: what is the company?

The company is an organisation which enables management to control through deskilling labour

In *Labor and Monopoly Capital*[33] Braverman argues that the division of labour promoted by Fredrick Taylor's management theories (known as Taylorism) was consciously adopted by management whose goal was to disempower labour and thereby to secure its own position. Taylorism was famously adopted by Henry Ford in American car production and Fordism became synonymous with Taylor's model for organising manufacturing. Fordism involved dividing the process of production into a series of simple tasks which simultaneously increased production and deskilled labour.

In contrast to the Blair–Stout thesis, for Braverman this process of deskilling does not make labour less valuable to capital in the productive process. Labour is always exploited for financial gain by capital (mainly shareholders in the context of companies). Labour does not become more significant to companies when it becomes skilled; it is always central to profit making. However, by investing intelligence in machinery and removing intelligence from the worker, management is able to assert more control over labour by making it more easily replaceable. Labour process theory, by looking at labour and who controls that labour, surmises that by deskilling labour and by withholding knowledge about the processes of

---

[30] A. Johnston, *EC Regulation of Corporate Governance* (Cambridge University Press, 2009), p. 64
[31] Ibid, p. 65, citing M. Blair, *Ownership and Control: Rethinking Corporate Governance for the Twenty-first Century* (Brookings Institute, 1995).
[32] Johnston (n. 30), p. 65.
[33] Free Press, 1974.

production, management is able to protect its own position and organise production around its own needs. Deskilling, from labour's perspective, is dehumanising, uncreative and demoralising. However, as deskilling also makes labour more vulnerable to replacement, management is able to extract more work, for longer hours and for low wages from its existing workforce. Thus from this perspective, labour is more exploited and more vulnerable (risk-bearing) than skilled labour, which retains some bargaining power – again the opposite of the Blair–Stout thesis. Indeed, from a common sense perspective it would be difficult to argue that unskilled, poorly paid labour, and often child labour, used by the multinational companies set out in Chapters 5 and 6, is not both central to profit making and highly exploited.

Karl Marx: what is the company?[34]

The company is an organisation designed to enable capital to extract value from labour

From a Marxist perspective, capitalism is a form of production in which capital and the holders of capital seek to extract value from labour. The company is a particularly effective mechanism for achieving this because the key claimants of surplus (shareholders) do not have to actively engage in this process and can claim the surplus through the simple possession of shares. The controversial nature of this political relationship is neutralised by its transformation into a piece of property, the share. The level of skill possessed by workers is irrelevant in terms of labour's use to capital. Labour can be utilised to profit the company so long as it takes under the average socially necessary labour time required to produce a particular product or service.

Labour is exploited at all levels of expertise, and disciplining labour in order to enhance that exploitation is always part of the management process. The discipline of labour is first performed by entrepreneurs, but later in capitalism and the development of the company it can be undertaken by skilled paid employees, the managers and directors. In and around the company there are varying kinds of capitalists with different methods of extracting value. These include finance capitalists (banks and money lenders who claim interest), industrial capitalists (who control production and claim remaining profit), merchant capitalists (who sell products at a greater price then they purchase them for) and rentier capitalists (who make money from ownership of titles such as shares, a claim to dividend). The law protects their contractual and property interests. From a Marxist perspective the company is a locus of the class conflict between capital and labour. In a company, shares will accrue high dividends and increase in value so long as labour is effectively exploited.

---

[34] See in particular Karl Marx's *Capital* Volumes I–III.

William Lazonick: what is the company?

The company is a historically developing organisation which usurps the market in its ability to coordinate production, discipline labour and enhance value

In Lazonick's words, 'the historical experience of capitalist development demonstrates the growing importance of organisational coordination relative to market coordination in the value-creation process'.[35] If the company could harness organisational coordination then it could transcend the limitations of the market. Using the example of British companies, Lazonick shows how failing to embrace good organisational techniques meant that value creation was severely compromised. He argues that underdevelopment of managerial skills continued to pervade British industry up until the 1970s with family control continuing to be the norm, with the addition of Oxbridge-educated 'outsiders'. The inner-circle elitism which characterised British management meant that they were removed from the productive process. 'As British companies grew in size in the interwar period, organizational segmentation between top management and the rest of employees became the norm and remained characteristic of British managerial structures even into the 1960s and 1970s.'[36] As a result, organisation of production became a matter for craft workers and unions in conjunction with shop-floor production. This generally involved 'squeezing as much productivity as possible out of existing technologies'[37] and working harder, to protect industries which they were bound to, by dint of their non-transferable skill base. This strategy worked for a relatively long period but was bound to meet objective limitations. By the 1960s decades of chronic lack of reinvestment began to show. Paradigmatically, 'the British automobile industry had reached the technical and social limits of the utilisation of its resources'.[38] It could not compete with the German and Japanese car industry.

However, for Lazonick the company is also a site of power and conflict. Team production in the context of the company, he argues, accentuates the power inequality between the capital owners and labour. In contrast, when workers determined their own work patterns there was more equality. However, once a form of corporate capitalism emerged, 'the hierarchical – "authoritarian," "dictatorial," "Fiat" – relations of the capitalist enterprise are designed to resolve the conflict in favour of the representative of capital, the claimants of the residual.'[39]

In this respect in particular, Lazonick takes issue with Alchian and Demsetz's non-hierarchical contractual model. First, the idea that there is equality in the team is belied by the fact that the monitor can hire and fire. This bestows him with

---

[35] W. Lazonick, *Business Organisation and the Myth of the Market Economy* (Cambridge University Press, 1994, 1st edn 1991), p. 59.
[36] Ibid, 48–9
[37] Ibid, 46.
[38] Ibid, 47.
[39] Ibid, 184.

considerable authority, unless there are no costs to the 'input' or team member in moving jobs. Alchian and Demsetz's solution is that long-term contracts are not inherent to the firm and labour can move freely with minimal costs in doing so. Lazonick points out that while labour mobility might deal (in theory) with the costs issue for labour, it entirely undermines the solution Alchian and Demsetz present for the issue of shirking. That is, if there are no costs to the input (labour) in moving then there are equally no incentives not to shirk. Furthermore, Lazonick argues, capitalist production relies on committed labour and will provide inducements to have more commitment from its workforce. Conditions of perfect labour mobility (necessary for Alchian model) are not conducive to the capitalist whose own financial commitment is fixed in machinery, raw material and other resources. Inducements for labour to be committed are designed to be a loss to labour if they are fired, which necessarily gives the monitor power.

Furthermore, argues Lazonick, in the examples used by Alchian and Demsetz to demonstrate the historical emergence of team production and thus the problem of shirking, they describe team productive processes (like the factory) that become successful precisely because they are authoritarian and because there is fiat. For example, the putting-out system (working from home) for weaving where inputs were organised through the market were, historically, usurped by the factory system. Alchian and Demsetz argued that this was because it became more efficient to share centralised equipment and work as a team, involved in different tasks. However, Lazonick argues that the fixed capital requirements for the factory system were much higher for the capitalist than when weavers tended to their own machinery. Furthermore, the capitalist had to offer many inducements to workers to leave their independent working practices and work in a factory. The reason factories became more productive than home working was because they enabled better discipline and time management of workers; 'it was the closer supervision of the workers afforded by the factory setting that, *despite* its higher capital costs, ultimately made it more profitable than domestic industry.'[40] Historically, employees submitted to this only when they had little choice, such as those Irish immigrant workers entering American factories in the 1840s.[41] 'Once a dependent labor force could be recruited, time discipline could be imposed within the factory setting with positive impacts on unit costs.'[42]

Thus the organisational features of the company, which in particular encompass the idea of authority and hierarchies, are successful precisely because they enable the exercise of power by capital over labour. There are costs for capital in the organisation of production in this way, but those costs are offset by the higher returns to capital.

---

[40] Ibid, 187.
[41] Ibid.
[42] Ibid.

5. IS COMPANY LAW IMPORTANT?

a. Yes, company law is important

In 'Saving the world with corporate law?', Kent Greenfield argues that corporate law is important and can be made more important through thoughtful reform. Company law reform could ensure that the wealth-creating capacity of corporations is fully utilised, that their wealth is spread to all stakeholders throughout society and that the tendency for corporations to create 'negative externalities' such as pollution and injury is redressed. He argues that these social goals should be met through corporate law itself because this is more efficient than using other forms of regulation such as employment law which provides some protection for employees.

Greenfield notes that the notion of the corporation as a public institution has been eradicated, leaving only shareholder interests as the corporation's goal and the purpose of corporate management:

> 'the "internal" regulation of corporate governance – for example, the legal imposition on managers and directors of fiduciary duties of care and loyalty – is used almost exclusively to protect shareholders (or the firm itself). "External" regulations, such as minimum-wage laws, environmental regulations, and consumer safety rules, are used to protect other stakeholders.'[43]

To further exacerbate this myopic corporate goal, serving the interests of shareholders has been interpreted as maximising shareholder return, a short-term policy which does not encompass the long-term stability or the productivity of the corporation. Thus Greenfield argues that there is a conflict between what external regulation attempts to do in creating fair distribution and stability and what the corporation aims to do internally; 'there is a tension between the internal and the external regulation of the corporation. The internal regulation, intended to protect the shareholders, has long been interpreted to impose a duty on the managers to maximise the return to the shareholders.'[44]

It is oft noted that the justification for this focus on shareholders alone in the internal governance of corporations has been very influenced by the finance economists' notion of efficiency. This holds that by focusing on one stakeholder (the shareholder), management can be more efficient, thus producing more wealth which is better for society as a whole. Greenfield argues that this position is absurd in that it essentially claims that 'corporate managers best advance society's interests by ignoring them'.[45] The clearly better way to advance society's interests would be to give managers a wider remit which encompasses the interests of all stakeholders, including the wider community, and to take more creative decisions

---

[43] K. Greenfield (with D.G. Smith), 'Debate: Saving the world with corporate law?' (2008) 57 *Emory L. J.* 947 at p. 960.
[44] Ibid, 960.
[45] Ibid, 966.

which directly address the needs of society. This wider remit would allow managers to address how corporations produce, which currently entails huge environmental damage and human rights abuses. Indeed, he notes, there are huge incentives for management to externalise costs in these ways by utilising human and natural resources with scant regard to the harm caused. Further, he argues, having managers whose duty was to return the wealth of production (which currently accrues to shareholders only) to all stakeholders would be a more efficient system of redistribution than, as currently, through the medium of tax and welfare policies. It would reduce the transaction costs involved in post-dividend clawbacks. It would also, one might speculate, reduce the tax lost to the public purse through tax avoidance schemes. Thus, as a matter of public policy, Greenfield argues, 'because the central purpose of the corporation is to create wealth, broadly defined, it is likely to be more efficient for the corporation to distribute wealth among those who contribute to its creation, rather than the government redistributing wealth after the fact'[46] through taxes or other welfare policies. The issue of distribution of corporate profits is thereby extracted from the current management–shareholder nexus and placed with public policy.

Greenfield also argues that much of the success of the corporation in creating wealth is due to its hierarchical organisational structure within which roles are rationally allocated. In particular, by allocating top-level decision making to a group of professionals, the board, corporations harness the creative and productive skills of the most effective individuals.[47] However, this too could be improved by recomposing the board with a more diverse set of stakeholders (representing different interests). More diversity, he argues, improves decision-making capabilities and 'the capacity of the board would increase with a more pluralistic makeup'.[48] In asserting this, Greenfield utilises research from Cass Susstein which shows that diversity and dissent in decision making improves the quality of the decisions, whereas conformity between decision makers increases the chances of errors.[49]

Thus Greenfield, though critical of many corporate activates and corporate goals, sees social progress within the corporate economy as being achievable by enhancing those many positive aspects of the corporation and utilising them for social ends. Reform of corporate law itself is essential to achieve this. 'The most powerful reason to accept changes in corporate governance is not to address the failures of the firm. Rather, the central reason to adjust corporate law is to take advantages of the success of the corporation in order to achieve important gains in social welfare.'[50]

---

[46] Ibid, p. 974.
[47] In promoting the board as the most efficient form of organisation, Greenfield cites Bainbridge (n. 26).
[48] Greenfield (n. 43), 953.
[49] C. Susstein, *Why Societies Need Dissent* (2003), cited by Greenfield (n. 43) at p. 981.
[50] Greenfield (n. 43), 974.

b. No, company law is not (really) important

Brian Cheffins argues that company law is fairly insignificant in constituting the company when compared with the greater impact of the market. In forwarding this argument, he chiefly focuses on the emergence of dispersed shareholding in both the UK and the US. This came about, he argues, because of the facility and security created by stock exchanges, not the law.[51] In downplaying the importance of company law, he takes issue with the 'law matters' thesis of La Porta et al. They argued that there is a correlation between high levels of share dispersal and good legal protections for minority shareholders, and that the implication of this correlation is that when minority shareholders have good legal protections (such as from the self-dealing of controlling shareholders or management), they are more likely to invest. They concluded from this evidence that if more jurisdictions introduced legal protections for minority shareholders, they would encourage more widely held investment. Cheffins disagrees. He (rightly) points out that this evidence does not actually prove a causal relationship between shareholder protection and more share dispersal. He argues that historically in both the UK and US, share dispersal preceded any attempt to create effective laws to protect minorities. Indeed, historically, laws which protect shareholders are passed in response to identifiable rises in share dispersal in recognition that this larger minority will require more legal protection. So, in the US, wide share dispersal emerged at the same time as New Jersey's corporate laws were the least hospitable to minority shareholders. They were laws which favoured controlling shareholders and management to such a degree that most of the major corporations in the US incorporated or reincorporated in New Jersey.[52] Originally attracted by the ability to have holding companies in New Jersey law (which also had the effect of marginalising small investors), corporations largely left New Jersey when it introduced new anti-trust legislation. Instead they incorporated or re-incorporated in Delaware, the state that had largely copied New Jersey corporate law (but not its anti-trust legislation).

By the 1920s family ownership was receding and share ownership became increasingly dispersed as ordinary households began buying corporate shares. This share dispersal occurred, notes Cheffins, when most of the big corporations operated under Delaware's corporate laws, which were inhospitable to minority shareholders. It was not, therefore, the law which attracted investors but an expectation of 'fair dealing', which was further underpinned by the role of the New York Stock Exchange:

> 'The regulatory efforts of the New York Stock Exchange (NYSE) provided investors
> with a market-orientated reason to expect "fair dealing". From before 1900, the
> NYSE saw itself as "a guardian of the financial quality of the issuers listed on it".

---

[51] B. Cheffins, 'Law as Bedrock: The Foundations of an Economy Dominated by Widely Held Public Companies' (2003) 23(1) *Oxford J. Legal Studies* 235.
[52] J. Seligman, 'History of Delaware Corporation Law' (1976) 1 *Del. J. Corp. L.* 249.

Hence, the NYSE would reject applications to list by corporations that lacked an adequate earnings track record or operated in a "high-risk" industry such as petroleum and mining.

   The NYSE also sought to build and protect its reputation by improving standards of corporate disclosure. At the turn of the century, when many listed companies remained family-dominated, the original proprietors were reluctant to abandon their instinct for secrecy. In 1909, however, the NYSE imposed a requirement that listed companies distribute annual financial reports to their shareholders and from that point onwards carried out a strong campaign to improve the quantity and quality of disclosure. These efforts yielded results, since Berle and Means said in their 1932 book that the NYSE's regulations largely accounted for a continuous flow of information reaching the market.'[53]

Of course, as the Wall Street crash was to show, that sense of fair dealing was an illusionary one – and more law was required in order to restore more confidence in the stock market.

   Cheffins also promotes his 'company law is not that important' argument through the example of the UK. Here the law was equally inhospitable to minority shareholders, he argues. The common law in *Foss v Harbottle*[54] provided little protection for the minority shareholder. However, from around the 1950s, shares began to become more widely dispersed and the old family ownership of companies dwindled. Shareholding became dispersed without any change in the law in respect of minority protection. Indeed, the key reforms to minority protection, the introduction of petitions in respect of unfairly prejudicial conduct (now section 994 of the Companies Act 2006), were introduced sometime *after* the rise of share dispersal following the privatisation of the UK nationalised industries, when the number of shareholders trebled from 3 million to 9 million.[55] In response to the rapid rise in shareholders, the London Stock Exchange's status was changed from that of a private organisation to that of statutory regulator of listed equities obliged to set out and oversee listing rules for companies which traded their shares publically. Cheffins argues that this reflects John Coffee's assertion that laws are only passed which protect minority shareholders *after* they substantially increase in number. Thus in the UK:

'The timing of the change to the Stock Exchange's status lends credence to the thesis that broadly based share ownership creates an hospitable environment for the enactment of legislation designed to assist outside investors. This is largely because the regulatory overhaul occurred at a time when the country's "investor class" was growing in strength largely as a result of share offerings carried out by companies that Margaret Thatcher's Conservative government were privatising. The number of individuals owning shares in the UK rose from approximately three million to nine million during the mid-1980s. The Thatcher Government was

---

[53] Cheffins (n. 51), 241.
[54] *Foss v Harbottle* (1843) 2 Hare 46, Ct of Chancery.
[55] Cheffins (n. 51), 245.

aware of this growing constituency and was prepared, despite being imbued with a free-market ideology, to legislate in instances where capitalism was likely to yield results to which potential supporters would take exception.'[56]

Thus Cheffins finds no instance of the law encouraging wide share dispersal. Instead, in the UK and US, share dispersal occurred in a legal environment which was hostile to minority shareholders. The single most compelling reason for minority shareholders emerging in substantial numbers was the better functioning of the stock markets. And, once the market had facilitated wide share dispersal, the law recognised the need for better legal protections for minorities. Thus, from Cheffins' perspective, while the law creates recognisable order it cannot affect substantial change. Corporate activity remains a creature of the market rather than of the law. In contrast, Greenfield sees the law as something which can change the nature of the company and how it operates in society. The market is ordered by and subject to the law. Moreover, it is the law relating to companies which is most effective in determining change in company activity.

CONCLUSION

Theorists who embrace the finance economist's model of the company view company law as having only a very peripheral impact on the nature of the company. For these theorists it is the market or the demand of efficiency that determines business forms. Indeed, some theorists reduce that form down to contracting individuals only. The company is successful because it mimics the market while simultaneously reducing some of the transaction costs of the market. The company also accommodates and addresses the 'irrational' choices of market players. Company law is successful in enhancing the economy, as opposed to restricting it, when it accommodates market efficiencies. For example, when company law provides a standard form contract it reduces the cost of bargaining, as in Easterbrook and Fischel's analysis. Cheffins, in downplaying of the importance of company law, falls into this category. In his analysis it is the market which is effective, not the law. Successful law responds to the market; unsuccessful law tries to control the market, hampering its development.

However, the market is itself the legal exchange of legally constructed property forms. The market in shares was not possible without limited liability or laws enabling the restructuring of company capital, making shares more transferable because they were in smaller denominations. The exchange of the share would not be possible without its legal construction as a property form, a thing that could be exchanged in a market dealing only with financial property because the share had been reconceptualised as financial property distinct from actual real property. Thus market activity is itself an expression of the legal construction of ownership

---

[56] Ibid, 244–5.

rights and responsibilities within the company, without which the market could not exist.

In contrast to the finance economists' approach, legal theorists emphasise the importance of company law and many see reform of company law as key to changing society. The company is a legal form whose activities are determined by the law and whose activities can be changed by changes to the law. These theorists embrace a more entity approach to the company. It is an organisation with distinct organisational characteristics. The latter view is shared by organisational theorists who see organisational structure as determinative of the effectiveness of the company in terms of its competiveness or in its ability to extract value from labour. The law has a clear role in the creation of the company's organisational structure. Thus the 'company law is important' debate is intrinsically interwoven with the debate on what the company actually is.

It is perhaps unsurprising that economists tend to think that the market determines the shape of the company or that lawyers tend to elevate the law. However, it is important to recognise the political imperative of the various positions. The finance economist's position, which has dominated thinking on the company over the last 30 years (at least), promotes the ideology of neoliberalism. It promotes the interests of investors and airbrushes other company participants out of the picture. The company is a description of the activities of self-maximising individuals who should largely be free from the state to self-maximise. In contrast, legal theorists and organisational theorists tend to join up society with the company. What the company is allowed to do, and should do, is intrinsically connected to how society should operate for its members. There is a range of political positions within this which are more or less socially concerned, more or less concerned with intervention and more or less concerned with company law reform. Thus the question of 'what is the company' is one that is always answered from a political perspective. Furthermore, that perspective is dynamic and will inform the holders' position in debates on the future shape of the company.

Further Reading

L. Bebchuck and J. Fried, *Pay Without Performance: The Unfulfilled Promise of Executive Compensation* (Library of Congress Cataloguing in Publication Data, 2004).

A. Chandler, *The Visible Hand* (Belknap Harvard, 1977).

J.R. Commons, *Institutional Economics: Its Place in Political Economy* (Transaction Publishers, 1990).

J. Dine and A. Fagan (eds), *Human Rights and Capitalism* (Edward Elgar, 2006).

T. Hadden, *Company Law and Capitalism* (Weidenfeld and Nicolson, 1972).

R. Kraakman et al., *The Anatomy of Corporate Law* (Oxford University Press, 2004).

A. Johnston, *EC Regulation of Corporate Governance* (Cambridge University Press, 2009).

L.E. Talbot, 'Polanyi's Embeddedness and Shareholder Stewardship: A contextual analysis of current Anglo-American perspectives on Corporate Governance', *Northern Ireland Legal Quarterly*, Winter 2011.

L.E. Talbot, *Progressive Corporate Governance for the 21st Century* (Routledge, 2012).

T. Veblen, *Absentee Ownership* (Transaction Publishers, 1976, first published 1923); *Theory of the Leisure Class: An Economic Study of Institutions* (Cosimo, 2004, first published 1903).

2

ARE SHAREHOLDERS THE COMPANY'S OWNERS? CLAIMS IN LAW AND CLAIMS IN IDEOLOGY

The question of whether shareholders own the company is one of the key debates in company law and one that directly impacts on the purpose of corporate governance. The debate illuminates the contradiction between the legal position on shareholder claims and the ideological position. The law maintains that the claims of ordinary shareholders are limited to a right to dividend if dividend is declared, a right to vote at general meeting and a right to any residual surplus upon liquidation. It is no more extensive than that. Indeed, the law has been keen to limit the boundaries of the ordinary share, especially when in the early part of the 19th century the share became uncoupled from the actual assets of the company. Historically, as this chapter discusses, the law has consistently attempted to stabilise that which the ordinary share is and has frowned on mechanisms which undermine the surety of the ordinary share. For example, the law has discouraged nil or partly paid shares but where they exist has ensured that the partly paid share contains the same rights as the fully paid share. In contrast, other forms of investments in the company have enjoyed much less stability. The so-called 'preference share' is used as an example on this point.

The first part of this chapter takes the view that what a shareholder owns is quite clear in law. Whether one imputes that which shareholders own in law as constituting them as the owners of the company as a whole is an ideological position, rather than a logical conclusion of the legal position. In fact, the law undermines the idea of shareholders as owners of the company. The law is clear that what shareholders own is not the company. So when directors fulfil their fiduciary duty to the company, that duty is not principally to shareholders, even where they are called 'the owners'. Thus even in the leading cases where the courts have held out the shareholders as the company owners, a directors' duty has been held to be to the company (as distinct from shareholders) and thus fulfilled by pursuing the interests of others involved in the company.

The chapter then goes on to consider those areas of law which give credence to the counter debate that shareholders are the owners. This includes the many parts in company law which make changes to the company subject to shareholder consent. The argument here is that although the separation between ownership and control in the company means that shareholders have devolved the day-to-day running of the company to the board of directors, shareholders still retain power over substantial changes made to the company and in respect of decisions which involve the directors' self-interest. The chapter concludes with a critical analysis of the argument that shareholders are owners because they contribute capital to the company.

This chapter is thus organised around three main propositions:

Proposition 1: Shareholders are not the owners of the company because what they own is not the company

Proposition 2: Shareholders are the owners of the company because of the legal rights they hold in the company

Proposition 3: Shareholders are the owners of the company because they contribute capital to the company

PROPOSITION 1: SHAREHOLDERS ARE NOT THE OWNERS OF THE COMPANY BECAUSE WHAT THEY OWN IS NOT THE COMPANY

a. They do not own the company's assets

Under the Companies Acts a share is defined as a 'share in the company's share capital',[1] not the company itself. The shareholders have a residual claim upon the company itself upon liquidation, after all other higher priority claimants. It has been a longstanding understanding in company law that the company share is an entitlement to the surplus created by the assets of the company but not an entitlement to the assets themselves. The assets are distinct from the profit that may be made using them. This has been the orthodox view of the share since at least 1837, when in *Bligh v Brent*,[2] the company share was defined as a personal entitlement to profit, but not a claim on the company's assets. Under the Companies Act 2006 (CA 2006) a member's share in a company is classed as personal property.[3] It is a *chose in action*. Being the registered member with a share confers certain legal rights and privileges, but does not give the member possession of a physical object.

The following extract looks at the judgement in *Bligh v Brent* and its significance:

'Prior to this case, company shares were legally conceived as equitable interests in the whole concern, tangible assets and profits, much as one would expect in a

---

[1] Companies Act 2006, s. 540 (1), as also defined in the Model Articles for a private company limited by shares.
[2] (1837) 2 Y & C 268.
[3] CA 2006, s. 541.

partnership arrangement.[4] Early judgments merged shareholders' property interests with those of the company[5] – "the corporation held its assets as a trustee for the shareholders, who were in equity co-owners".[6] So, in the cases assessed by 19th century scholar Samuel Williston involving the Statutes of Mortmain and Frauds and transfers involving real estate, which hinged on whether a property interest in the share was realty or personalty, it was always found that the nature of the share depended on the nature of the corporate property.[7] Williston noted that "if the shareholders have in equity the same interest which the corporation has at law, a share will be real estate or personalty, according as the corporate property is real or personal".[8] So, in respect of the fraudulent or mistaken transfer of shares, the acquisition by a *bona fide* purchaser for value was protected precisely because shareholders were not legal but equitable owners. A transfer made without the knowledge of the original shareholders entitled them to relief only.

This conception of the share, which inter alia made shareholders liable in equity for their company's debts as co-owners of the assets and liabilities, ceased with *Bligh v Brent* noted Williston. The plaintiff's assertion that the interest of the *cestui que trust* was co-extensive with the legal interest of the trustee was entirely in line with previous authorities.[9] However, the court held the shares in the company to be personalty rather than realty regardless of the company's assets.[10] In his judgment, Baron Alderton stated that shareholders had no claim on the assets but only the surplus that those assets produced. As such he described shares as a property which was a claim to profits and distinct from the tangible property that created those profits: the company owning the former, the shareholder the latter.'[11]

So *Bligh v Brent* decoupled the share from the company's assets, enhancing its fluidity and capacity to be exchanged. It established that whatever it is that shareholders do own, it is not the company assets. The same point underpins the cases on the doctrine of separate corporate personality, which consistently maintain that it is the company which owns the assets, not the shareholders. For example, in *Macaura v Northern Assurance Co Ltd*[12] the sole director and shareholder of a limited company was unable to claim for fire damage to the company's property on his own personal insurance. A claim could only be made on the company's own insurance, as a shareholder had no 'insurable interest' in the company's assets. In deciding the case in

---

[4] S. Williston, 'History of the Law of Business Corporations Before 1800 – Part II' (1888) 2 *Harv. L. Rev.* 149.
[5] Ibid.
[6] Ibid, 150.
[7] Ibid.
[8] Ibid.
[9] This judgment was subsequently adopted in America. It is interesting to note that *Bligh v Brent* (1837) 2 Y & C Ex 268 involved a charter company whose assets were in fact mainly personalty rather than realty – so arguably this decision was less ground-breaking than might at first appear. However, the judges' definition of a share continued to inform subsequent cases.
[10] Under the terms of a will, the nature of shares, either personalty or realty, determined who could take them.
[11] L.E. Talbot, *Progressive Corporate Governance for the 21st Century* (Routledge, 2012), pp. 17–18.
[12] [1925] AC 619.

this way the court was faithfully following the principles laid down in *Salomon v Salomon*.[13] The company was a separate legal being which required its own insurance. The company owned itself. The rights granted to shareholders did not add up to ownership of the company.

Following *Bligh v Brent*, shareholders came to own something which was distinct from the identifiable assets and liabilities of the company. It was a new property form, and therefore its boundaries needed to be established. The share needed to be concretised, or reified, as a piece of property. This required clarity as to what this new form of property consisted in. The law provided this clarity in the form of the many rules shaping the contours and setting the boundaries of the share.

b. The law has carefully fixed those limited claims

Shares in a limited company with a share capital must each have a fixed nominal value (CA 2006, s. 542(1)). In limited companies, shares may be issued as nil paid, partly paid, fully paid or at a premium. However, nil or partly paid shares have been problematic historically, partly because they undermine the nature and value of the share. This has in turn inhibited the liquidity of the share and enabled dangerously speculative investment. Indeed, nil or partly paid-up shares are only successfully used in a business which is registered as a company but where the business operates as if it were a partnership. In this situation, shareholders manage the company and distribute profits according to the proportion of shares owned, but do not use the issue of shares to raise capital. Such companies as these organise ownership and control in ways that are indistinguishable from partnerships.

Today shares are mainly fully paid up, so that their value as a piece of property is clear. When, in the days before *Bligh v Brent*, a share represented a fraction of the companies' tangible assets, then it was conceptually straightforward to ascertain its value. However, decoupled from tangible assets, valuation becomes more complex because it is an assessment of what the profits may be in the future. That complexity is considerably enhanced when the share is not paid up. As a paid-up share, it, at least, had a value which was paid upon issue, based on assessment of future profits. Partly or nil paid shares, at their worst, left both value and liabilities unresolved. The unpaid part of the share was a debt which the holder of the share would have to pay if the company required that person to do so. The company could make a call upon that share at any time, or it may not. If the original share price was very high but the paid part was very small, the shareholder was effectively subject to de facto unlimited liability.[14] Shareholders had no way of knowing whether their potential (and often huge) liabilities on shares would be realised or not. This undermined the stability of the share market because it undermined

---

[13] [1897] AC 22.
[14] Williston (n. 4) noted that the company's ongoing right to make 'leviations or calls for payments from its members' meant that members had de facto unlimited liability.

share value and it undermined a clear sense of liabilities. All of this undermined the ability of the share to be easily transferable.

As a result of this, in the early period of the market in shares, the judiciary routinely struck down companies which issued largely unpaid shares, which, it was felt, fuelled speculative bubbles.[15] In *Joseph v Pebrer*,[16] the court found that the company's use of nil and partly paid shares rendered the company illegal under the Bubble Act 1720 notwithstanding that the business itself was a respectable enough endeavour and that the earlier decision in *Rex v Dodd*[17] had held that all businesses not 'injurious to the public' would be exempt from the Bubble Act. Unpaid shares were evidently injurious to the public:

'The real value of the share could not be properly calculated and in this case the company claimed to have £2 million of capital when only £40,000 was paid up. In his judgment Abbott CJ stated that: "The traffic in shares of this kind must be highly injurious, as what is gained by one person must be lost by another; whereas, in commerce, every party may be a gainer". Thus, transferability was injurious precisely because it tended to disguise the fact that much of the company's value was in uncalled capital, making it difficult for an investor to judge the real value of his investment. With an eye firmly on the South Sea Bubble, Guerny CJ stated that: "this is one of those dreadful speculations which inflicted so great an injury in this country about a century ago, and which, if not checked, would do similar injury now".'[18]

Often, the use of uncalled capital, or partly paid shares, was for the benefit of the controlling shareholders and managers (industrialists) and to the detriment of outside investors. Having uncalled capital enabled industrialists to get injections of capital when and if the business needed it:

'Jefferys's study of share denominations covering the period from the passage of the limited liability Act until 1885, concluded that when companies still had need of additional financing, partly paid shares were issued but when they did not, fully paid shares were issued. Thus true limited liability came not with the Act but "the needs of industry and trade".[19] The use of large denomination shares with small initial payments differed from industry to industry. Iron, coal, steel, shipbuilding and engineering tended to have large denomination shares with uncalled capital, whereas cooperative mines and cotton mills had low denomination fully paid up shares, which were owned by the workers.[20] Jefferys notes that: "Of the 3720 companies formed between 1856 and 1865 inclusive and believed still to be in existence

---

[15] Bishop C. Hunt, 'The Joint Stock Company in England 1830–1944' (1935) 43 *Journal of Political Economy* 331, 17.

[16] 3 B & C 639 (1825).

[17] (1808) 9 East 516.

[18] Talbot (n. 11), p. 14.

[19] J.B. Jefferys, 'The Denomination and Character of Shares 1855–1885' (1946) 16 *Economic History Review* 45.

[20] Ibid, p. 46.

in the latter year, only 597, or 16%, had shares below £5 in value; the remainder ranged between £5 and £5000 ... more than thirty companies had share denominations of £1000 and over".[21]

Further indications that uncalled capital undermined use of the share as a piece of transferable property are provided by evidence on other uses of partly paid shares. Shares were frequently used, not as a way of raising capital from the investing public, but as way of allocating power and entitlement amongst a small group of people. These people were in practice, if not in law, partners in a partnership. In these 'quasi-partnerships' the uncalled capital, frequently part of very large denomination shares, indicated an effective continuation of the partnership principles:

'Large denomination shares were held by "quasi-partners" who managed the quasi-partnership which had been incorporated as a company. In these companies creditors would expect payment from the shareholders/quasi-partners utilising uncalled capital (de facto unlimited liability) to the same effect as if they were relying on the unlimited liability (de jure unlimited liability) of partners in a partnership. The quasi-partnership nature of these companies is also evidenced by David Chadwick, company promoter,[22] in a Select Committee in 1877 on amending the Companies Acts. He stated that when businesses incorporated as limited liability companies they almost always sold the ordinary shares to an exclusive group of friends.[23]

Furthermore, it was common practice to evaluate the creditworthiness of a company through reference to the creditworthiness of the large denomination shareholders whose shares would have a large proportion of uncalled capital. Indeed, the presence of uncalled capital was common in business practice because it was thought to designate a stable company, in which credit could confidently be extended. David Chadwick stated: "In the case of a trading company I think it is very prudent and very proper to have 25 to 33 or 40% uncalled out of the subscribed capital; without that they cannot stand in the market with proper credit."[24][25]

Later in the 19th century, the judiciary aimed to stabilise uncalled capital where it continued to be a feature of companies' shares. Though uncalled capital might be used, it could be better quantified so as to dispel the uncertainties of investors' liabilities. Uncalled capital was designated as a debt owed to the company. If a share was nil paid or partly paid, a company could make calls on the uncalled, or unpaid for part of a share as the shareholder 'is liable in respect of all moneys unpaid on his shares to pay up every call that is duly made up him'.[26] Likewise, in the current legislation, 'Money payable by a member to the company under its

---

[21] Talbot (n. 11), p. 45.

[22] David Chadwick supported the 1876 Bill to amend the Companies Acts 1862 and 1867.

[23] R. McQueen, *A Social History of Company Law: Great Britain and the Australian Colonies 1854–1920* (Ashgate, 2009), 179.

[24] J.B. Jefferys (n. 19).

[25] Talbot (n. 11), p. 25

[26] *Birch v Cropper* (1889) 14 App Cas 525, HL.

constitution is a debt due from him to the company.'[27] Furthermore, in insolvency, the unpaid part of any share is treated as an asset of the company and the outstanding amount must be paid to the liquidator. This makes the purchase of a share, a purchase of a particular commodity for a set price. Money outstanding will be a debt but the share buyer still possesses the rights of other shareholders regardless of this debt.

Thus case law clarified the nature and extent of shareholders' claims on dividends and of their claims to the residue of any liquidated assets of the company in the context of partly paid shares. These claims, the courts held, are determined by the number of shares that a shareholder possesses and not how much has been paid on the shares. It also followed from this reasoning that a shareholder's rights would not be extended by making payments in response to a call on unpaid capital. In the 1889 case of *Birch v Cropper*, Lord Macnaghton stated that the shareholder 'does not by such payment acquire any further or other interest in the capital of the company. His share in the capital is just what it was before. His liability to the company is diminished by the amount paid.'[28] Furthermore, in respect to the shareholder's claim to the residue upon liquidation, 'the rights and interests of the contributories in the company must then be simply in proportion to their shares.'[29] Lord Macnaghton stated that the fixed claims of shareholders derives from the Companies Acts. They did not possess additional benefits or otherwise because their investment was subject to some risk – as other judges in this case argued. Shareholders bought a set of entitlements and the nature and limit of those entitlements were set out in statute.

c. The law did not extend this fixity to other investors

Rather than describing the ownership right of shareholders in an expansive and non-exhaustive manner, from which a wider claim of ownership might be winkled out, the law, as noted above, has actively determined the nature and extent of a shareholder's entitlement. This approach has enabled the share to exchange as an identifiable property but it has also, paradoxically, inhibited a wider description of shareholders as the owners of the company. In contrast to the fixity of the arrangements and entitlements accruing to ordinary shareholders, other non-ordinary shareholders are often subject to uncertainties in their entitlements.

The Companies Act 2006 defines different classes of shares thus: '... shares are of one class if the rights attached to them are in all respects uniform.'[30] A company may create different classes of shares with differing rights if it has power in its constitution to do so. The different rights will usually be set out in the articles but may be held in a shareholders' agreement. Ordinary shares are defined in the

---

[27] Companies Act 2006, s. 33(2).
[28] *Birch v Cropper* (1889) 14 App Cas 525 at 543.
[29] Ibid at 545.
[30] CA 2006, s. 629(1).

Companies Act 2006 as 'shares other than shares that as respects dividends and capital carry a right to participate only up to certain specified amount in a distribution'.[31] They typically have three basic rights attached:

(a) one vote for each share;[32]
(b) a right to a dividend if declared (after any preference shareholders); and
(c) in a solvent winding up, right to return of capital, after preference shareholders, with an unlimited right to participate in surplus funds.

The position in relation to ordinary shares is therefore clear. Once one leaves ordinary shares, however, there may be difficulties in determining whether a share is a member of a particular class. In *Cumbrian Newspapers Group Ltd v Cumberland & Westmoreland Herald Newspapers & Printing Co. Ltd*,[33] Scott J discussed whether certain rights in articles were class rights for statutory purposes. The plaintiff shareholder company, which held ordinary shares, had rights which included the right to appoint a director so long as it held at least 10% of the issued shares. In judgment, Scott J stated that rights or benefits conferred by articles can be classified into three categories:

(a) rights or benefits attached to a particular shares-class, such as 'dividend rights and rights to participate in surplus assets on a winding up' and voting rights;
(b) rights or benefits conferred on individuals, not in their capacity as shareholders of a company but connected with the administration of the company's affairs or the conduct of its business;
(c) rights or benefits that although not attached to any particular shares are nonetheless conferred on the beneficiary in his capacity as a shareholder.[34]

The most common form of a modified share, in the sense set out in section 560, is the preference share. Typically, preference shareholders may only vote in their own class meetings and may only vote in general meetings in special circumstances such as when their dividends are in arrears. They usually have a priority right to an annual dividend at a fixed rate and there is a presumption that the dividend is cumulative.[35] Preferential shareholders usually have a preferential right over ordinary shareholders to the return of their share capital in a solvent winding up, but they do not usually have a preferential right to a share in any surplus in a

---

[31] CA 2006, s. 560(1).

[32] Although weighted voting rights may be given: *Bushell v Faith* [1970] AC 1099.

[33] [1987] Ch 1.

[34] In this case the first category did not apply because the rights were conferred on condition of holding 10% of the shares, rather than a quality of the shares themselves. The second category constituted rights attached to a particular shareholder, independent of the nature of the share itself. These rights did not constitute class rights and were amendable by special resolution. Again, this did not cover the situation in the case. It was, rather, the third category that was relevant. The rights conferred on the plaintiff were *qua* a member of the company and they could not be enforceable by the plaintiff if he did not own 10% of the issued shares. The court ruled that these did amount to class rights. Thus class rights may be rights annexed to particular shares or intrinsic to those shares.

[35] *Webb v Earle* [1875] LR 20 Eq 556; *Staples v Eastman Photographic Materials Co.* [1896] 2 Ch 303.

solvent winding up unless they have an express right. These rights seem clear enough. However, the entitlements attached to preference shares are notoriously uncertain. The entitlements may change. Preference shareholders may be bought out whether they like it or not. Rights which preference shareholders possess may be interpreted in a detrimental way for the rights holder. Often this will mean that the preference shareholder will not enjoy the same legal protections as ordinary shareholders in respect to any variations on their rights.

The detrimental interpretation of preferential shareholder rights can be seen in numerous cases. What appears to be a class right belonging to preference shareholders has been interpreted by the court as something else. For example, when the company has sought to change the terms of the preference shareholders' entitlement, the courts may interpret the amendment as falling short of an actual variation. In *White v Bristol Aeroplane Co. Ltd*[36] the company wished to increase the capital of the company by a bonus issue to the ordinary shareholders of both preference and ordinary shares. The existing preference shareholders argued that this would 'affect' the existing preference shareholders' voting rights since their votes would thereby be diluted. However, the court held that although the proposed amendment affected the enjoyment of their voting rights, it did not alter or even affect the right itself.[37] In the context of preference shares, a class right is not varied by making it worthless through acts which render a right irrelevant. For example, in *Dimbula Valley (Ceylon) Tea Co Ltd v Laurie*,[38] a right for preference shareholders to participate in surplus assets on winding up was not deemed to have been varied by the act of distributing the surplus to ordinary shareholders before winding up. The right continued unvaried, although the enjoyment of the benefits of that right had ceased. There are also a series of cases where the repurchase of preference shares against the wishes of the owners were not deemed to be a variation but merely an expression of their entitlement as preference shareholders to have their capital repaid before ordinary shareholders.[39]

The consequence of these interpretations of the rights of preference shareholders is that they have been denied the statutory protection given to classes of shares to cover the situation when a company resolution purports to vary those rights. The law requires that if a company attempts to amend or vary[40] a class right, then that class must consent to the variation.[41] Furthermore, if only a minority of the

---

[36] [1953] Ch 65.

[37] See also *Re John Smith's Tadcaster Brewery Co. Ltd* [1953] Ch 305.

[38] [1961] Ch 353.

[39] *House of Fraser plc v ACGE Investments* [1987] AC 387 and on liquidation *Re Saltdean Estate Co. Ltd* [1968] 1 WLR 1844.

[40] Under section 630 of the CA 2006: 'Any amendment of a provision in the articles for the variation of the rights attached to a class of shares, or the insertion of any such provision into the articles, is … treated as a variation [or an 'abrogation'] of those rights.'

[41] Under section 630 a variation is only permitted if made in accordance with the provisions in the company's articles or, where there are no such provisions in the articles, if the holders of shares of that class consent to the variation in accordance with the statutory provisions (CA 2006, s. 630(2)). That consent must be made either by the holders of at least three-quarters in nominal value of the issued shares of that class consenting in writing to the variation or by a special resolution passed at a separate general meeting of the holders of that class.

affected class object to the variation, they still retain a special right to object to the variation.[42] These are valuable protections, which enable minority shareholders to protect their interests against the company vote. However, as the case above indicates, because the company amendments which have affected preference shareholders have been held to fall short of an actual variation, preference shareholders have not been able to enjoy these protections. As a result, their rights may be varied by special resolution under section 21(1) of the CA 2006 and they have no redress. In contrast, ordinary shareholders have clarity in respect of the nature of the rights they possess.

d. What shareholders own is not the company even when they are termed the 'owners'

Notwithstanding that company law is clear on the entitlements of shareholders and that these entitlements do not denote ownership of the company per se, where a case needs to make reference to shareholder entitlements, the courts will often assert that shareholders are the owners. However, the key case cited on this point for over a century in English company law involved a decision which was against the interests of the shareholders in question and which explicitly *narrowed* the scope that ownership. Interestingly, the same thing happened in America. The key case there involved (at least in large part) a decision which was against the interests of the shareholders and further limited the scope of what was a shareholder's entitlement more generally. In both cases, after asserting the ownership of shareholders, the courts decided the cases on the basis that directors must make decisions in the interests of the company as a whole, and in so doing will consider the interests of employees, creditors and the wider community as well as considering the interests of shareholders.

i. The English case: *Percival v Wright*[43]

The case was an action to set aside the sale of shares in a limited company. The company secretary had been approached by a number of shareholders who wished to sell their shares and requested his help and advice on their disposal. It was a private company, so the shares could not be valued in and sold on the stock market. Furthermore, the company's memorandum provided that the shares could not be sold without the approval of the board of directors. The plaintiff shareholders stated the price they would accept and the company chairman wrote to their solicitor offering to purchase the shares. A sale was agreed. The chairman disclosed that the shares would be divided into three lots, two of which would be held by two other directors. After the transaction was completed, the shareholders discovered that the board had been approached by a third party, a Mr Holden, who had

---

[42] CA 2006, s. 633.
[43] [1902] 2 Ch 421.

offered a considerable sum for the entire undertaking with the intention of selling the company onto a new company. Although no firm offer had ever been made by Mr Holden and although negotiations fell through, the court was not convinced that the board seriously entertained his offer.

The plaintiffs argued that the directors were in a fiduciary position in relation to them and should have disclosed the negotiations with Holden. They argued that the company should be understood as 'merely the sum of the shares',[44] which at law belonged to the company but in equity belonged to the sharehold-ers. Accordingly, they were the beneficiaries of the company and the directors were 'trustees of the sale of the undertaking'.[45] Counsel contended that the direc-tors were under a duty to disclose all related negotiations to the beneficiaries. Furthermore, they argued, 'in this respect the shareholders *inter se* are in the same position as partners … If managing partners employ an agent to sell their business, he cannot purchase the share of a sleeping partner without disclosing the fact of his employment. Incorporation cannot affect this broad equitable principle.'[46]

However, Swinfen Eady J held that the directors owed a duty to act in 'the best interests of the company as a whole', and that directors were not 'trustees for indi-vidual shareholders'.[47] The doctrine of separate corporate personality established that the company was distinct from shareholders. The interests of both may coin-cide but they could not be conflated. Directors represented the interests of the company and those interests might well be contrary to the wishes of shareholders. Swinfen Eady J set out established authorities on the definition of directors' duties in the context of the modern company with separate corporate personality as being trustees of the companies' assets. 'Directors are the mere trustees or agents of the company – trustees of the company's money and property – agents in the transactions which they enter into on behalf of the company.'[48] The directors' duty to the productive assets also explains the strict rules on self-dealing in English law. The judge concluded that the nature of incorporation alters the position of share-holders so that they are not like partners and cannot conjoin themselves with the business so as to make a director's fiduciary duty which is owed to the company, one that is owed to them also.

Swinfen Eady J rejected the proposition that though incorporation affected the relations of the shareholders to the external world, and the company thereby becoming a distinct entity, the position of the shareholders *inter se* was not affected, and was the same as that of partners or shareholders in an unincorporated company.[49]

---

[44] Ibid at 423.
[45] Ibid.
[46] Ibid.
[47] Ibid.
[48] *Great Eastern Ry Co. v Turner* (1872–3) LR 8 Ch App 149, quoted in *Percival* at p. 425.
[49] Ibid.

Thus, the court effectively reasoned that though they may be the owners, it was not a form of ownership which entitled them to exercise the usual rights of owners. It was an ownership with limited entitlements, and it was only those entitlements that directors were obliged to consider, when acting in the best interests of the company. In considering the best interests of the company, directors might equally consider other interests connected with those productive assets, such as those of creditors, consumers and employees.

ii. The American case: *Dodge v Ford*[50]

The classic American case setting out the shareholder primacy claim that the corporation should operate in shareholders' interests as the owners is *Dodge v Ford*. It concerned the management of Henry Ford in Ford Motor Co. and the entitlement of substantial minority shareholders, the Dodge brothers. The minority shareholders challenged the board of directors on three of its decisions. The first was the decision to cease paying 'special' high-rate dividends, the second was the board's decision to invest more in the business and the third to reduce the price of the Ford cars. The Michigan Supreme Court held that 'a business corporation is organised and carried on primarily for the profit of its stockholders', thus making the shareholder primacy point fairly succinctly. Accordingly, it upheld the paying of special dividend to the Dodge brothers. However, it did not agree with the trial court that an injunction should be granted to stop management investing profit in the business and reducing the price of its vehicles. These two decisions were management decisions in line with the decisions the board is bound to make in respect of the productive assets of the company when fulfilling its fiduciary duty to act in the interests of the company.

Many contemporary scholars have pointed to the *non*-shareholder primacy elements to this decision.[51] The court, while making strong statements about shareholder primacy, simultaneously accepted that the corporation engaged wider concerns than that of producing value for shareholders. Company directors owed a duty to the company, and in fulfilling that duty they could consider issues like the development of a wide customer base, product development and competitiveness, even where those concerns might run contrary to the desires of shareholders, as they did in this case. In particular, the short-term interests of shareholders to dividend should be secondary to the need to develop and protect the productive assets of the company for the long term.

This judgment is also interesting in historical context. This was a time in America when management power rather than shareholder power was of huge concern to judges like Brandeis and Cardozo and to many politicians. Scholarship in this period was extremely concerned with the power of big business, but the concern was with director primacy, not the primacy of shareholders. Such dominance could

---

[50] (1919) 170 NW 66.
[51] P.M. Vasudev and S. Watson, *Corporate Governance After the Financial Crisis* (Edward Elgar, 2012), 101.

manifest in all sorts of ways, including, as in this case, restricting dividends. Yet even as the judiciary were alert to the potential problem of an overpowered management – and Henry Ford is a classic example of that kind of all-pervading management force – they continued to uphold the principle that a shareholder's ownership claims were limited.

So what these cases indicate is that even where the courts are making the legal case for shareholder ownership, they delineate it very narrowly. For the most part, they prioritise decision making which is not in the interest of shareholders. Thus, paradoxically, in making the case for shareholder ownership, they necessarily make the case for their effective non-ownership of the company.

e. Shareholders are termed owners because of an historical accident

Paddy Ireland maintains that the root cause or justification for distinguishing a shareholder who makes a money contribution from a creditor who does the same, is that the shareholder is said to have risked his capital whereas the creditor has not.[52] A shareholder has invested his capital in the corporation whereas the creditor has merely lent his money for a limited period of time. The importance of risk, in distinguishing the two, has long historic origins, which Ireland traces back to the moral abhorrence and legal prohibitions against money lending, or usury. For the most part, usury was defined as charging more than 5 per cent interest on loans and the penalties were harsh. During the Elizabethan period this was increased to 10 per cent, which indicated the basic problem of usury laws for British capitalism. Anti-usury laws were a firmly entrenched in British society both through the Christian church and its accompanying anti-Semitism; it was part of the moral fabric of British society.

On the other hand, capitalism required capital and that meant extensive borrowing, but the limits on interest set by the usury laws made lending unattractive. According to Ireland, the judiciary responded to this conundrum in an interesting and innovative way. Throughout the 18th and part of the 19th century, British capitalism was rapidly developing. The usury laws retained a general application but certain financial institutions were explicitly exempted from its provisions. Individuals, however, were not exempted and could not on the face of it invest in business for a good rate of return. The partnership was the dominant vehicle for business during this period and investment was crucial for business development. Thus, following the decision in *Grace v Smith* (1775), the judiciary adopted a practice of construing investors in partnerships as partners, even though they were not declared as such and played no part in the business. By construing them thus, investors could enjoy high rates of return without incurring the penalties of the usury laws. Investing capital was sufficient to qualify as 'business in common with a view to profit', the later statutory definition of a partnership,

---

[52] P. Ireland, 'The Myth of Shareholder Ownership' (1999) 62(1) *Modern Law Review* 32.

which retained enjoying the profit as prima facie evidence of partnership. Partners, who merely invested in the partnership, were morally exempted from the usury laws because, unlike the usurer, they were risking their capital. Partners owned and controlled the business; they were all equally entitled to the firm's profits and personally responsible for the firm's debts.

Ireland maintains that when early companies evolved from the roots of partnership law, the same values which construed an investor in a partnership as a partner likewise served to construe an investor in a company as an owner. In early companies formed under the Joint Stock Companies Act 1844, this was more understandable as the few hundred companies formed under this Act did not provide for members' limited liability and members retained some proprietary connection to the company assets. They were not dissimilar to partnerships. However, as company law responded to the changing nature of the company and its shareholders, it developed as a distinct area of law with distinct principles. This, perhaps, should have been a time when the notion of shareholder as owner/partner was abandoned, but it was not. It was this failure to fully shake off the values of partnership law which allowed pure investors to be partners to avoid the usury laws, which Ireland asserts is the reason why shareholders today retain their status as owners. Thus, notwithstanding the fundamental differences between a general partner and a modern shareholder, the latter continue to be regarded as the *raison d'être* of corporate governance procedures.

PROPOSITION 2: SHAREHOLDERS ARE THE OWNERS OF THE COMPANY BECAUSE OF THE LEGAL RIGHTS THEY HOLD IN THE COMPANY

It could be argued that shareholders are the owners of the company because they exercise, or at least have the legal power to exercise, considerable power over the company through their control over the agents of the company, the board of directors. The principle source of their control over the board is the articles of association, but many acts of the boards or individual directors will also require additional shareholder approvals, including directors' own remuneration. The board is also bound to communicate to its shareholders through the medium of the company accounts and reports. Directors of listed companies comply with or explain their lack of compliance with the UK Corporate Governance Code and with the listing rules, instruments designed to promote the interests of shareholders.

The articles of association are often understood as a statutory contract in which the shareholders agree that directors can manage the company subject to limitations on their authority in the articles and the requirements of the Companies Act. The centrality of the articles of association in English company law is in many ways unique. It was originally a feature of commonwealth countries which took their starting point from English company law, but was later abandoned. Nonetheless, it has been a powerful basis for those who argue that shareholders are indeed the owners of the company. It seems to posit a contract between shareholders and the company as being the principle organising force in the company.

Susan Watson takes issue with the ideological significance frequently attached to the fact that, in English company law, directors' legal authority derives from the articles of association, rather than, as in other common law countries, from statute.[53] The origins of directors' authority in English company law has led to the conclusion that company law is (and should be) 'shareholder centred'. Watson instead argues that company law assumes that directors do operate independently on behalf of the company, *as if* their powers were derived from statute. The connection of director authority to the company constitution is, she argues, an 'anomaly brought about by the drafters of the original Joint Stock Companies Act 1856 using as a precedent existing deeds of settlement'.[54] It has no further significance than that, and directors' practice in Britain does not differ from those of other jurisdictions. Indeed, she argues, there is a constant theme throughout company law history of the centrality of the management powers of the board of directors.

Historically, she argues, a separate management in control of the business was an attractive proposition for investors. This was evident in the popularity of corporations chartered to engage in merchant trade from the 16th century. And, when the Bubble Act 1720 restricted chartered corporations,[55] many investors continued to require a centralised management arrangement and did so using the deed of settlement company form. This was a legal innovation which created an unincorporated association with trustees and a separate management (directors) who acted on behalf of the association. The directors were appointed through the deed and derived their powers from the deed, which generally included the power to manage all of the company's affairs. These forms of organisations flourished, argues Watson, precisely because investors wanted a central management. They did so despite the strong stand taken against them by the judiciary.[56] Deed of settlement companies continued to be popular after the repeal of the Bubble Act, and although they were treated in common law as partnerships, in terms of their management, there was little to separate unincorporated joint stock companies from the incorporated form. Watson cites an explicit statement of this in *Burnes v Pennell*,[57] where the House of Lords stated that '[a]ll who have dealing with a joint stock company know that the authority to manage the business is conferred upon the directors, and that a shareholder, as such, has no power to contract for the company. For this purpose it is wholly immaterial whether the company is incorporated or unincorporated.'[58]

---

[53] Vasudev and Watson (n. 51), 48.

[54] Ibid, 49.

[55] This was a political outcome of the Bubble Act rather than a legal one. Charters could be granted but Parliament was wary of doing so.

[56] Although it should be noted that this strong stand only really appears in the 19th century with *Rex v Dodd* 103 Eng. Rep. 670 (1808).

[57] (1849) 2 HL Cas 497.

[58] Vasudev and Watson (n. 51), 54.

Watson illustrates her argument by an examination of the raft of company legislation passed in the 19th century. The Joint Stock Companies Act 1844 empowered directors to act. The Act included no standard articles of association and therefore no assertion of shareholders giving authority to directors through that mechanism. The Companies Clauses Consolidation Act 1845 redressed that somewhat by including a provision that directors exercised their powers subject to the power of the members at annual general meeting. The Joint Stock Companies Act 1856 did not include that section. However, neither did it contain the 1844 provision bestowing the power to manage on directors. Instead the power to manage was put into the articles of association. So, at first, directors' authority derived from statute, then the statute identified the general meeting as bestowing authority and finally, in 1856, the law took the current position that authority to act is derived from the articles of association. So why did the legislature turn from statute to articles?

Watson argues that the corporate form came to be seen as an important vehicle for outside investment, having previously been viewed as a legal form that needed to be highly regulated. The 1844 Act contained so many requirements that 76 per cent of proposed registrations under the Act were abandoned before completion. The 1856 Act was intended to make incorporation much easier and to mirror the organisational form which had succeeded in facilitating outside investment, the established deed of settlement company. Watson argues that from the 1856 Act there was 'a statutory adoption of the deed of settlement form'[59] because the legislature wanted to legitimate large investment vehicles. Companies formed under the 1856 Act were clearly intended to attract investment and to compete with continental legal forms that were enabling of investors. The Act was therefore always conceived as creating a business form for many investors, raising large sums of capital and managed by a separate board. The legislature envisaged a separation of ownership from control model – a public company. That the clause empowering directors to act was in the articles rather than a freestanding section merely reflected the long-established drafting method of deed of settlement companies. The later use of incorporation under the Companies Acts for small concerns as private companies was a 'happy' chance in which a factual reuniting of ownership and control took place. Watson concludes that the derivation of director power through the articles is an historical anachronism which most common law jurisdictions have abandoned in favour of statutory powers.[60] This anachronism has more recently gained much ideological significance in the works of those claiming that shareholders are the owner-principals and that directors are the shareholders' agents. However, Watson maintains, the law in fact treats directors' powers and duties as statutory powers and duties.[61]

Whatever one might think about the anomalous nature of the articles of association, shareholders do, in fact, retain a great deal of legal power in respect of the

[59] Ibid, 56.
[60] She notes the New Zealand Companies Act 1993.
[61] As in the UK Companies Act 2006, ss. 171–177.

articles. Changes to the constitution (including those to the articles) are made by a shareholder resolution, usually by a special resolution. Shareholders may vote to change the name of the company.[62] A company may only amend its articles of association by special resolution,[63] unless they have been 'entrenched' either at the company's formation[64] or by an amendment to the articles following unanimous agreement by the shareholders.[65] Shareholders may still, however, amend an entrenched provision by unanimous agreement.[66] Furthermore, members can resist some alterations. They are not, for example, bound by any alteration to the articles made after they become members if it requires them to subscribe for more shares or to increase their liability to contribute to the company.[67]

Shareholders' consent is sought at major turning points or changes in a company's life. Their consent is required if the company is changing from a public to a private company, or vice versa.[68] Consent is required for an allotment of shares or disapplication of pre-emption rights[69] and for a reduction of share capital, repurchase of shares or giving financial assistance. Shareholders' approval is required for defensive measures taken once takeover is imminent.[70] The Listing Rules require shareholder consent for Class 1 transactions – acquisitions exceeding one quarter of the company's assets, transactions entered into by directors with their company and some share option schemes and long-term incentive plans.[71]

Shareholders' consent is required for a range of transactions between directors and the company.[72] Civil remedies are imposed in respect of a failure to get members' approval for transactions or loans or service contracts. These sections also stipulate the consequences of not gaining member consent. Long-term service contracts (over two years) require member approval,[73] and failure to get this approval will allow the company to terminate the contract at any time following reasonable notice. In respect of substantial property transactions,[74] members' approval is required when the company buys or sells a non-cash asset from or to a director of the company or a director of its holding company, or from or to a person connected with a director of the company.[75] Under Listing

---

[62] Companies Act 2006, s. 78 following a special resolution.

[63] Ibid, s. 21

[64] Ibid, s. 22(2)(a).

[65] Ibid, s. 22(2)(b).

[66] Ibid, s. 22(3)(a) or by a court order under s. 22(3)(b).

[67] Ibid, s. 25.

[68] Ibid, ss. 90 and 97.

[69] Ibid, ss. 561 and 567.

[70] The Takeover Panel, *The City Code on Takeovers and Mergers (The Takeover Code)*, Rule 21.3 <http://www.thetakeoverpanel.org.uk/the-code>.

[71] Financial Conduct Authority (FCA), *The Listing Rules*, Rule 9.4 <http://fshandbook.info/FS/html/FCA>.

[72] Under the Companies Act 2006, ss. 188–226, transactions which require the approval of members are drawn together in one chapter.

[73] Ibid, ss. 188 and 189.

[74] Ibid, s 191 defines substantial as 10 per cent of the company's net assets and more than £5,000 or the transaction is worth more than £100,000.

[75] Ibid, s. 190. Without approval the transaction is voidable unless restitution is impossible (ibid, s. 195).

Rule 11, shareholder approval is required if a party to the transaction is a 10 per cent vote holder.

Loans, quasi-loans and credit transactions require member approval. Payments for loss of office will only be valid with member approval and this includes compensation or 'golden handshakes'.[76] Unapproved payment is held on trust for the company, and the director who authorised the payment must indemnify the company. Although directors may make provisions for employees or ex-employees on cessation or transfer of the business, they may not rely on this section to make payments for themselves or to former directors or to shadow directors. Such payments may only be made following a resolution of members unless articles allow such authorisations to be made by the board.[77] Political donations require member consent and this covers payments to registered political parties, independent candidates and organisations.[78] Finally, where there is conflict of interest between the director personally and the interests of company under section 175 (corporate opportunities), member approval is required for the director to avoid liability.

In setting out many of the key instances when shareholder approval is required, it may be feasible to argue that the law gives shareholders the power one would attribute to owners. Thus shareholders are the owners by dint of their legal powers. On the other hand, authority to act on behalf of the company is possessed by the directors either through the (anachronistic – as Watson claims) articles of association or by statute. And, as the cases noted earlier show, a director's authority is to be exercised for the benefit of the company and not just the shareholders.

Shareholders are not involved in managing the day-to-day business of the company. They invest in a business undertaken by others. As such they possess legal powers that are appropriate to outside investors but not powers appropriate to owners of the whole undertaking. This includes powers relating to the protection of the company, such as ensuring the 'trustees' do not diminish the company's assets either through self-dealing or by making unreasonable and substantial changes to the company capital. As I will argue in the next chapter, shareholders' legal powers as they stand are undesirable (at least in respect of large companies) and have a highly deleterious effect on corporate governance. However, even as the law stands, the powers that shareholders possess are mechanisms to promote and protect the interests of a particular financial investment. This is enabled either directly in respect of powers to thwart a proposed variation of their rights, or indirectly by rights to ensure that the assets which produce the profits (in which they do have a property interest) are protected.

---

[76] Ibid, ss. 215–222.
[77] Ibid, s. 247.
[78] Ibid, s. 367.

PROPOSITION 3: SHAREHOLDERS ARE THE OWNERS BECAUSE THEY CONTRIBUTE CAPITAL TO THE COMPANY

The final proposition on the question of shareholder ownership is that shareholders are the owners because they contribute the capital which is the productive assets of the company and without which the company would not exist. Their entitlement as owners comes from their contribution to company capital. They are owners because the company is the embodiment of their financial contribution and they are entitled to expect management to protect and enhance that investment in their interest, as owners. No other person connected to the company is connected by dint of their contribution to capital. Employees contribute their labour for a wage, creditors contribute loans in the expectation that the repayment agreement will be met, suppliers expect payment for deliveries in line with their contract with the company. Shareholders, however, contribute capital in exchange for ownership rights. This potentially powerful argument is based on, essentially, a contractual relationship, and does not rely on anything outside a simple exchange relation. However, it is wrong, and it is wrong because, for the most part, shareholders do not contribute capital to the company.

First, the vast majority of shares owned are bought on the secondary share market. The initial share offerings which could be said to constitute a company's start-up capital or expansion capital is a tiny proportion of the whole share market. Furthermore, companies as a whole *buy back* more shares which are in issue than the amount of shares which are offered as initial share offerings. '[I]n 2009 ... 214 UK companies distributed cash by repurchasing stock.'[79] Increasingly, over the last 30 years, companies have relied on debt to expand and not equity. They have also relied on debt to finance takeover activity.

It is an interesting phenomenon that as management has been under increasing pressure to enhance shareholder value, it has engaged in an activity which undermines part of the shareholders' claim to ownership status. Since the late 1970s when corporate governance imperatives shifted to shareholder primacy, buy backs were liberally utilised as a method for enhancing share values. They both increase dividends by decreasing the number of shares to which dividend accrues and enhance the value of those shares as dividend earners and as residual claims on company assets. Working on figures in the United States, William Lazonick shows that during the 1950s–1970s the pay-out ratio (the ratio of dividends to after-tax adjusted corporate profits) averaged at about 40 per cent, still high, he notes, by international standards. However, from the late 1970s onwards the pay-out ratio significantly increased. In 1980, when profits declined by 17 per cent, dividends rose by 13 per cent, a pay-out ratio of 57 per cent.[80] Pay-out ratios were

---

[79] M. Siems and A. de Cesari, 'The Law and Finance of Share Repurchases in Europe' (2012) 12 *Journal of Corporate Law Studies* 33, 46.
[80] Henwood's work also concurs with these figures. D. Henwood, *Wall Street: How It Works and For Whom* (Verso, 1998), p. 73.

further enhanced through buying back of shares using profit, so that in most of the 1980s more stock was retired than issued. In 1987, following the crash, there were 777 corporate announcements of buy backs. 'In 1989, when dividends had risen to $134.4 billion, stock repurchases had increased to over $60 billion, increasing the effective pay-out ratio to over 81 per cent.'[81] Similarly, Mitchell notes that companies 'spent more money on stock buy outs ... than on investment in capital production'.[82]

Henwood vigorously debunks the myth that shareholders capitalise the company:

'... the stock market contributes virtually nothing to the financing of outside investment. Between 1901 and 1996, net flotations of new stock amounted to just 4% of nonfinancial corporations' capex. That average is inflated by the experience of the early years of the century, when corporations were going public in large number; new stock offerings were equal to 11% of real investment from 1901 through 1929. Given the wave of takeovers and buybacks in recent years, far more stock has been retired than issued; new stock offerings were –11% of capex between 1980 and 1997, making the stock market, surreally, a negative source of funds.

But if you exclude that period, and look at only 1946-1979, stocks financed just 5% of real investment. This is true of most other First World countries; in the Third World, the figures are more like those of the early twentieth century in the U.S., but again that's because firms are going public for the first time, not because existing ones are raising funds through fresh stock offerings.'[83]

Using buy backs to enhance shareholder value is also on the increase in the EU, as a recent articles indicates:

'Over the years, the importance of repurchases as transactions to distribute cash to shareholders has dramatically increased both in the US and in the EU. For instance, Grullon and Muchaely find that in the US the ratio between repurchases and dividends was equal to 13.1% in 1980 and amounted to a far larger 113.1% in 2000. US evidence for more recent years is offered by Skinner, who documents that firms paid out more cash through repurchases than dividends in 2005. For the EU, von Eije and Megginson report that the share of repurchases in total payout (ie the sum of repurchases and dividends) increased from 17% in 1989 to 34% in 2005.'[84]

In this piece Siems and de Cesari assess the effect of the EU law on market abuse in relation to share repurchases. Such purchases (or at least open market stock repurchases) became subject to regulation because they put information into the market in a way which may have the effect of distorting the market. Siems and de

---

[81] W. Lazonic and M. Sullivan, 'Maximising shareholder value: a new ideology for corporate governance' (2000) 29(1) *Economy and Society* 13, 23.
[82] L.E. Mitchell, 'Financialism: A (Very) Brief History' <http://papers.ssrn.com/sol3/papers.cfm?abstract_id= 1655739> p.10.
[83] Henwood (n. 80), 72–3.
[84] Siems and de Cesari (n. 79), 37.

Cesari found that buy-back activity actually increased after the introduction of regulation to arrest market abuse.

The EU Market Abuse Directive (MAD)[85] was introduced to add to the rules on insider trading rules relating to manipulating the market price of shares. Thus the Directive might have deterred buy backs. To redress this, the European Commission passed a Regulation on buy backs.[86] Prior to MAD, some EU countries had no general prohibition on market manipulation at all (Ireland, Czech Republic, Netherlands), and in others the 'safe harbour'[87] provision was very wide or the law was generally more liberal (France, Greece, Sweden, UK, Bulgaria, Italy, Romania). In the other countries the rules were stricter. Latvia always defined repurchases as market manipulations, and in Austria, Denmark, Lithuania, Malta, Portugal and Spain there was a prohibition and no 'explicit safe harbour'. The authors expected that after the Regulation, there would be decreases of buy backs in the former countries and increases in the latter countries. In fact, in The Netherlands, France, the UK and Italy (as well as those expected to increase their buy-back activity, Austria, Denmark, Portugal and Spain), 'the proportion of companies that execute repurchases become larger after the MAD Implementation year'. Furthermore, 'for a substantial number of countries, the increases in companies' propensities to purchase own stock are very large. Relative positive changes are particularly noteworthy in Italy (+420% = (26% – 5%)/5%), France (+300%) and Austria (+93%).'[88] The writers put this down to a 'legal placebo effect',[89] or legal certainty in uniformity which was absent before MAD. They argue that, 'in the present case, it can be said that the passing of the new EU-wide safe harbour had sent a positive signal regarding repurchases, making companies more aware about the possibilities to repurchase their own shares.'[90]

While the legal placebo argument may have some mileage, the overwhelming reason for increases in buy backs is the pursuit of shareholder value. Share buy backs are a tried and tested mechanism for returning value to shareholders, and companies that adhere to shareholder primacy governance are likely to avail themselves of them. Companies in the UK and US were first to do so; they are now being followed by companies in Europe. Share buy backs promote shareholder value but paradoxically they remove a key justification for the pursuit of that shareholder value, that of shareholders contributing the working capital of the company and therefore being the owners. This factual basis for this argument has been absent in the UK and US for many decades. The *Financial Times* recently reported that in

---

[85] 2003/6/EC (MAD).
[86] European Commission Regulation 2273/2003 on buy-back programmes and stabilisation of financial instruments.
[87] A 'safe harbour provision' refers to a legal provision that specifies that certain conduct will be deemed not to violate a given rule.
[88] Siems and de Cesari (n. 79), 47.
[89] Ibid, 56.
[90] Ibid.

2013 US companies in the S&P 500 index spent $448.1bn on share repurchases.[91] At the end of the year Kraft Foods, 3M and Boeing revealed their plans for extensive share repurchases. Many companies are making large profits which they do not want to spend on actual production. It is safer to enhance share value by share repurchases. So with the equity market playing small part in contributing capital to the company, a new role is being carved out for shareholders to justify their ownership claims. This we will examine in the next chapter.

CONCLUSION

During the 19th century the share became an independent property form which was separate from the company assets. The changes in the law which enabled it to become independent, discussed here, include the reconceptualisation of the property of the share[92] and the concretisation of the boundaries of the property of share which also enabled a more accurate valuation. This has enabled the share to become highly transferable, a financial product quickly exchangeable on the stock market. As such, the share has enabled investors to chase profit and to avoid being bound to the ups and downs of a particular business. Indeed, as noted in the following chapter, the norm for investors is to spread investment widely and to exit rapidly if the market signals poor company performance.

However, in the process of developing a quickly transferable property form which enables investors to chase the profits of business, the issue of ownership has been left somewhat messy and unresolved. The law is clear that shareholders do not own the company, yet it is considered common sense to call them the owners. Indeed, it may even be dangerously radical to suggest that they are anything less than owners. This is true today, more than ever, as the discussion on shareholder stewardship in the next chapter indicates. And, should anyone think that this debate is of academic interest only, this recent event shows how acutely important and controversial it really is.[93]

In Norway from February 2013, abating sometime in April, an intense and often torrid debate played out involving the two largest financial newspapers, *Dagens Næringsliv* and *Finansavisen,* and sister paper *Kapital*[94] (used for the scandalous and utterly baseless 'revelations'), numerous lawyers, shareholders, chief executives, Oslo University and other miscellaneous commentators. Most of the participants lined up to accuse one Oslo University academic, Professor Beate Sjåfjell, of numerous intellectual, moral and political wrongs. She was accused

---

[91] 'US group's share buybacks at highest level since financial crisis', Arash Massoudi and Ed Crooks, *Financial Times*, 19 December 2013, p. 17.

[92] See Williston (n. 4).

[93] I am very grateful to Professor Beate Sjåfjell for her assistance in preparing this section of the conclusion.

[94] For a list of all the newspapers involved in this debate, see <http://www.jus.uio.no/forskning/omrader/ selskaper/arrangementer/selskapsrettsforumet/050313-eierskapsmyten-forum.html>.

inter alia of professional incompetence, inappropriate use of professional status to promote dubious political opinions, mysteriously fixing the promotion system and of having a flawed doctoral thesis. All of these accusations were pure fiction. Many participants called for her resignation or, at minimum, for the university to censor her opinions. *Finansavisen* editor Trygve Hegnar stated (more than once) in his newspaper that Professor Sjåfjell was a witch who would have been burnt at the stake in the 16th century. Journalists called her colleagues and friends for any negative or salacious personal insights. Apparently, what Professor Sjåfjell had to say was too controversial and too wrong-headed to be exposed to the public and she should be stopped by any means. So who is Professor Sjåfjell and what was she saying?

Professor Sjåfjell is a softly spoken, hard-working scholar who works in the field of company law. An experienced and committed teacher, she has written numerous articles and books and leads a highly regarded research project on the subject. Her 'sins' were to articulate the company law position on shareholders in Norway (a subject she is more than qualified to speak on), much in the way as has been set out in this chapter. To view the bundle of rights possessed by share-holders as *not sufficient* to constitute the entitlement of owners of the whole enterprise (the position she takes) was a heresy that hit right at the heart of landed interests. Landed interests responded by showing they would stop at nothing to muddy the name of a respectable academic in order to promote their ideological position.

Oslo University did not in fact censor Professor Sjåfjell's views though the debate had persistently posed the question of 'whether professors and other academics ought to be free to put their academic status and authority behind state-ments in the public realm also in cases where such utterances involve political issues.'[95]

Tom Colbjørnsen President at BI Norwegian Business School noted that although he and Oslo University had been pressed to reprimand Professor Sjåfjell, they had rightly declined to do so. He drew a distinction between Professor Sjåfjell's public views (which were her own and should not be interfered with by her employer) and her academic views, which were monitored by open debate and the desire to retain academic reputation.[96]

My own view is that when one is discussing one's area of expertise there is no proper distinction between a political and professional position. Academic research is the pursuit of truth and often that truth has political implications. Allowing a distinction between the political and the professional is dangerous to the process of debate and the betterment of society which that debate seeks. In

---

[95] Norwegian Business School, *Academic Freedom in the Public Realm* (2013) <http://www.bi.edu/about-bi/The-organisation/Presidents-page/Presidents-blog/Dates/2013/04/academic-freedom-in-the-public-realm/>.
[96] Ibid.

Professor Sjåfjell's words, 'Trying to stop an academic debate by asking for censorship is the opposite of what we need to achieve progress.'[97]

The debate continues.

Further Reading

The argument that shareholders cannot be considered the owners of the company has many proponents. I tend to cite Adolf Berle in *Modern Corporation* (Transaction Publishers, 1991) on this point but other key publications include T. Veblen, *Absentee Ownership Business Enterprise in Recent Times: The Case of America* (Transaction Publishers, 1977, first published 1923).

S. Bainbridge, 'Director Primacy and Shareholder Disempowerment' (2006) 119(6) *Harvard Law Review* 1735.

L. Bebchuk, 'The Case for Increasing Shareholder Power' (2005) 118(3) *Harvard Law Review* 833.

L. Bebchuk, 'The Myth of the Shareholder Franchise' (May 2007) 93(3) *Virginia Law Review* 675.

J. Charkham and A. Simpson, *Fair Shares: The Future of Shareholder Power and Responsibility* (Oxford University Press, 1999).

L.C.B. Gowe, 'Some Reflection between British and American Corporation Law' (1956) *Harv. L.* 9(8) 1372

P. Hall and K. Thelen, 'Institutional Change in Varieties of Capitalism' (2009) 7(1) *Socio-Economic Review* 7.

L. Stout, 'Bad and Not-So-Bad Arguments For Shareholder Primacy' (2001–2002) 75 *Southern California Law Review* 1189.

L.E. Talbot, 'Why shareholders shouldn't vote: a Marxist-progressive critique of shareholder empowerment' (2013) 76(5) *Modern Law Review* 791–816.

S. Worthington, 'Shares and Shareholders: Property, Power and Entitlement: Part 1' (2001) 22(9) *The Company Lawyer* 258.

S. Worthington, 'Shares and Shareholders: Property, Power and Entitlement: Part 2' (2001) 22(10) *The Company Lawyer* 307.

---

[97] Ibid.

3

SHOULD SHAREHOLDERS HAVE POWER OVER THE COMPANY?

Over a century ago Veblen wryly noted that shareholders are engaged in the 'pursuit of something for nothing', an inactivity which modern society perversely conceives as superior to getting something from engaging in actual productive activity! In his words, 'Any person who falls short in this pursuit of something for nothing, and so fails to avoid work in some useful occupation, is a shiftless ne'er-do-well; he loses self-respect as well as the respect of his neighbours and is in a fair way to be rated as an undesirable citizen.'[1] However, the current consensus in Europe and in the United States is that shareholders should do a *little* for something and so shareholder power should be increased and it should be exercised forcefully, meaningfully and responsibly by shareholders.[2] I argue here that they should not do more, nor should they have power over the company. Indeed, Veblen's 'something for nothing' scenario is much to be preferred to the current position on shareholder power and activism.

This chapter discusses the initiatives to increase shareholder power as a new (or renewed) approach to corporate governance. I criticise these initiatives on the grounds that shareholders are uniquely *unsuited* to exercise powers within the company if what is sought is governance which will enhance stability, productivity and sustainability – goals which the proponents of this position seek. The first section critically assesses a number of initiatives to increase shareholder power and shareholder monitoring of the company. The second section looks at why shareholders cannot be stewards. The third section considers shareholder empowerment in respect of director remuneration, why the legislation put forward to achieve this in the UK has been watered down and why it was misconceived in any case. The final section considers and describes in detail a current and key paper examining the equity market, corporate governance and the obstacles to shareholder governance, the Kay Review 2012. This is a Review which looks likely, at the point of

---

[1] T. Veblen, *Absentee Ownership: Business Enterprise in Recent Times: The Case of America* (New Edition, Transaction Books, 1997), 13.

[2] Shareholders, in this context, are invariably institutional shareholders and through the chapter they will be referred to as 'shareholders', 'institutional shareholders', 'investors' and 'institutional investors'.

writing, to define reform in the area of shareholder governance in the UK and beyond. This chapter invites the reader to consider the Review in the light of the criticism of the shareholder governance project voiced in the first parts of the chapter and those noted throughout the discussion of the Review.

1. SHAREHOLDER EMPOWERMENT AND GOVERNANCE

a. Can shareholders contribute positively to corporate governance? Or alternatively if directors are the baddies, are shareholders really the goodies?

The financial crisis has invigorated the discussion around the enhanced role that shareholders might play in corporate governance. The belief that shareholders have a positive role to play in corporate governance, and moreover that they might contribute to more sustainable company activity, has taken hold in Europe and in the United States. In this section I will demonstrate how this approach has manifested itself in the UK and in Europe through initiatives and reports since the crisis, which I will describe chronologically. I will argue that these approaches are utterly misguided. Not only should shareholder governance not be pursued, but the existing powers possessed by shareholders (such as voting powers) should be removed. I examine arguments which show why shareholders cannot be trusted with the governance of organisations which affect so many other stakeholders.

The first initiative to recreate shareholder governance in the UK examined here is the Stewardship Code 2010. The idea behind the Stewardship Code is to attempt to define responsibilities for large shareholders and those in the investment chain who act on behalf of shareholders. The Code is intended to inculcate responsible attitudes to investment so that shareholders and their representatives could have a greater, and positive, impact on corporate governance. The first Stewardship Code was introduced following the specific recommendation of the Walker Review[3] that a Code for investors should adopt the 2009 Institutional Shareholders' Committee[4] (ISC) Code on the Responsibilities of Institutional Investors.[5] This Code set out best practice for institutional shareholders when engaging with the companies in which they have invested. It encouraged greater engagement in governance by shareholders. The aim of the ISC Code was to reduce the practices which contributed to the financial crisis, including risky decision making and short-termism. The Financial Reporting Council in its review of

---

[3] The Walker Review, published in 2009, proposed reforms to the governance of banks and other financial institutions post-crisis. It recommended more shareholder involvement in governance monitoring and the adoption of the 2009 ISC Code by institutional shareholders through the United Kingdom corporate governance codes.

[4] Now the Institutional Investor Committee <http://www.iicomm.org/index.htm>.

[5] Institutional Shareholders' Committee Code 2009 <http://www2.warwick.ac.uk/fac/soc/law/research/clusters/regulationandgovernance/govdc>.

the Combined Code opted for this approach and recommended a Stewardship Code which would cement institutional shareholders' role as the company's monitor.[6]

The ensuing Stewardship Code published in 2010 was organised around loose, non-legal language involving expectations, encouragement and principles.[7] The principles, seven in all, require institutional investors to:

'1. publicly disclose their policy on how they will discharge their stewardship responsibilities.
2. have a robust policy on managing conflicts of interest in relation to stewardship and this policy should be publicly disclosed.
3. monitor their investee companies.
4. establish clear guidelines on when and how they will escalate their activities as a method of protecting and enhancing shareholder value.
5. be willing to act collectively with other investors where appropriate.
6. have a clear policy on voting and disclosure of voting activity.
7. report periodically on their stewardship and voting activities.'

Compliance follows the 'comply or explain' model first introduced by the Cadbury Report.[8] Cadbury initiated a process where companies that wished to be listed on the London Stock Exchange must report on how they have complied with the relevant corporate governance code, or if they have not complied they must explain where and why they have not done so. In the context of the Stewardship Code, the 'listing' in not on an exchange but on the Financial Reporting Council's website in which investment firms publish their commitment to the Code.[9] Comply and explain compliance is also required to be evidenced on firms' own websites.

Later that year the European Commission Green Paper on the corporate governance and remuneration policy of financial institutions was published.[10] This set out the key problems which needed to be addressed so that corporate governance could enable stability and sustainability. It noted that the various mechanisms which attempted to ensure good corporate governance (such as the Codes) were not sufficiently specific and the principle-based regime they utilised gave the users

---

[6] Financial Reporting Council (FRC) *Consultation on a Stewardship Code for Institutional Shareholders* (January 2010). No longer available but referred to at <https://frc.org.uk/Our-Work/Codes-Standards/Corporate-governance/UK-Stewardship-Code/Additional-information-on-the-Stewardship-Code.aspx>. Sir David Walker, *A Review of Corporate Governance in UK* banks and other financial industry entities (July 2009) <http://www.audit-committee-institute.be/dbfetch/52616e646f6d4956f9ed6cb8ae5277dbec35c233bab54a5b/walker_review_consultation_160709.pdf>.

[7] Financial Reporting Council (FRC), *The UK Stewardship Code 2010* (July 2010) <https://frc.org.uk/Our-Work/Publications/Corporate-Governance/The-UK-Stewardship-Code.pdf>.

[8] <http://www.ecgi.org/codes/documents/cadbury.pdf>.

[9] Financial Reporting Council (FRC), *UK Stewardship Code Statements* (2012) <http://www.frc.org.uk/Our-Work/Codes-Standards/Corporate-governance/UK-Stewardship-Code/UK-Stewardship-Code-statements.aspx>.

[10] EU Commission Green Paper of 2010 on financial companies' corporate governance and remuneration polices, COM (2010) 284 final.

'too much scope for interpretation'.[11] The rules were non-binding and they failed to be clear about the responsibility to be executed by the users. Boards were poorly monitored and did not exercise or even understand effective risk management.

The Paper was also critical of shareholders, noting their demands for short-term profits and their indifference to the 'company's long-term viability'.[12] As a result, the Paper noted that shareholders 'may even be responsible for encouraging excessive risk-taking in view of their relatively short, or even very short (quarterly or half-yearly) investment horizons'.[13] This was a problem not just in financial companies, but it was a problem evidenced in all companies where there is a presumption of 'effective control by shareholders'.[14] This short-termism in corporate governance goals was also exacerbated by performance-related remuneration for company management, a form of remuneration which is designed to align managers' interests with those of shareholders. As I have argued elsewhere, performance-related pay (in its many forms) intends to make what is good governance for shareholders (short-termism and high profits) good governance for managers. In so doing it incentivises a shift away from the kinds of decisions which enable sustainability because often those decisions do not produce the short-term profits desired by shareholders.[15] The Paper also noted that shareholders were not concerned with actual engagement with corporate governance because it was costly. A combination of portfolios of different shares to spread risk and the assurance that managers were incentivised to pursue shareholder value was (and remains) a much more cost-effective approach for shareholders.

Given this assessment of the nature of shareholders and the incentives of managers, one might have thought that this Paper would suggest ways in which managers may be steered away from pursuing a corporate governance which shareholders required and of reducing the mechanisms by which shareholders could ensure that directors would stick to that agenda, but no. Instead, perversely, the Paper suggested that giving yet more power to shareholders might redress the problem. Institutional shareholders should then be encouraged to utilise this power through mechanisms such as advisory or mandatory voting on director remuneration and to engage in corporate governance. Ways in which they could do so included engaging shareholders through use of discussion platforms, requiring shareholders to disclose their voting practices and the remuneration policy for their financial intermediaries, and finally requiring shareholders to adhere to Stewardship Codes. It also emphasised the importance of Member States establishing mandatory or optional votes on directors' remuneration.

---

[11] Ibid, 6.

[12] For a good review of the literature on how short-termism is the dominant feature of investors, see C. Helms, M. Fox and R. Kenagy, 'Corporate Short-Termism: Causes and Remedies' (2012) 23 *International Company and Commercial Law Review* 45.

[13] COM (2010) 284, 8.

[14] Ibid.

[15] L.E. Talbot, 'Of Insane Forms: Building Societies from Collectives to Management Controlled Organisations to Shareholder Value Organisations', *Journal of Banking Regulation*, pp. 1–36, April 2010.

The EU Commission Corporate Governance Framework Green Paper 2011 which followed the 2010 Paper was specifically focused of the corporate governance of non-financial EU listed companies. The 2011 Paper concurred with the 2010 Paper's analysis of the negative impact of shareholders.[16] It also further developed the critique of the imperatives of the capital market which tended to insist upon short-termism, including that financial intermediaries' effectiveness was tested on their short-term performance.[17] The 2011 Paper, like the 2010 Paper, proposed more transparency between market players and, equally perversely, argued for more shareholder power, and encouragement to exercise that power.[18] While the Paper criticised the inventive structures for financial players as perpetrating destructive short-termism, it did not suggest scrapping them. Instead it suggested more transparency in the incentive structures and more power for institutional investors in relation to these incentives.[19] It concerned itself with the problem of getting shareholders to actively engage in corporate governance while avoiding the charge of 'acting in concert'.[20] Both Papers took the view that by replacing the old shareholder primacy pursuing management with more shareholders, they could encourage a corporate governance which is less shareholder orientated; a curious reversal which sees shareholders as somehow self-sacrificing.

b. Why shareholders cannot be good stewards

In a 2011 paper I argue that the idea of shareholder stewardship is fundamentally misconceived:

'Shareholder stewardship is a paradox because shareholders lack the central quality that underpinned previous conceptions of stewardship, namely a detachment from share ownership and therefore a detachment from a sectional interest in profit. This detachment was thought to enable the steward to pursue a wider public interest.[21] Previous conceptions of stewardship viewed non owning professional management as worthy stewards of the company's best interests, precisely because they *were* non owning, trained professionals.[22] Directors could be good stewards because they were personally motivated by a wide range of concerns including personal achievement, good employee relations, product development and economic stability.[23,24]

---

[16] The EU Corporate Governance Framework (COM (2011) 164), 11.

[17] Ibid, 12.

[18] Ibid, 15.

[19] Ibid, 13.

[20] Ibid.

[21] E.M. Dodd, 'For Whom are Managers Trustees?' (1932) 45 *HLR* 1145.

[22] A.A. Berle, *The American Economic Republic* (Harcourt: Brace and World, 1963).

[23] T. Donaldson and J. Davis, 'Boards and Corporate Performance – Research Challenges and Conventional Wisdom' (1994) 2 *Corporate Governance: An International Review* 151.

[24] L.E. Talbot, 'Polanyi's Embeddedness and Shareholder Stewardship: A Contextual Analysis of Current Anglo-American Perspectives on Corporate Governance', *Northern Ireland Legal Quarterly*, Winter 2011.

Stewardship involves both a desire to be active in corporate governance and a desire to do so for selfless and socially responsible goals. The problem with institutional shareholders in respect of stewardship is that if they are ever active, it is always for selfish and socially irresponsible reasons. Alternatively they are inactive. Pension funds have largely chosen to be inactive because being active is too costly. As Bainbridge says, 'institutional shareholders will prefer liquidity to activism. For fully diversified institutions even the total failure of a particular firm will not have significant effect on their portfolio, and may indeed benefit them to the extent they also hold stock in competing firms.'[25] Being active by monitoring the corporate governance of the firm in which they invest would be expensive and would involve skills which they do not specialise in. The risk of not monitoring an investment is therefore dealt with by having extensive portfolios which spreads risk. Looking at the same phenomenon from the opposite angle, Wong argues that it is excessive portfolio diversification which makes monitoring more difficult. 'Large portfolios ... give rise to difficulties in monitoring – particularly the resource-intensive engagements between institutional investors and boards of directors contemplated by stewardship codes in the UK and other markets – and weaken an "ownership" mind set.'[26]

In the UK, institutional shareholders spread investments throughout all the largest companies. In 2008, 84.3 per cent of pension funds investment in UK equities was invested in the FTSE 100 companies.[27] In the US, Professor Bushee argues that the majority (61 per cent) of institutional investors approach investment in this way.[28] He calls them quasi-indexers, characterised by a highly diversified portfolio and low levels of engagement with companies. Indeed, their inactivity extended to their activity on the equities markets, as Bushee found they were also infrequent traders. Thus in respect of these investors, the market for corporate control can be said to be thoroughly ineffective. In 2008 UK pension funds owned around 12.8 per cent of all UK equity value,[29] and insurance companies 13.4 per cent.[30] So although these institutional shareholders are clearly large, they choose not to be stewards and to engage in any steward-like activity.

Similarly, Bainbridge argues (in respect of US investors) that institutional shareholders do not like to vote and there is virtually no incentive to be activist.[31] He argues that, 'Because institutional investors generally are profit maximizers, they will not engage in an activity where costs exceed its benefits.'[32] Indeed, he argues,

---

[25] S. Bainbridge, 'The Case For Limited Shareholder Voting Rights' (2006) 53 *UCLA L. Rev.* 601, 631.

[26] S. Wong, 'Why stewardship is proving elusive for institutional shareholders' (July 2010) *Butterworths Journal of International Banking and Financial Law* 406, 407.

[27] Office for National Statistics, *Share Ownership Survey 2008*, 9. This is up from the 2006 survey where pension funds held 77.3 per cent in FTSE 100 companies.

[28] B. Bushee, 'The Influence of Institutional Investors on Myopic R&D Investment Behaviour' (1998) 72 *Acct. Rev.* 305.

[29] Office for National Statistics Statistical Bulletin, *Share Ownership Survey 2008*, 2.

[30] Ibid.

[31] Bainbridge (n. 25) at p. 630, quoting B. Black, 'Shareholder Activism and Corporate Governance in the United States', 3 *The New Palgrave Dictionary of Economics and the Law* 459.

[32] Bainbridge (n. 25), 630.

it is in line with efficient capital theories that they are non-activist because 'the best investment approach is passive indexing, which in fact has become a widely followed strategy among both individual and institutional investors'.[33]

The alternative approach to corporate governance taken by institutional shareholders is that of active engagement in order to feed a rapacious appetite for short-term profits at the expense of sustainability. Hedge funds provide the key example of this kind of activity. For example, Bratton's study in the US showed that the strategies used by hedge funds to profit-maximise had the effect of undermining the companies' capital base and created instability. These strategies included increasing leverage, returning capital to shareholders and selling corporate assets.[34] Bushee's study showed that these kinds of investors, which he calls 'transient investors', represent 31 per cent of total institutional investors. Transient investors turned over 70 per cent of their portfolios each quarter year. These sorts of investors were very attendant to what companies were doing, because this enabled them to take a hit and run approach to investment, influencing company decisions for personal gain and then selling. Only a small percentage of investors in Bushee's study were steward-like, the so-called 'dedicated investors' (8 per cent of total institutional investors) whom he defined as those who held onto at least 75 per cent of their stock for at two years.

Another obstacle to institutional investors being good stewards, argues Wong, is that they 'use inappropriate metrics that promote short-termism'. Quarterly reviews of fund managers' performance is the norm and this means that they must make quick returns rather than considered, long-term investments. This has a knock-on effect to the companies in which the fund managers invest, so that 'investment managers focus on delivering short-term returns, including pressuring investee companies to maximise their near-term profits'.[35] Thus where fund managers are used, pressure for short-term profits will prevail. The funds themselves will not engage in governance and their representatives pressure for short-term gains. Furthermore, Wong argues, lengthening the share ownership chain has weakened the 'ownership' mindset and that the increasingly large number of financial intermediaries has 'lessened the sense of accountability between ultimate investor and investee company'.[36] This chain involves its own agency problems throughout, which have resulted in a 'cascading set of performance measures'.[37] These are designed to monitor intermediary performance but instead they increase the number of short-term performance metrics throughout the chain. Far from enabling a more responsible sense of ownership, institutional shareholders have massively increased share turnover. In 1980 the average time to hold shares was five years whereas today it is less than five months.

---

[33] Ibid, 632.

[34] W. Bratton and M. Wachter, 'The Case Against Shareholder Empowerment' (2010) 158 *University of Pennsylvania Law Review* 653.

[35] Wong (n. 26).

[36] Ibid, 407.

[37] Ibid, 408.

Thus the experience of institutional shareholder activity in the UK and the US is that shareholders do not want to be stewards, and the interests that they serve are not the interests of the company. The company is a means of extracting value and whether that undermines the long-term sustainability of the company is of no matter. What institutional shareholders want is liquidity, either because they want to spread their investment widely (as in the case of pension funds and insurance companies) or because they want to leave the company as soon as the maximum value extraction has been achieved, as in the case of active funds. Most institutional shareholders rely on information provided by the market, such as indexing and share price, when making investment decisions, rather than engagement with the company. Institutional shareholders are happy to pay lip service to stewardship but it is simply against their nature to actually act as stewards. Thus it is no surprise that although over 250 asset managers, asset owners and service providers have signed up and stated their support for the Code (designed to promote responsible long-term investment in the company's interest),[38] the Financial Reporting Council admitted in March 2012 that there was little engagement beyond that.[39]

There is much evidence that the Stewardship Code 2010 did not change the behaviours of institutional shareholders and their representatives. For example, the TUC's annual study of the voting of fund managers showed that in the first year after the introduction of the Stewardship Code, there had been no shift from their traditional voting patterns.[40] Traditionally, fund managers (on average) voted against directors' remuneration reports but in favour of proposals to restructure company capital (more complex proposals). Following the Stewardship Code, 43 per cent voted in favour of directors' remuneration reports [41] and 70 per cent voted in favour of proposed changes to company capital.[42] Furthermore, affiliations remained unchanged. Fund managers, such as JP Morgan, tend to vote in favour of management resolutions while others, such as PIRC and Co-operative Asset Management, tend to vote against management.

Yet these figures only cover the 21 respondents to the survey.[43] Larger surveys have revealed much greater inactivity.[44] This indicates that the Stewardship Code has not changed fund managers' behaviours. Those that were inactive are still inactive, and those that were active are still active and still active in the same way.

---

[38] FRC (n. 9). Those signing up were mainly asset managers; there is little interest from pension funds.

[39] Baroness Hogg speech, ICGN conference, 20 March 2012.

[40] Trade Union Congress, Fund Manager Voting Survey (2011) *A survey of the voting and engagement records and processes of institutional investors* < http://www.tuc.org.uk/economy/tuc-20303-f0.cfm>.

[41] Ibid, 55.

[42] Ibid, 59.

[43] The Survey notes that respondents had not changed their approach since the Stewardship Code nor increased resources devoted to stewardship precisely because they thought that they already fulfilled the Code's requirements. The Code was to instruct *other* investors.

[44] PIRC, which looked at the votes in 300 annual general meetings, found that the average vote against remuneration reports was only 7.64 per cent in the first six months of 2012. R. Sullivan, 'Shareholder Spring' Muted', *Financial Times*, 26 August 2012 <http://www.ft.com/cms/s/0/0a1e41c4-ed42-11e1-95ba-00144feab49a.html#axzz24faJwrxv>.

c. Responses to the reality of shareholder stewardship

The lack of progress on making stewards of institutional investors led to a rethink that was incredibly radical, but was treated as if this was a natural and logical development from the previous position. The Financial Reporting Council reconceptualised stewardship as being the art of self-serving. In the 2011 review of the UK Corporate Governance Code and the Stewardship Code,[45] shareholder stewardship was described as enhancing *shareholder* value rather than enhancing and protecting the value of the company in a long-term, sustainable way. Indeed, the consultation document stated that the term stewardship had been mistakenly associated with 'socially responsible investment'.[46]

The Financial Reporting Council reasoned that as institutional investors owed a duty to their beneficiaries and fund managers to their clients, they could only fulfil that duty by enhancing shareholder value. Thus stewardship was *in fact* the pursuit of shareholder value. This is an unsurprising assumption from the perspective of institutional investors; however, the purpose of the Stewardship Code was to go further than the instinctive motivations of institutional shareholders so as to build more sustainability into companies' activity. Stewardship was conceived to redress the motivations which contributed to the financial crisis. Now they were forced to accept the ideological assumption (against all evidence to the contrary) that shareholders would pursue a new form of clear-sighted sensible shareholder value.

In order to properly express the 'true' nature of stewardship, the Financial Reporting Council proposed a small redefinition of stewardship. To that end it proposed that a definition of stewardship should include the objective of 'protecting and enhancing shareholder value' which would underpin all of the Code's principles.[47] Thus, the Stewardship Code 2012 now states that, 'So as to protect and enhance the value that accrues to the ultimate beneficiary, institutional investors should ...'[48], followed by the seven principles.[49]

As an alternative to simply redefining stewardship and carrying on business as usual, Simon Wong set out a number of ways in which the barriers to institutional shareholders being good stewards could be removed.[50] He argues that 'excessive portfolio diversification' makes monitoring more difficult. This is based on a business model of passive funds which could be discouraged through regulation and incentives. Furthermore, by having less diversified portfolios, freeloading would be reduced and genuinely good performers would be rewarded and poorer companies

---

[45] Financial Reporting Council, *Developments in Corporate Governance 2011. The Impact and Implementation of the UK Corporate Governance and the Stewardship Codes* (2011) <http://www.frc.org.uk/FRC/media/Documents/Developments-in-Corporate-Governance-20117.pdf>.

[46] Ibid, 5.

[47] Ibid, 11.

[48] FRC (n. 9).

[49] Principle 4 is reworded so as not to repeat the requirement to escalate stewardship activities to increase shareholder value as this is now otiose given that this goal underpins all the Principles under the 2012 Code.

[50] Wong (n. 26).

would need to improve to gather investment – in other words low diversification would enhance the market in corporate control.

The long investment chain, he argues, instils irresponsibility, but this chain could be quickly reduced by eliminating unnecessary links by having, for example, in-house investment, rather than outsourcing in the chain. Additionally, he argues, fiduciary duties would need to be reconceptualised to enhance qualitative measures such as sustainability rather than quantitative measures such as share value. Fiduciary duties are currently, and problematically, he argues, assessed purely in financial terms. In general, he says, performance indicators should be calculated over longer periods. Wong's approach has many similarities with the Kay Review discussed later in this chapter.

d. Other shareholder empowerment initiatives: director remuneration

Director remuneration has been a hot topic since the early 1990s, if not before. There is a voluminous literature on the subject (some noted in the further reading section), almost exclusively arguing that directors of large companies are paid too much. The concern with remuneration prompted the Greenbury Report on corporate governance[51] and the changes to company law which introduced a shareholder advisory vote in 2002. The latest initiative has dovetailed with the political agreement that shareholders must be empowered. So, partly in response to the EU Green Paper 2011, which noted the importance of shareholder monitoring of director remuneration, the start of 2012 saw every major party in Britain coming out in favour of reform. Labour argued for 'more responsible and better capitalism' and its business secretary, Chuka Umunna, highlighted executive pay as one the principle obstacles to this.[52] The coalition Government announced policies on executive pay, which included introducing new rules requiring companies to publish 'more informative remuneration reports' for shareholders.[53] They proposed that the law should be changed to make director remuneration subject to a mandatory shareholder vote.[54] This would upgrade the 'advisory vote' on the directors' remuneration report under current legislation in place since 2002, now under section 439 of the Companies Act 2006. Vince Cable, the Secretary of State for Business, has been at the forefront of this new weapon in the armoury of radical shareholder governance. He introduced the Enterprise and Regulatory Reform Bill to Parliament in May 2012 (in which the amendment to the Companies Act on director remuneration was included), saying it was designed to address:

---

[51] <http://www.ecgi.org/codes/documents/greenbury.pdf>.
[52] 'Labour calls for "responsible and better" capitalism', *British Broadcasting Corporation* (January 2012) <http://www.bbc.co.uk/news/uk-16454102>.
[53] 'Cable Wants Binding Shareholder Vote on Executive Pay', *The Telegraph* (January 2012) <http://www.telegraph.co.uk/finance/financialcrisis/9033712/Cable-wants-binding-shareholder-vote-on-executive-pay.html>.
[54] 'Cameron Promises Powers to Limit Executives' Pay', *British Broadcasting Corporation* (January 2012) <http://www.bbc.co.uk/news/uk-16458570>.

'the disconnect between directors' pay and long-term company performance by giving shareholders of UK quoted companies binding votes on directors' remuneration. This will encourage shareholders to be more engaged and companies to listen to what they say.'[55]

This new invigoration of shareholder power was further conceived as a way in which the true beneficiaries of corporate activity would finally be able to assert their ownership rights. In the words of Simon Walker, Director General of the Institute of Directors:

'The introduction of a binding shareholder vote on executive pay policy provides shareholders with an excellent opportunity to assert their interests as owners. This is not about having a bun fight for its own sake, but allowing the people who own a company to have a real say over a company's performance against longer-term strategic objectives.'[56]

Yet despite the reformers claim to radically empower shareholders, the end result has been rather lukewarm, with a shareholder vote being required only every three years. Section 79 of the Enterprise and Regulatory Reform Act 2013[57] requires a quoted company to give notice of an intention to move an ordinary resolution to approve a directors' remuneration policy (at the accounts meeting in the first financial year of becoming a quoted company or one held no later than three years after the first financial year). If the remuneration policy was not subject to an advisory vote at the last accounts meeting, the company must give notice to move an ordinary resolution approving it. Any changes to the remuneration policy must be passed by ordinary resolution within three years.

Given the critique of shareholders' influence on the company offered by the chapter thus far, this legislative reform is highly undesirable. However, notwithstanding that, these are not really radical measures to bring directors to heel at all. So why is there such a discrepancy between the zeal of the reformers and its manifestation in law? I would argue that it is this. There is a great deal of difference between the rhetoric of shareholders' empowerment and the reality. The rhetoric states that shareholders are the key element of corporate governance reform and that their activity will create stability and sustainability in the economy and act as a bulwark against financial crisis. The reality is that they are self-serving and the financial crisis is the result of bolstering shareholder interests, not an expression of its failure. Furthermore, if financial crisis resulted from the pursuit of shareholder value when company management lay in the hands of professionals with training and experience, the pursuit of shareholder value by untrained and inexperienced institutions is likely to make the situation much worse. Thus the law in this area is muted, managerial authority is largely

---

[55] U. Flynn, 'Enterprise and Regulatory Reform Bill Published', *Department for Business Innovation & Skills* <http://news.bis.gov.uk/Press-Releases/Enterprise-and-Regulatory-Reform-Bill-published-67a68.aspx>.
[56] Cited in 'Cable floats new proposals to control boardroom pay' (2012) 33(5) *Comp. Law.* 142.
[57] Changes introduced here will form a new section 439A of the Companies Act 2006.

retained but management is focused more keenly on shareholders' self-serving requirements.

In the light of this reality, the notion of shareholder stewardship is reconceived. And, in the light of this reality, shareholder control over directors' remuneration is delayed – every three years, rather than annually. Because when shareholders are judging what they think constitutes good director performance, they are thinking about share value. And, if they are allowed to vote on that every year, directors will continue to pursue short-term horizons. Three years, from the point of view of long-termism, gives some breathing space. Reformers hold onto the rhetoric of shareholder empowerment without operationalising too much of its reality.

I would go further. Directors, like most people doing a job they would choose, are motivated by what they are incentivised to do: doing the job well. If doing the job well is enhancing shareholder value then that is what they will do. If it is being socially responsible then *that is* what they will do. Directors are much more likely stewards than shareholders. Stewardship theory maintains that stewards are motivated by intrinsic rewards that are not easily quantifiable. Shareholders' motivation is very easily quantifiable! Directors, on the other hand, are motivated by a range of human rewards: the enjoyment of power, the pleasure of creativity, the thrill of the deal, the human relationships. This is not to say that shareholders are selfish people per se; it is just that shareholders *qua* shareholders are selfish. It goes with the role. In life we have many roles and some of those roles are less than edifying. To give you an example, in my role as an academic I am passionate and hardworking. I thrill at the detailed interrogation of ideas. I will always do more than is required of me and I love to do so. I am quite the angel! However, when it comes to my role as an investor (or at least someone looking to put a few pounds in a deposit account for the children), I am a total philistine. I want the highest interest rate and that is the sum total of my analytical and moral interest in the matter. Investors *qua* investors will always be at their worst. However, if you pay directors to hold the balance of power within the organisation, appropriately rewarding all the interests, in the context of a system which gives them all a voice, they will do that well. In the next section I consider one of the initiatives to effectively retain a shareholder-orientated system while locating and redressing mechanisms in the system which contribute to short-termism.

2. THE KAY REVIEW OF UK EQUITY MARKETS AND LONG-TERM DECISION MAKING (FINAL REPORT, JULY 2012)

a. Though shareholders are driven by short-termism, can they be encouraged to embrace long-termism?

In June 2011 Vince Cable announced that the economist Professor John Kay would undertake a major review of the UK equity market. The purpose was to ensure that the long-term interests of shareholders (represented by pension and insurance funds) were protected and to address the problem of short-termism by investors such as hedge funds. The overall aim was to ensure sustainability in the economy by enabling long-term investment projects such as the development of new technologies. In Vince Cable's words, 'In particular, we need to examine how the equity investment regime can be recalibrated to support the long-term interests of companies and the underlying beneficiaries such as pension fund members.'[58]

In July 2012, after just over a year of consultation and research, the Kay Review Final Report was published. The Review made an extensive assessment of the characteristics of the UK equity market that leads it to short-termism and made recommendations as to how the equity market might be encouraged to 'support sustainable long-term value creation' instead.[59]

The Review argues that short-termism in the equity market encourages undesirable decision making in business, which it summarises as 'a tendency to underinvestment, whether in physical assets or in intangibles such as product development, employee skills and reputation with customers, and as hyperactive behaviour by executives whose corporate strategy focuses on restructuring, financial re-engineering or mergers and acquisitions at the expense of developing the fundamental operational capabilities of the business.'[60]

The Review identifies two key issues which may redress this short-termism. First, the re-establishment of trust between market players and, secondly, the realignment of the currently misaligned incentives of those market players. They are seen as interrelated. The Review notes that the equity market is not (and indeed has not been for some time) a significant source of financing for companies. In the previous chapter this was noted as a reason for debunking the idea that shareholders should be called the owners because they contributed the working capital. The Kay Review takes a different position. It argues that this development means that the role of the market (which includes shareholders) should now be that of governance and stewardship. The purpose of the market should be to monitor how capital is utilised within companies, rather than how capital is allocated between companies. Having reconceptualised the role of investors thus, the Review then sets out why doing so is problematised by the fragmentation of ownership relations within companies, which has seen a huge growth in intermediaries engaging in the exchange of securities, and with the rise of foreign investors. It rightly notes that this fragmentation has been viewed as unproblematic because of bad theory. This bad theory is the efficient market hypothesis which, it explains, has exacerbated the market's tendency to short-termism and lack of long-term investment. In their words of the Review's authors:

---

[58] T. Bawden, 'Vince Cable Appoints Top Economist to Review UK Equity Markets', *The Guardian* (June 2011) <http://www.guardian.co.uk/business/2011/jun/21/corporate-governance-stock-markets>.

[59] Department for Business, Innovation and Skills, The Kay Review of UK Equity Markets and Long-Term Decision Making – Final Report (2012), p. 9 <http://www.bis.gov.uk/assets/biscore/business-law/docs/k/12-917-kay-review-of-equity-markets-final-report.pdf>.

[60] Ibid, 10.

'We question the exaggerated faith which market commentators place in the efficient market hypothesis, arguing that the theory represents a poor basis for either regulation or investment. Regulatory philosophy influenced by the efficient market hypothesis has placed undue reliance on information disclosure as a response to divergences in knowledge and incentives across the equity investment chain. This approach has led to the provision of large quantities of data, much of which is of little value to users. Such copious data provision may drive damaging short-term decisions by investors, aggravated by well-documented cognitive biases such as excessive optimism, loss aversion and anchoring.'[61]

The Kay Review Principles therefore are orientated around establishing meaningful and responsible relationships between all market players, underpinned by principles of stewardship, which the Review assumes involves a high level of long-termism, notwithstanding that the 2012 Stewardship Code seems to have moved away from that assumption.[62] It emphasises that a director's duty is to the company – much in the terms described in *Percival* and *Dodge*, discussed in Chapter 2. It also emphasises that a financial intermediary's duty is to their client. However, the Review assumes that there is no conflict in these two duties and that somehow, ultimately, the financial intermediary is not interested in high returns as soon as possible but has a conjoined interest with directors in the long-term productive health of the company in which they have invested. The use of the phrase 'generally prevailing standards of decent behaviour' makes many Panglossian assumptions.

In terms of concrete recommendations to underpin trust and stewardship, the Review identifies the adoption of existing standards by all intermediaries and company directors, and for regulatory authorities to apply fiduciary standards to all actors in the investment chain from directors to fund managers. The recommendations specific to company directors is that they consult long-term investors over appointments and disengage from the sorts of activities which encourage short-termism in investors, such as announcements. The Review further recommends that directors adopt remuneration packages which are linked to the achievement of long-term goals.

The problem with these recommendations seems to be that the Review does not have a solution to the likely scenario of directors consulting investors and those investors choosing short-term profits over long-term profits. Does the director ignore the shareholder, and if so at what cost to that director given the greater powers bestowed on shareholders, such as in the recent reform of section 459 noted above. Furthermore, the privileging of long-term investors over short-term investors seems to fly in the face of the company law premise and doctrine that all shareholders are equal. While I am all for flying in the face of doctrine, there seems to be no recognition that this is what is being proposed and that it will present profound difficulties.

---

[61] Ibid, 11.
[62] L.E. Talbot, 'Why shareholders shouldn't vote: a Marxist-progressive critique of shareholder empowerment' (2013) 76(5) *Modern Law Review* 791–816.

Kay Review Principles

1. All participants in the equity investment chain should act according to the principles of stewardship, based on respect for those whose funds are invested or managed, and trust in those by whom the funds are invested or managed.

2. Relationships based on trust and respect are everywhere more effective than trading transactions between anonymous agents in promoting high performance of companies and securing good returns to savers taken as a whole.

3. Asset managers can contribute more to the performance of British business (and in consequence to overall returns to their savers) through greater involvement with the companies in which they invest.

4. Directors are stewards of the assets and operations of their business. The duties of company directors are to the company, not its share price, and companies should aim to develop relationships with investors, rather than with 'the market'.

5. All participants in the equity investment chain should observe fiduciary standards in their relationships with their clients and customers. Fiduciary standards require that the client's interests are put first, that conflict of interest should be avoided, and that the direct and indirect costs of services provided should be reasonable and disclosed. These standards should not require, nor even permit, the agent to depart from generally prevailing standards of decent behaviour. Contractual terms should not claim to override these standards.

6. At each stage of the equity investment chain, reporting of performance should be clear, relevant, timely, related closely to the needs of users and directed to the creation of long-term value in the companies in which savers' funds are invested.

7. Metrics and models used in the equity investment chain should give information directly relevant to the creation of long-term value in companies and good risk adjusted long-term returns to savers.

8. Risk in the equity investment chain is the failure of companies to meet the reasonable expectations of their stakeholders or the failure of investments to meet the reasonable expectations of savers. Risk is not short-term volatility of return, or tracking error relative to an index benchmark, and the use of measures and models which rely on such metrics should be discouraged.

9. Market incentives should enable and encourage companies, savers and intermediaries to adopt investment approaches which achieve long-term returns by supporting and challenging corporate decisions in pursuit of long-term value.

10. The regulatory framework should enable and encourage companies, savers and intermediaries to adopt such investment approaches. (Kay Review, p. 12)

In respect of investors, the Review recommends the creation of an investors' forum 'to facilitate collective engagement by investors'. Financial intermediaries should make full disclosure of their fees and all income earned from stock lending, and they should align their remuneration and incentive policies with the (assumed) long-term interest of clients. In respect of government and government-related organisations, the Department for Business, Innovation and Skills (BIS) should keep the effectiveness of merger activity under review and the Law Commission should assess how fiduciary duties can be applied to financial intermediaries. Regulators along with government should review their metrics and models of assessment including risk assessment models, so as to avoid a slavish, uncritical attachment to one model. Finally, the government should find a 'cost effective means for individual investors to hold shares directly on an electronic register'.[63]

For all of the above, quarterly reporting obligations should be removed and effective, meaningful 'narrative reporting' should be used.

b. The Kay Review on why companies have become wedded to short-termism

The Review highlights what it calls 'hyperactivity' as the root cause of short-termism, something that is manifested in the decisions directors make in respect of restructuring or merger activities right through to the hyperactivity of high frequency traders. Hyperactivity is designed to achieve dramatic short-term results with high rewards. The result of this has been a downward trend in research and development and an increase in financial holdings. Indeed, finance and financial holdings have come to replace productive assets. The Review looks at the examples of ICI and GEC, whose business trajectories went from being established industries to ones dominated by the imperatives of hyperactivity. In the 1990s both bowed to pressures to enhance financial, as distinct from productive targets. However, in both cases, their failure to reach productive targets ultimately led to a failure to achieve in the former too. Neither company exists today. 'Both companies reacted to weaknesses in their operating activities by trading in businesses rather than by trading in chemicals or electrical goods. Both were influenced in these decisions by external financial advice and by market perceptions of their activities as reflected in the rating of their stock.'[64]

Following other similar examples offered by the Review of this shift to financialisation or of risky profit-enhancing strategies, the Review concluded that shareholders were complicit in these decisions. This is quite right and I have often argued that it is wrong to characterise these share value-enhancing activities as driven by managerial greed, or some inherent recklessness. At root it is a response to shareholder demand.[65] However, what is more curious is the Review's conclusion that if shareholders' engagement with directors was improved, that drive for long-term strategies would also follow. The Review states that:

'The issue that concerns us is not whether there is too much or too little shareholder engagement. It is whether the messages that managers and shareholders convey to each other, at meetings and through the share price, provide a framework within

---

[63] Kay Review (n. 59), p. 13.
[64] Ibid, p. 18.
[65] Talbot (n. 62).

which companies and their boards can make balanced assessments of the measures needed to promote the success of the company in the long-run. Shareholder engagement is neither good nor bad in itself: it is the character and quality of that engagement that matters.'[66]

It concluded that shareholders would be more likely to engage in governance rather than to utilise the stock market for a quick exit if the communication between directors and shareholders were improved: 'We believe equity markets will function more effectively if there are more trust relationships which are based on voice and fewer trading relationships emphasising exit.'[67] However, it surmised that much of the problem with communication between shareholders and directors arises from structural changes in the way shares are now owned. Increased diversity of ownership and increased liquidity has meant that shareholders have less knowledge of the company and less trust in the company. The distance of shareholders from the company is the result of the rise of equity markets which have facilitated and encouraged diversification and liquidity.

In the past, diversification and liquidity has proved beneficial for both shareholders and companies. It freed shareholders to pursue the greatest returns and it enabled companies to raise capital and attract investment where success was anticipated. However, the Review suggests, this is now an outmoded model for business. First, it is outmoded for shareholders because the intermediation which accompanies liquidity and rapid exchanges have created their own problems: 'capable and knowledgeable intermediation will be costly, and savers who employ intermediaries place their funds in the hands of managers whose interest may not be aligned with their own.'[68] This is what economists call information asymmetry and agency costs. Secondly, while in the past the equity market has been an important mechanism to raise capital and a rational way to move capital to its most effective use, this is no longer the case. Recently the equities market has not been an important source of income for new investment. Mitchell and Lazonick noted the dominance of a debt model for reinvesting from the later 1980s. The Kay Review notes the large companies now have huge retained funds which they can use for reinvestment but do not utilise. And, although there was a small rise in new share issues in 2009, this was largely caused by banks who were required by their regulators to reduce their leverage (and the UK government was the principal provider of such capital).[69] Debt and retained earnings are the most popular form of financing. 'Even companies in sectors that have large capital requirements – such as oil and utilities – make little or no use of primary equity markets, relying instead on debt and internal funding.'[70] The Review argues that the reasons are 'the nature of the financial intermediation itself'.

---

[66] Kay Review (n. 59), 20.
[67] Ibid, 21.
[68] Ibid, 22.
[69] Ibid, 23.
[70] Ibid, 24–5.

Raising finance from shareholders involves engaging in a difficult arrangement because the degree of shareholder separation from the company has created a huge gulf between the profits shareholders expect and the profits the company can reasonably deliver.

Kay argues that these expectation problems derive from the length of the intermediary chain: 'the gulf in expectations results from information asymmetry and principal-agent problems.'[71] Savers do not understand the information given to them, or they are misinformed. This leads to inaccurately valued shares. On the other hand, the attempt to equalise information by having diversified financial institutions which can disseminate the information has seen the rise of an ethos 'which emphasised transactions and trading over relationships'.[72] The transformation from 'voice to exit' in economic relations also permeated to managers who 'came to see themselves as traders engaged in the management of a portfolio of businesses to which they owed no particular attachment'.[73] This was in contrast to the relationships of trust which (apparently) underpinned the City of London and contrary to the closely held ownership of shares still prevalent in the rest of Europe.

There is also a marked decrease in companies buying the shares of other companies. Companies do not seem to be trying to extend the number. As the Office for National Statistics states:

> 'The value of acquisitions in the UK by other UK companies (domestic investment) fell between Q2 and Q3 of 2012, from £1.0 billion to £0.5 billion. This is the lowest quarterly value reported since Q2 2009. The most significant transaction recorded in Q3 2012 was the acquisition of Woodstock Target 10 Limited by Trilliam Bidco Limited.
>
> The number of domestic acquisitions decreased significantly between the second and third quarters of 2012 (Figure 6). There were 47 acquisitions of UK companies by other UK companies in Q3 2012, compared with 79 in Q2 2012. Within these transactions there were 40 acquisitions of independent companies (85% of the total number of deals) and seven transactions by company groups involving their subsidiaries (15%).
>
> Annual comparisons of Q3 data between 2011 and 2012 reflect a sharp decline in domestic M&A activity, where both the number and value of domestic transactions fell considerably. There were 97 deals in Q3 2011 compared with 47 in Q3 2012, the lowest number reported since Q2 2009. This may be evidence of continued caution by UK companies to undertake equity capital transactions during the current economic climate.'[74]

So what we can surmise thus far is this. Companies do not use shareholder investment to reinvest in production, but they pursue short-term returns anyway

---

[71] Ibid, 26.
[72] Ibid, 27.
[73] Ibid, 27.
[74] <http://www.ons.gov.uk/ons/dcp171778_289733.pdf>.

because shareholders, largely through their intermediaries, rapidly exit and sell their shares (bringing down their value) when those returns fall. By engaging in buy-outs and not having new share issues, the value of the remaining shares is enhanced which is also good for shareholder value. Despite this, shareholders feel short-changed, perhaps because of the claims made by various financial interme- diaries throughout the chain – notwithstanding that the system of financial inter- mediaries was designed to pool expertise and maximise returns. So, it seems to me that, objectively speaking, we have a system which, by and large, works best for shareholders,[75] even though they may feel disappointed with the returns and feel that their interests are not being met. Thus, one of the questions must be, will an increased sense of trust that the system is working for them be enough to entice shareholders to be company stewards and long-term investors?

As equity markets are no longer important in terms of effective allocation of capi- tal (although that could be encouraged still), the role of the market, through market intermediaries, needs to be reconceived. The Kay Review envisages this role being in the creation of good corporate governance through the adoption of a steward- ship role. 'The effectiveness of modern equity markets depends almost entirely on their effectiveness in promoting these goals of stewardship and governance.'[76]

The Review spends some time assessing the barriers to stewardship of this kind and notes that the changes in the structure of shareholding in the UK are not conducive to old-fashioned hands-on ownership relations. As the Review shows, there have been two key shifts in share ownership patterns. First, a shift from private shareholding to institutional shareholders and, secondly, a shift from institutional shareholding to overseas investors. The current proportion of pension and life insur- ance funds has dropped to around 20 per cent of total equity markets. Foreign investors own over 40 per cent and individual investors own around 11 per cent. However, within those groups, profit is shared by the many financial intermediaries who are appointed for their specialisms. Institutional investors mainly utilise special- ist asset managers; private shareholders frequently hold shares through nominees in nominee accounts'[77] Thus, from company to shareholders, there is likely to be a long chain of intermediaries, which include nominee shareholders who are not the bene- ficiaries, fund managers, fund holders and specialist proxy voting service providers.

Thus the Review states:

> '3.7 The decline in the role of the individual shareholder has been paralleled by an explosion of intermediation. Between the company and the saver are now inter- posed registrars, nominees, custodians, asset managers, managers who allocate funds to specialist asset managers, trustees, investment consultants, agents who "wrap" products, retail platforms, distributors and independent financial advisers.

---

[75] D. Stockman, 'State-Wrecked: The Corruption of Capitalism in America' (2013) *The New York Times*. Article noting the rise in the stock market <http://www.nytimes.com/2013/03/31/opinion/sunday/ sundown-in-america.html?smid=fb-share&_r=0>.
[76] Kay Review (n. 59), 28.
[77] Ibid, 29.

Each of these agents must employ its own compliance staff to monitor consistency with regulation, must use the services of its own auditors and lawyers and earn sufficient to remunerate the employees and reward its own investors.'[78]

The Kay Review takes the view that the rise in intermediaries is partly attributable to the lack of trust within investment, and the need for more monitoring within it. The 'principal driver of the growth of intermediation has been the decline of trust and confidence in the investment chain. The role of custodian came into being because the asset manager could not be trusted to hold shares on behalf of the ultimate shareholder.'[79]

Table 3.1 Historical Trends in Beneficial Ownership (Percentage Held)[80]

	1963	1975	1981	1991	2001	2008	2010
Rest of the world	7	5.6	3.6	12.8	35.7	41.5	41.2
Insurance companies	10	15.9	20.5	20.8	20	13.4	8.6
Pension funds	6.4	16.8	26.7	31.3	16.1	12.8	5.1
Individuals	54	37.5	28.2	19.9	14.8	10.2	11.5
Other	22.6	24.2	21	15.2	13.4	22.1	33.6

However, the Review hints that the fragmentation may not be as complete as the statistics suggest. For example, the foreign owner may be a parent company whose subsidiaries and beneficiaries are still, in fact, 'non foreign'. The Review cites BlackRock, a US firm and the largest asset manager in UK equity market with £530 billion but still managed in London for many UK beneficiaries, as an example of this.[81] Statistics from the Cass Business School survey of ownership in the FTSE 100 showed that 69 per cent of equities were held by charities, financials, government, hedge funds, investment funds, investment trusts, company holdings, and unclassified funds:

'The holdings of these asset managers in UK companies are principally run from London. Major sovereign wealth funds also have London offices. London is the world's largest centre for asset management (although if funds managed from Boston and San Francisco are added to those of New York, the total of funds under management in the United States is greater). Investment in UK business is a relatively small part of that total of funds under management. It is, however, the part of greatest significance for the economic performance of the UK. The dominant players in the equity investment chain today are professional asset managers, and the dominant players in UK equity markets are London based asset managers.'[82]

---

[78] Ibid, 30.
[79] Ibid, 30.
[80] Ibid, Table 1, 31.
[81] Ibid, 31.
[82] Ibid, 32.

Within this latter category, Kay presents useful analysis of the different activities of asset managers, arguing that there is a distinction between asset managers who engage in long-term investment strategies (investors) and traders who attempt to make money through short-term holdings (traders). The latter account for the vast majority of equity market turnover, though they represent a smaller percentage of equity holders. 'Hedge funds, high frequency traders and proprietary traders are responsible for 72% of market turnover (but a small proportion of shareholding).'[83] Problematically, the activity of traders puts pressure on investors to adopt similar value-creating strategies precisely because they deliver what shareholders want, higher short-term returns. This undermines their ability to systematically assess the long-term prospects of companies at a deeper analytical level which would enhance their stewardship skills and the economy as a whole:

> 'from the perspective of long-term decision-making by savers and companies, what matters is value discovery, *i.e.* activity which yields insight into the fundamental value of a company's shares. Investors, in the words of the IMA,[84] *"tend to hold (equities) for the long-term based on their analysis of a company's prospects and underlying performance."* Only the process of analysis can acquaint investors with the long-term prospects of a company, and only as a result of analysis will companies receive relevant signals from the market about the direction of the business.'[85]

c. Kay Review recommendations to encourage shareholder long-termism

The solution to the many real obstacles to long-term investment strategies which are contained within and perpetuated by the market in equities are, the Review argues, resolvable through the re-establishment of trust-based relationships. These would replace impersonal transactions between participants who act on the basis of incentives which tend to enhance short-termism. Taking the term 'investing' to designate long-term investing over the term 'trading' to designate short-termism, the Review seeks to promote investing by engaging trust in each part of the investment chain. To this end the Review makes a number of recommendations.

Recommendation 1: The Stewardship Code should be developed to incorporate a more expansive form of stewardship, focusing on strategic issues as well as questions of corporate governance.[86]

The Review sees the implementation of this as being achieved by shortening the investment chain and encouraging those in the investment chain to act more

---

[83] Ibid, 38.
[84] Investment Management Association.
[85] Kay Review (n. 59), 39.
[86] Ibid, 45.

collectively and to have more expertise; 'relationships should be fewer and deeper'.[87] Changing the market structure, it says, is more effective than regulation. However, regulation and good practice incorporated in the Corporate Governance Code and in the Stewardship Code 'can establish a framework which encourages trust'[88] and punish abuses of trust. The nature of those good practice statements are set out in the second recommendation.

Recommendation 2: Company directors, asset managers and asset holders should adopt Good Practice Statements that promote stewardship and long-term decision making. Regulators and industry groups should take steps to align existing standards, guidance and codes of practice with the Review's Good Practice Statements.[89]

This would be achievable by promoting a 'culture of stewardship throughout the investment chain'[90] but particularly in respect of directors' relationship with the company. In strengthening the investment chain and enhancing asset manager engagement with the long-term prospects of the company, the Review suggests that an independent body should be established so that asset managers can begin to work collectively rather than competitively. This leads the Review to Recommendation 3.

Recommendation 3: An investors' forum should be established to facilitate collective engagement by investors in UK companies.[91]

The remit of this forum is to encourage assets managers to meet the need of both ends of the investment chain: companies and savers, through this forum and through the adoption of the Good Practice statement which is set out on page 72.

On the other hand, asset holders should also adopt a Good Practice statement which would assist asset managers to achieve the aims of long-termism. The Review sets out Good Practice as reproduced on page 73.

Underpinning this re-establishment of relations is the expectation that equity markets will decline in importance and that this will make the relationships between intermediaries all the more important. In line with this approach and with the Stewardship Code, the Review also recommends that companies should 'consult their major long-term investors over board appointments', including non-executive as well as executive positions.[92] The Review also hoped to re-engage small retail investors into the activity of the companies in which they invested by reducing the use of nominee shareholders, and for the government to 'explore the most cost effective means for individual investors to hold shares directly on an

---

[87] Ibid, 46.
[88] Ibid.
[89] Ibid, 48.
[90] Ibid, 48.
[91] Ibid, 51.
[92] Ibid, 63. As noted earlier, there are problems with this approach.

Good Practice Statement for Asset Managers

Asset Managers should...

1. recognise that they are in a position of trust managing client money and should act at all times in the best long-term interests of their clients, informing them of possible conflicts of interest and avoiding these wherever possible.
2. operate within a culture of open dialogue with their clients – building an agreed understanding of investment objectives and risks, which is informed by their investment expertise.
3. provide information to clients, including information on investment performance, in a way which is clear, timely, useable and relevant to the long-term creation of value in the investee companies, and therefore to clients' investment objectives.
4. disclose fully all costs that fall on investors in a way that investors can understand.
5. ensure that income generated from lending securities is rebated in full to the fund, with any related costs disclosed separately.
6. adhere to the investment strategy agreed with clients.
7. prioritise medium to long-term value creation and absolute returns rather than short-term returns from market movements when making investment decisions.
8. build an ongoing relationship of stewardship with the companies in which they invest to help improve long-term performance – recognising that engagement goes beyond merely voting.
9. make investment decisions based on judgments about long-term company performance, informed by an understanding of company strategy and a range of information relevant to the specific company, and avoiding reliance on single measures of performance.
10. be prepared to act collectively to improve the performance of their investee companies.
11. be paid in line with the interests and timescales of their clients. Specifically remuneration should not be related to short-term performance of the investment fund or the performance of the asset management firm. Instead, a long-term performance incentive should be provided in the form of an interest in the fund (directly or via the firm) to be held until the manager is no longer responsible for that fund. (Kay Review, p. 53)

---

electronic register'.[93] To further promote the aims of long-termism, Recommendation 6 states that: 'Companies should seek to disengage from the process of managing short term earnings expectations and announcements.'[94] This recommendation also links to Recommendation 11 – 'Mandatory IMS (quarterly

---

[93] Ibid, 85.
[94] Ibid, 64.

Good Practice Statement for Asset Holders

Asset Holders should...

1. recognise that they are in a position of trust managing client money and should act at all times in the best long-term interests of their clients, informing them of possible conflicts of interest and avoiding these wherever possible.
2. operate within a culture of open dialogue with beneficiaries – building an agreed understanding of investment objectives and risks.
3. provide information to beneficiaries, including information on investment performance, in a way which is clear, timely, useable and relevant to clients' investment objectives.
4. be proactive in setting mandates for asset managers based on open dialogue about agreed investment objectives.
5. set mandates which focus managers on achieving absolute returns in line with beneficiaries long-term investment objectives, rather than short-term relative performance benchmarks.
6. recognise that diversification is the result of diversity of investment styles.
7. review performance no more frequently than is necessary, and with reference to long-term absolute performance.
8. encourage and empower asset managers to engage with investee companies as a means of improving company performance to deliver investment returns. (Kay Review, p. 53)

---

reporting) obligations should be removed'[95] – and Recommendation 12 – 'High quality, succinct narrative reporting should be strongly encouraged'.[96]

The Review states that the level of 'Regulatory obligations in the equity investment chain should be raised to fiduciary standards'.[97] This includes asset managers (Recommendation 8[98]) and company directors who are understood in the Review to owe a duty to protect the productive assets of the company.[99] This is in contrast to the duty as it is currently set out in section 172 of the Companies Act 2006, which is either a big step forward on the part of the Review, or a failure to grasp the current legal position. To link personal incentives to the undertaking of a fiduciary function, the Review recommends that financial incentives should be linked to the achievement of long-term value. The stated principle is that: 'Market incentives should enable and encourage companies, savers and intermediaries to adopt investment approaches which achieve long-term returns by supporting and challenging corporate decisions in pursuit of long-term value.'[100]

---

[95] Ibid, 74.
[96] Ibid, 74.
[97] Ibid, 65.
[98] Ibid, 67.
[99] This reflects the Andrew Keay's EMS model discussed in Chapter 1.
[100] Kay Review (n. 59), 77.

The Review Directions which follow from that principle are that: 'any bonuses paid in the equity investment chain should be closely related to the agent's performance in determining long-term value, and the ability to realise the value of the bonus should be related to the realisation of that long-term value. Rewards should reflect long-term value creation rather than the amount or volume of transactions.'[101]

Its specific recommendation in respect of directors' performance-related pay is that companies should structure directors' remuneration to relate incentives to sustainable long-term business performance. Long-term performance incentives should be provided only in the form of company shares to be held at least until after the executive has retired from the business. (Recommendation 15)[102]

In respect of asset management firms:

> 'Asset management firms should similarly structure managers' remuneration so as to align the interests of asset managers with the interests and timescales of their clients. Pay should therefore not be related to short-term performance of the investment fund or asset management firm. Rather a long-term performance incentive should be provided in the form of an interest in the fund (either directly or via the firm) to be held at least until the manager is no longer responsible for that fund.' (Recommendation 16)[103]

These recommendations seem very problematic. If long-termism is *really* what shareholders want, then they would have it now. They do not have it because they do not want it (perfectly rationally). If, on the other hand, Kay is arguing that long-termism is an endogenously generated value for society as a whole, any recommendation must be about liberating directors from shareholders' interests and redefining their relationship to the company seen as a whole.

The Review concludes that in the post-1970s shift to globalisation, deregulation (followed by re-regulation) has created an equity market which serves the interests of financial intermediaries, such as asset management firms, which have grown in number and profitability, at the expense of savers, investors and companies. Paradoxically, while the equity market has become an insignificant source of funding for companies, company directors are more bound to follow and respond to market share price – the movement of which is the source of financial intermediaries' wealth. The result has been a profound shift away from long-term investment strategies for companies and returns for savers. The Review's solution to this is to change the role of asset manager from competitive, self-serving profit maximiser to that of mentor to companies in which long-term investments are held. By shortening the investment chain, realigning incentives, reducing liquidity to levels which facilitate medium-term investment and not electronically manufactured high-speed liquidity, and by introducing codes of

---

[101] Ibid, 77.
[102] Ibid, 79.
[103] Ibid, 80.

conduct, the Review hopes to 'rebuild the equity investment chain on the basis of trust relationships'.[104]

CONCLUSION

The Kay Review provides an excellent analysis of the current relationships and incentives in the equity markets and of corporate governance, which chimes with much of the academic criticism of our corporate governance system over the last few decades. Where it open to criticism analytically is in its assumption that shareholders' real interests are in long-termism, which I believe is a profound mistake.[105] Furthermore, the notion that what is missing in corporate governance is trust seems fanciful. The Review simultaneously takes the sensible, reasoned and evidenced position that the investment chain is long because of the expertise required to effectively extract value for shareholders and then takes the unreasoned, unevidenced position that shareholders do not want this. Instead, Kay maintains that shareholders would prefer to have a close stewardship relationship with the company, cut out the middle man, pursue long-termism and accept small profits. It seems unlikely that shareholders will want to do more in order to receive less. Shareholders may be unhappy, but that is because they think the intermediaries, especially directors, are not properly pursuing shareholder value and are taking too much for themselves. They are not unhappy because of the long-term effects on the economy and their lack of involvement in improving that.

There is no doubt that as a society we need to set different motivations into company activity but we cannot expect shareholders to do this. Kay falls at the last hurdle in embracing this, preferring to blame the intermediaries, rather than the shareholders. But it is not just the Czar's advisors, it is the Czar. Because of this failure to take the analysis to its logical conclusion, Kay's recommendations attempt to address the wrong problem. As the first part of this chapter argues, shareholder empowerment and their promotion in corporate governance is a regressive step that will not deliver shareholder stewardship or long-term investment. Recommendations to create stability in the economy must address the problem of shareholder power. They must seek to remove it, not to enhance it. Ensuring managers' compliance with the long-term interest of the economy must come from reorienting their professional goals and in the last resort from public enforcement.

---

[104] Ibid.

[105] See Talbot (n. 62). I argue that shareholder empowerment initiatives are motivated by an impulse to solidify their entitlement as owners at a time when the public is subject to an extensive austerity programme. By introducing strategies to make shareholders active and reconnected to ownership, all their attendant entitlements may be re-legitimated. If that is true, this would affect Kay's reform.

Further Reading

I. Anabtawi and S. Lynn, 'Fiduciary Duties for Activist Shareholders' (2007–2008) 60 *Stanford Law Review* 1255.

L. Backer, 'Director Shareholder Democracy: Reflections on Lucian Bebchuk' (2006) 2 *Corporate Governance Law Review* 375.

S. Bainbridge, 'Director v Shareholder Primacy in the Convergence Debate' (2002–2003) 16 *Journal of Transnational Law* 45.

S. Bainbridge, 'Director Primacy and Shareholder Disempowerment' (2006) 119(6) *Harvard Law Review* 1735.

L. Bebchuk, 'The Case for Shareholder Access to the Ballot' (2003) 59 *Business Law* 43.

B. Black, 'Shareholder Passivity Reexamined' (1990) 89 *Michigan Law Review* 520.

W. Bratton and M. Wachter, 'Shareholders and Social Welfare' (2012–2013) 36 *Seattle University Law Review* 489.

S. Deakin, 'The Coming Transformation of Shareholder Value' (2005) 13 *Corporate Governance* 11.

S. Gillan and L. Starks, 'A Survey of Shareholder Activism: Motivation and Empirical Evidence' (1998) 2 *Contemporary Financial Digest* 10.

C. Rademeyer and J. Holtzhausen, 'King II, Corporate Governance and Shareholder Activism' (2003) 120 *South African Law Journal* 767.

L. Stout, 'The Mythical Benefits of Shareholder Control' (2007–2008) 30 *Regulation* 42.

4

THE BOARD OF DIRECTORS: EFFECTIVE MANAGEMENT OR A REFLECTION OF SOCIAL INEQUALITY AND PREJUDICE?

INTRODUCTION: WHAT IS THE BOARD?

One of the key manifestations of a company's separate corporate personality is the existence of a board of directors, which is the company's decision-making body. The board of directors is responsible for all decisions relating to the business of the company, its organisational and financial strategies and its resource decisions, including human resources. The existence of a board which acts for the company is yet another manifestation of the limited nature of shareholders' ownership. While shareholders may own an entitlement to dividends, they do not own the company *per se* and so they do not generally speak for the company. It is only in *extremis*, when the board is breaching its duty to the company *and* profiting by doing so,[1] that the shareholder may seek the court's permission to act on the company's behalf in place of the board. When a shareholder seeks to directly represent the company, this is known as a derivative action because the shareholder is deriving that right from a wrong done to the company. Such an action, in that it so radically departs from the governance norm of the board representing the company, has traditionally been highly controlled by the courts, as Cheffins notes (see Chapter 1). Derivative actions enact Alchian and Demseltz's vision that shareholders will monitor the managers because they will personally gain from enhancing any residual returns.[2] Alchian and Demseltz view monitoring as a fluid mechanism; the law significantly restricts its use.

The rule in *Foss v Harbottle*, established in 1840,[3] which maintains that only the company can sue in respect of a wrong done to it, always applied unless the wrong

---

[1] Breaching a duty to the company but profiting by doing so has not been sufficient cause for a derivative action under the common law; *Pavlides v Jenson* [1956] 2 All ER 518.
[2] Discussed in Chapter 1.
[3] *Foss v Harbottle* (1840) 2 Hare 461.

done to the company was a fraud and those committing the wrong were in control. The statutory derivative action introduced by the Companies Act 2006 retains this restrictive approach in most respects. In particular, the court will decide at an early stage in the process not to give permission for the action to continue if it does not consider it to be in the company's interest.[4] In short, the ability for shareholders to represent the company is extremely constrained in law and the board's capacity to act for the company cannot generally be usurped.

However, having secured the board as agent for the company, the law does not then determine the shape of the board of directors. This is a matter for the company constitution which sets out the breadth and limits of the directors' authority. The law subjects the board to a number of duties intended to ensure the fiduciary character of the directors' duty to the company, which are now held in the Companies Act 2006. There is no law setting out the maximum number of directors though there is a minimum. The UK Corporate Governance Code 2012 (and previous Codes) recognises the board as the highest managerial authority with a monitoring function at the top of the managerial hierarchy, but the law is silent on most matters relating to the board. Given that freedom for heterogeneity, boards of directors are remarkably homogenous.

Here is a little experiment. Close your eyes and think of the board of directors sitting around the table (or board as it was). Who do you see? My guess is that you see a room full of mainly white men. Perhaps you see one ethnic minority director and/or one woman but no more than that. We think of the board of directors as composed of a particular set of people and we are largely correct in that assumption. So, is it important? Well it is certainly important from a social equality perspective. Being a company director of a substantial company is a good job with a great deal of influence and personal reward. It is not a position that rightfully belongs to one sector of society. But it may also be important from the perspective of company reform and board effectiveness. Reform of the company partly depends on the receptiveness of the board of directors to that reform. So who makes up the board may affect that receptiveness to reform. But it may not. Board members may simply perform their roles in line with their position in the company hierarchy (making their ethnicity, class or gender irrelevant). Alternatively, their socio-economic position in society may significantly influence their decision making.

In this chapter, I will examine the board of directors as a decision-making group located within a hierarchy. This is, in part, an institutional enquiry, in part a psychological one. In pursuing the question I will look at work by Stephen Bainbridge,[5] in which he argues that the board of directors acts in a way particular to its role in a group at the top of a hierarchy. He considers a number of experiments which assess the character and efficacy of group based decision making. These suggest that there is something very particular and superior about the way in which groups make decisions when compared to individual decision making.

---

[4] Companies Act 2006, s. 263.
[5] Professor of Law at UCLA School of Law.

Alternatively, do directors' decisions reflect their pre-determined social positions, or does the board as an institution subordinate individual diversity to something akin to Goffman's total institution,[6] such that the institution determines roles and individuals perform then uncritically in the same way? I will examine this question by looking at two categories of people in a particular social context: one historical and one contemporary. The historical example relates to boards of directors in Germany c. 1870–1930, a period which saw the rise of corporate capitalism and the introduction of the supervisory board in German companies from 1884. The supervisory board was composed of investors at a time when the banks were particularly intertwined with the development of industrial companies. The particular board members I will consider are male Jewish bankers. In so doing I will consider the effect of anti-Semitism. The contemporary example is women on the board, and how gender affects their role on the board, as well as their access to the board in the first place. In so doing I will consider a number of initiatives to increase the number of women on the board.

1. GROUP DYNAMICS AS DETERMINING DECISION MAKING IN THE BOARD

Bainbridge is a key proponent of the desirability of an independent board of directors. He argues that the separation of ownership from control in large corporations has a strong efficiency basis because it enables authority based decision making, 'a central agency to which all relevant information is transmitted and which is empowered to make decisions binding on the whole'.[7] This central agency acts as an efficient mechanism to gather and critically evaluate all available information. This is particularly important when there are many parties with conflicting interests in the corporation, such as labour and investors. In the corporate context, a consensus based decision, which relies upon shared self-interest, is not possible. The conflicting interests of parties such as labour and investors may only be resolved by authority based decision making, an authority which lies outside the conflicting parties. The desirability of such an authority, Bainbridge argues, is recognised in law which empowers directors to manage the company. In the US context this is present in the Model Business Corporation Act and the Delaware Code, in which shareholders have very little power. In the UK it is recognised in the articles of association which empower directors to manage on behalf of the company.

Bainbridge sees the efficiency argument for a board of directors starting with a recognition that corporations work with many hierarchal layers of teams because this way of organising is 'a high value adaptive response to the transaction costs

---

[6] E. Goffman, *Asylums: essays on the social situation of mental patients and other inmates* (1961).
[7] S. Bainbridge, 'Why a Board? Group Decision-making in Corporate Governance' (2002) 55 *Vand. L. Rev.* 1, 4.

associated with organising production within a firm'.[8] It is also an effective way of transmitting information. Furthermore, it also helps overcome the problem of 'bounded rationality', noted by both new institutional economists and behavioural economists, discussed in Chapter 1. Bounded rationality may be experienced by individual actors, who may be motivated by rational self-interest but cannot gather and process the amount of information needed to make the most efficient decisions. Group decision making transcends this and so, in the business organisation, 'branching hierarchies are an efficient adaption to bounded rationality' so that 'such an organisation system gets reliable information to the right decision maker more efficiently than any other organisational system'.[9]

These branching hierarchies also help counter some of the problems of team production. Demsetz's argument, noted in Chapter 1, is that the company is engaged in team production and team production creates a metering problem, where some members carry the burden of the team's activities while others shirk. In a corporation, argues Bainbridge, this is managed by ex post governance, as ex ante contracting would not be capable of covering all eventualities. That governance is achieved by delegating responsibility throughout the corporate structure.

> 'Creating such a branching hierarchy addresses the problems of uncertainty, bounded rationality, and shirking faced by monitors by breaking the firm team into discrete segments, each of which is more readily monitored than the whole. At each hierarchical level, the responsible monitor is responsible for supervising only a few individuals, which usefully limits and focuses his task.'[10]

The key areas for the board are policy making and in providing links to other resources and institutions. The board must also actively monitor management. This monitoring is ensured through a number of institutionalised mechanisms such as incentives like share options which, argues Bainbridge, has enhanced board independence. Furthermore, he argues, board independence is ensured by the courts as they will only allow the business judgement rule[11] to operate where there is actual evidence of effective board monitoring. He also cites the market in corporate control and increased shareholder litigation as enhancing board effectiveness and independence. Thus, today, he argues, boards are 'smaller than their antecedents, meet more often, are more independent from management, own more stock and have better access to information'.[12]

So while there are problems with groups, such as metering or 'social loafing' – 'the difficulty of motivating members of a team with non-separable outputs'[13] – evidence

---

[8] Ibid, 5.

[9] Ibid, 6.

[10] Ibid, 7.

[11] The business judgement rule in the US protects decisions (including negligently made decisions) made by directors so long as they are made honestly. However, it does not cover gross negligence in decision making.

[12] Bainbridge (n. 7), 4.

[13] Ibid, 11.

cited by Bainbridge from non-legal disciplines also suggests that groups are still more effective. 'Indeed, numerous studies have found that group decisions are not only superior to those of the average member, but also to those made by the very best individual decision makers in the group.'[14]

He cites experiments by Binder and Morgan[15] which show that group decision making was faster than individual decision making and further that the decisions groups made were better and contained less mistakes. This trend remained fairly constant in subsequent experiments where the tasks became more complex and specialised. Bainbridge also noted other experiments where the task involved 'a creative exercise of evaluative judgement with respect to complex problems having a range of solutions',[16] such as Miner's experiment to evaluate group performance in a winter survival exercise. Miner found that group decisions were better than individual ones on average (although he also found that groups were not as good as the best decision maker in the group). This experiment, Bainbridge argues, is very close to the boardroom experience as the participants were business students who knew one another and shared a single goal.

Many experiments cited by Bainbridge indicated that group decision making was superior to individual decision making because groups were better at the four key resources required for good decision making: observation, memory, computation and communication. Institutional memory was very effective. Groups were very adept at using information to address complex issues, and belonging to a group gave the actors the confidence and imagination to make bold decisions. Michaelsen, Watson and Black's experiments (cited by Bainbridge) also identified the synergies which emerged from group decision making:[17]

'group decision making may be an adaptive response to bounded rationality, creating a system for aggregating the inputs of multiple individual with differing knowledge, interests and skills. In the corporate context, the board of directors thus may have emerged as an institutional governance mechanism to constrain the deleterious effect of bounded rationality on the organisation decision making process.'[18]

Bainbridge also assessed evidence which shows that individuals' irrational decision making is not occasional, but rather individual decision making 'contains biases which systematically depart from that predicted by the traditional rational choice model'.[19] For example, individual decision makers have a tendency to herd (where the herd is everyone else in the field, the uncontroversial decision) and to make

[14] Ibid, 12.

[15] A. Binder and J. Morgan, 'Are Two Heads Better Than One? An Experimental Analysis of Group Versus Individual Decisionmaking' (2002) (National Bureau of Economic Research, Working Paper No. 7909).

[16] Bainbridge (n. 7), 17.

[17] L. Michaelsen et al., 'A Realistic Test of Individual Versus Consensus Decision Making' (1989) 74 *Journal of Applied Psychology* 834.

[18] Bainbridge (n. 7), 21.

[19] Ibid, 27.

choices which align to those of others despite information to the contrary that they may possess. This is because making a radically unexpected decision is too risky and the penalty for failure is too high. Herding can also result from bounded rationality and lack of information. Copying others or free-riding on other peoples' decisions can be a rational way of getting around that. Groups can counteract the tendency for herding because they give individuals the confidence to try a different course. As such, groups frequently encourage a more risky strategy which, Bainbridge argues, is appropriate for corporate boards. Conversely, some individual decision making might be overconfident, even reckless, in which case the group can temper opinions, provide alternative views, or identify faulty reasoning.

Group decision making, of course, has its own problems. Groups can encourage 'groupthink', that is when the group prizes cohesion and harmony over good (often controversial) decision making. This is indeed a problem which, Bainbridge argues, needs to be addressed in corporate governance:

> 'Boardroom culture encourages groupthink. Boards emphasize politeness and courtesy at the expense of oversight. The CEOs foster and channel groupthink through the exercise of their powers to control information flows, reward consensus, and discourage re-election of troublemakers.'[20]

However, this problem is not significant, argues Bainbridge. Indeed, it is significantly more desirable than an environment which allows overbearing and reckless decision makers to rule the roost. Group thinking in the boardroom context can create social norms which encourage good behaviours and reduce the tendency for self-serving in higher management. Also groups will create a group culture around particular corporate goals which is conducive to the corporations' success. As such, their activities will reduce agency costs.

Size matter when it comes to corporate boards. Much of the evidence presented by Bainbridge suggests that large boards are more effective than the (currently more fashionable) smaller board. In larger boards there will be more interlocking relationships which enable strategic alliances. The amount of knowledge resources that can be drawn on will be greater, and more diverse specialists can be used. In an increasingly complex business world, utilising board members mainly for their own specialism allows boards to transcend bounded rationality. As Bainbridge notes, 'specialism is a rational response to bounded rationality. The expert in a field makes the most of his or her limited capacity to absorb and master information by limiting the amount of information that must be processed through limiting the breadth of the field in which the expert specializes.'[21] That expertise is then disseminated to the group, for processing as a group. Specialism allows the group to rationally select which board member is best equipped to lead decisions on particular issues.

---

[20] Ibid, 32.
[21] Ibid, 43.

Thus Bainbridge concludes that although team production is subject to 'unique cognitive biases, such as group think, and unique sources of agency costs, such as social loafing ... with respect to the exercise of critical evaluative judgement ... groups have clear advantages over autonomous individuals.'[22] As most board tasks involve the need for critical evaluative judgement, the use of a group gives the corporations a clear institutional advantage over other business forms that do not have a team at the top of the management hierarchy.

There is, of course, significant opposition to the idea that the board of directors is an effective monitor. Some commentators have noted the tendency of the independent directors in the US (non-executive directors in the UK) to be subject to 'capture' where they cannot act independently because they are too impressed or sympathetic to the managing director's (or CEO's) viewpoint. Others have noted the tendency for the remuneration of top executive directors to have increased exponentially and blame too partisan remuneration committees on the board for such high awards.[23] However, these criticisms of the board share the same characteristics of Bainbridge's more favourable assessment. They understand individual board members as determined by a group dynamic within a particular institutional structure. They do not rely upon an analysis of the board as consisting of subjective personalities. This latter view is examined below.

2. THE BOARD AS COMPOSED OF SOCIO-ECONOMIC GROUPS

In this section I examine examples of when prejudice has affected the diversity and/or effectiveness of the board. These examples challenge the idea that the board is determined by its place in an institution and shows that socio-economic positioning may have significant impact on board decision making. This would indicate that a deeper sociological analysis of the people who make up the board is required if we are to understand why boards act in the way that they do and thus how they may respond to reform.

a. German boards and anti-semitism, c. 1870–1930

In this section I speculate that the socio-economic position of key members of the German supervisory board may have influenced their decision making on the board. There is strong circumstantial evidence from more current research indicating that bank representatives on the supervisory boards significantly underplayed their power. I surmise that the reason for this was that the board members were Jewish, acting in a period of burgeoning anti-Semitism. However, in order to substantiate this thesis, more research must be undertaken than is presented here. The material in this section is only a starting point to the debate. A keen research

---

[22] Ibid, 54.
[23] D. Kershaw, *Company Law in Context* (Oxford University Press, 2009), ch. 8.

student might want to examine further evidence in order to substantiate or refute this thesis.

The argument

Following the passage of Germany's 1870 company law,[24] a large number of businesses went public (known as the Founder's boom) and sold their shares on a stock exchange that had no listing rules for entry and where no prospectus was required. The number of public companies rose from around 200 before the Act, to 1,000 soon after.[25] A stock market crash followed in 1873 as a result of fraudulent or inflated share values and the joint stock company form fell into disrepute. Its use was later revitalised with the passage of the 1884 Act on joint stock companies which made specific requirements of incorporated companies, designed to protect the investing public from the earlier frauds. It also established the two-tier board consisting of a supervisory board and a management board. The management board would continue to make strategic business decisions, while the supervisory board (whose members were those with a financial stake in the company) was to monitor the management board and to exercise fiduciary responsibility toward the company. To emphasise the oversight function of the supervisory board, no member of it could simultaneously serve on the management board.

Banks were significantly represented on the supervisory board. Hilferding, in his masterpiece *Finance Capital*,[26] argued that it was in part through this that the banks dominated decision making in German corporations. In *Finance Capital*, Hilferding argued that banks became powerful because of their financial role in corporations. The first step was cartelisation which the banks promoted. Hilferding placed great significance on the fact that cartelisation in industry was matched by cartelisation in banking – 'from the outset the effect of advanced cartelisation is that banks also amalgamate and expand in order not to become dependent upon the cartel or trust.'[27] Banks' profits from their investment in industry were enhanced by cartelisation because reduced competition enabled price increases and enhanced profits. Thus, he argued, banks will 'work together to bring about this amalgamation even against the will of individual manufacturers'.[28] As banks invested an increasingly large amount of their funds in industrial companies, a large proportion of their funds became industrial productive capital. This capital becomes what Hilferding called 'finance capital'. Industrial

---

[24] Although the German empire did not exist until 1871, this Act (and other Commercial Codes) applied to those areas that became Germany.

[25] C. Fohlin, 'The History of Corporate Ownership and Control in Germany', 227, in R. Morck, *The History of Corporate Governance Around the World: Family Business Groups to Professional Managers* (University of Chicago Press, 2005).

[26] R. Hilferding, *Finance Capital: A Study in the Latest Phase of Capitalist Development* (Routledge, 1981, first published 1923), 223.

[27] Ibid.

[28] Ibid.

companies become dependent upon it and 'an ever increasing proportion of the capital used by industry is finance capital, capital at the disposition of the banks which is used by the industrialists'.[29]

To be sure, all capitalist development relied upon some money capital (loans); however in other economies this had a limited role. Industrial capital rapidly subordinated money capital. In contrast, in Germany, argued Hilferding, money capital reasserted its domination by becoming finance capital; 'the power of banks increases and they become founders and eventually rulers of industry, whose profits they seize for themselves as finance capital'.[30]

Hilferding further argued that it was the joint stock company which enabled the banks to dominate governance. In separating ownership from control and by transforming ownership into a commodity form, the joint stock company form allowed banks to purchase a significant proportion of stock and thus have direct access to industrial profits. Their financial power was enhanced by their profits from shares and the stability ensured by the cartelisation of industrial companies. Their deep involvement in industrial companies led the banks to construct an institutional framework which enabled them to monitor the company so as to ensure that the moneys lent were used properly and that the company was reaching optimum profitability and declaring high dividends. In Hilferding's words:

> 'the interest of the banks in the corporations give rise to a desire to establish a permanent supervision of the companies' affairs, which is best done by securing representation on the board of directors. This ensures, first, that the corporation will conduct all its other financial transactions, associated with the issue of shares, through the bank. Second, in order to spread its risks and to widen its business connections, the bank tries to work with as many companies as possible, and at the same time, to be represented on their board of directors. Ownership of shares enables the bank to impose its representatives even upon corporations which initially resisted. In this way there arises a tendency for the banks to accumulate such directorships.'[31]

In *Finance Capital*, Hilferding cited Jeidels' assertion that the banks engage in a 'systematic policy of placing their representatives on boards of directors'.[32] Jeidels' study evidenced enormous bank representation on the boards of industrial companies. Deutsche Bank had 221 representatives, 101 of whom were managing directors, Disconto-Gesellschaft had 92, including 21 managing director representatives. Darmstädter Bank had 51 representatives as managing directors and 50 ordinary board members. Dresdner Bank had a total of 133 representatives (53 of whom were managing directors), Schaaffhausen'scher Bankverein had 130 representatives (68

---

[29] Ibid, 225.
[30] Ibid, 226.
[31] Ibid, 121.
[32] Ibid, 398, n. 18, citing O. Jeidels, *Die Verhalnisse der deutchen Grossbanken zur Industrie*, p. 180.

of whom were managing directors) and Berliner Handels-Gesellschaft had 40 managing director representatives and 34 ordinary board members. In total, these top six banks held 751 board seats in industrial companies. Hilferding also noted the centralisation of power by banks through the boards. So, in 1909, there were 12,000 board positions, but 2,918 were held by only 179 people and 'the banking profession has the leading place'.[33] Furthermore, these positions were dominated by a small number of leading bankers. Karl Fürstenberg, director of the joint stock bank Berliner Handels-Gesellschaft since 1883, held 44 positions and Eugene Gutmann of Dresden Bank held 35 positions.

Hilferding's work presents the dynamics behind bank domination and the mechanisms by which it was achieved. The supervisory board institutionalises the relationship between management and investors (company and bank) where investors, particularly represented by the bank (or finance capital), can prevail on management to make decisions which will promote their interests. The structural power which the banks could exert defined board decision making.

However, Hilferding's characterisation of the dominance of finance capital and banks has since been criticised. Paul Sweezy, writing in the 1940s (interesting as well because it is his work rather than Hilferding's which now seems outdated), argued that Hilferding overestimated the importance of finance capital, stating that 'the dominance of bank capital is a passing phase of capitalist development, which roughly coincides with the transition from competitive to monopoly capitalism.'[34] In further developing his theory of monopoly capital with Paul Baran, Sweezy argued that in the United States corporations generated their own funds for reinvestment and did not depend on the financial markets.[35] The model of finance capitalism set out by Hilferding, they argued, was a distinctly German model and not one which was reproduced elsewhere. Indeed, they argued, the norm was toward monopoly capitalism not finance capitalism. However, Sweezy and Baran wrote this in the 1960s and the picture today is much closer to Hilferding's finance capitalism. Indeed, after the publication of *Monopoly Capitalism*, American companies changed their investment strategies. Neoliberal pro-shareholder governance meant that corporations stopped retaining funds for reinvestment and started distributing retained earnings as dividends. Reinvestment was met through the financial markets and so finance capitalism became firmly established.

However, though Hilferding's broad analysis of finance capitalism may be said to have contemporary relevance, his work has more recently been criticised on the narrower point of bank domination in the governance of companies. Caroline Fohlin's work asserts that the rise of joint stock companies was accompanied by cooperation between firms which ensured industrial power. Furthermore, individual

---

[33] Hilferding (n. 26), 399.
[34] P. Sweezy, *The Theory of Capitalist Development: Principles of Marxian Political Economy* (New York: Oxford University Press, 1942), 268.
[35] P. Sweezy and P. Baran, *Monopoly Capital: An Essay on the American Economic and Social Order* (Monthly Review Press, 1966).

industrial entrepreneurs 'possessed both the necessary equity and the personal authority to maintain solid control of their concerns'.[36] She argues that as late as 1907, the majority of companies remained entrepreneurial in that they were mainly owned by a small group of active owners. This remained the case as the *Aktiengesellschafts* (AGs)[37] increased in size and dominance. Amalgamation increased in the decades from the late 19th century until 'by 1927 virtually all of the 100 largest industrial enterprises had become groups – many in the form of holding companies'. The majority of the largest companies became managerial companies with outside shareholders. However, argues Fohlin, throughout this period, banks retained relatively small amounts of equity in industrial companies, though she acknowledges Reisser's observation that banks would tend to under-value their equity stakes for fear of appearing to speculate with savers' deposits.[38] However, if fear determined undervaluing it could equally determine banks' levels of actual ownership. And indeed, Fohlin calculates that from 1880 until World War I the equity holdings of the great banks did not exceed 11 per cent.

Fohlin also notes that board interlinks which were unconnected with banks (and therefore constituted a powerful network outside of the banks' control) also became a dominant feature. She calculates that in 1904 over half of all joint stock companies had board interlinks but that one-third of these had no banker on their board.[39] In Fohlin's study she shows that 'less than 22 per cent of firms had a bank director as chair or vice-chair of their supervisory boards'.[40] Indeed she argues there is no clear evidence to suggest bank influence in AGs and the speculative hypothesis yields no evidence either. So, 'if universal banks were providing advice their impact in the areas one would consider most important (such as profits) was small.'[41]

Fohlin does, however, admit that there was significant potential for banks to have influence on corporate governance though proxy voting. With the rise in size of AGs and the attendant powerlessness of smaller shareholders, proxy voting could redress their effective disenfranchisement. Thus, 'bankers could hypothetically build up significant stakes from many disparate small shareholders'.[42] Furthermore, until the shareholder law of 1937, banks frequently required customers to cede their voting power to the bank.

In the final analysis, though, Fohlin concludes that the low equity holdings by banks, the relatively small presence of bankers on the supervisory boards, the lack of evidence of the impact of banks' governance and the control entrepreneurial capitalists, and then later employee managers, held over their firms indicate that banks did not dominate or even significantly influence the governance of industrial

---

[36] Fohlin (n. 25), 227.
[37] *Aktiengesellschaft*, a corporation that is limited by shares.
[38] Fohlin (n. 25), 239.
[39] Ibid, 247.
[40] Ibid, 249.
[41] Ibid, 250.
[42] Ibid, 261.

companies. 'Traditional explanations of German bank-form relationships that focus on bank interventions in investment decisions and direct monitoring of debt contracts find little support in the available empirical analysis.'[43] However, if banks did not significantly influence industrial companies, why did they not? The great banks did sit on many supervisory boards, and even though their equity share was perhaps relatively small, they could potentially influence the company's affairs through proxy voting. Furthermore, they did advance huge loans to industrial companies. Indeed, Fohlin's earlier work indicated a huge rise in 'formalized bank involvement via interlocking directorates'[44] from the end of the 19th century. However, Fohlin finds no evidence of bank influence over corporate governance and contends that industrial capitalists dominated corporate governance.

Similarly, Fear and Kobrak's paper on the role and powers of German and American banks from 1870–1914 (a period of rapid capitalist development in both countries) concludes that American banks asserted a much greater influence on the corporate governance of non-financial companies even though, formally, German banks had much more power to do so. In both countries, 'banks acted as special intermediaries on the basis of their close relations with major corporations and their roles as gatekeepers on stock exchanges that issued and traded corporate securities. Banks substituted not for entrepreneurship but the lack of institutionalised trust in imperfect, nascent capital markets.' Academic work in Germany from that period testifies to the importance of banks to the stability of the exchange of stock. Emery, writing in 1898 and quoted by Franks et al., stated, 'a very interesting result of these practices is the development of the banks as independent markets for securities ... In this way an increasing volume of business is done outside the exchange.'[45] In both countries in this period, 'banks offered wide-ranging services as "gatekeeper" when equity and bond markets were in their infancies. Professional activities had not yet been divided into specialised firms.'[46] They retained this role until new accountancy practices, the securities market and credit rating agencies took over. However, Fear and Kobrack argue that although German banks had many roles and offered many diverse services, they did not control German companies. Rather, banks' various interconnectedness with industrial companies 'were considered regulatory and political virtues ... Above all, having a seat on the board of directors of client companies symbolised this fiduciary role and institutionalised relationship banking.'[47]

---

[43] Ibid, 261.

[44] C. Fohlin, 'The Rise of Interlocking Directorates in Imperial Germany' (1999) 2 *Economic History Review*, 307, 308.

[45] J. Franks, C. Mayer and H. Wagner, 'The Origins of the German Corporation – Finance, Ownership and Control' (2006) 10(4) *Review of Finance* 537, citing H. Emery, 'The Results of the German Exchange Act of 1896' (1898) 13(2) *Political Science Quarterly* 286.

[46] J. Fear and C. Kobrak, 'Banks on Board: German and American Corporate Governance 1870–1914' (Winter 2010) 84 *Business History Review* 703, 707.

[47] Ibid, 711–12.

Hilferding also recognised the banks' role in the marketing of securities. He argued that the more the 'capital resources of the bank and its interest in the share market increase, the more actively does it go into business on its own account. ... The bank ceases to be simply a middleman in securities trading and becomes a dealer itself.'[48] At the same time the large banks also take over part of the function of the stock exchange, and themselves become a securities market.[49] However, for Hilferding this activity did not replace their role in corporate governance.

Fear and Kobrak's study concludes that the power possessed by German banks was considerable, certainly greater than stated in Fohlin's work. They argue that a large percentage of companies in Germany had at least one banker on its board (23.3 per cent in 1896–1900, 40.9 per cent in 1914 and 59.4 per cent in 1928). However, few companies had three or more bankers on their boards (3.8 per cent in 1896–1900, 7.2 per cent in 1914, and 18.9 per cent in 1928).[50] What is distinctive about the German situation is the significant percentage of bankers who acted as president of the board (13.7 per cent in 1896–1900, 14.5 per cent in 1914 and 23.0 per cent in 1928[51]). However, Fear and Kobrak argue that despite their structural power, banks were required to act as 'careful diplomats' rather than activists. They did, on occasion, take a proactive role. For instance, Deutsche Bank was involved in the removal of the founder owners of Mannesmann when the company was in severe economic decline. But such instances were extremely rare. Generally, 'Deutsche Bank managers apparently had little involvement in the day-to-day management of companies.'[52]

Fear and Kobrak argue that the role of banks on the board was as monitor of company management in the interest of investors. Banks also provided more in-house credit and could provide professional advice. Their presence on the supervisory board merely underpinned the more personalised business world of this period rather than indicating a bank-orientated monitoring. Furthermore, they argue, the regulators saw banks as providing a brake on speculation and enhancing long-term stability. They note that this notion of dampening, or smoothing, inherently anarchic markets underlay much of German regulation, whether it took the form of 'creating cartels, shaping accounting policy that would enable companies to build hidden reserves, stabilising dividends or share prices, maintaining corporate interlocks, or having banks on board'.[53] Indeed, Germany's business cycles had relatively modest downturns, and in the main companies managed to avoid the savage round of job cuts experienced by American workers in similar downturns.[54]

---

[48] Hilfderfing (n. 26), 147.
[49] Ibid, 138.
[50] Fear and Kobrak (n. 46), 713. These percentages are fairly similar to the picture in the United States.
[51] Ibid, 713.
[52] Ibid, 724.
[53] Ibid, 717.
[54] Ibid, 722.

Fear and Kobrak also note that the regulatory power of banks in Germany was considerable. For example, regulation gave banks considerable control over the securities they issued, which extended to significant powers of intervention, should problems arise.[55] Their responsibility was viewed as one to the nation and economy as a whole, and to this end they were considered to owe a responsibility to productive capital rather than speculative capital.[56] German banks were heavily engaged in investment, corporate rescue and a range of other services for companies. They were also huge. Fear and Kobrak note that before World War I, 17 of Germany's top 25 joint stock companies were banks.[57] On top of this, banks wielded much of the voting power in companies, through proxies. It was common practice for banks' clients to cede their votes to their banks, or frequently banks required this as part of their contract with clients. So, 'with few exceptions, large banks cast the majority of votes at annual meetings'.[58]

The business culture at this time delineated certain roles for banks which were specific and restrictive. However, they did not reflect the power banks actually possessed by dint of their lending powers, issuing powers and voting powers. Business culture determined that 'bankers would not interfere with strategic investment decisions, but would instead support entrepreneurial decisions as finance specialists and supply lines of credit at attractive interest rates'.[59] Fear and Kobrak claim that banks concurred with this because they needed the industrialists' business. The state, on the other hand, relied on the banks to create stability in the stock market. 'Partly through legislation and partly through evolving business practice, large banks played a critical role as stock exchange regulators in a world where state supervision did not exist.'[60]

However, the reliance of business and the state on the considerable functions of the banks explains why business and the state required banks to act in a particular way, but not why the banks fell in with this so readily. This and Fohlin's evidence on the role of banks in industrial companies make clear that banks were punching well below their weight. Hilferding and Jeidels evidenced the huge power which banks possessed, which Hilferding utilised to develop his theory on finance capital. Fohlin and Fear and Kobrak acknowledge that power (with some reservations in respect of levels of equity ownership) but make clear that the banks did not utilise it. So, if they are right and Hilferding is wrong, did the banks' representatives act in accordance with their socio-economic position in German society rather than their economic and legal power? In the Anglo-American company the socio-economic group bankers and company board members belong to is the wealthy and well educated. This was also true in Germany in this period. However,

---

[55] Ibid, 725.
[56] Ibid, 725.
[57] Ibid, 727.
[58] Ibid, 728.
[59] Ibid, 731.
[60] Ibid, 731.

significant numbers of the leading bankers belonged to another group. They were Jewish and crucially they were Jewish during a period when anti-Semitism was significant and frequently underestimated.

After centuries of legal and political oppression marked by periods of violence and pogroms, the Jewish community in Germany in 1870 stood at about 1 per cent of the population. The Jewish population was still subject to legal control, such as limits on the total allowed to live in a city and the number of married couples allowed. There had never been a Jewish officer in the Prussian army. Violent outbursts against them still occurred, the worst up to that date being the so-called 'Hep-Hep riots' pogroms which swept through many Bavarian towns in 1819. However, following the establishment of the German state in 1871 and the stock market crash in 1873, anti-Semitism took on a new character. First, it became a respectable nationalised perspective and, secondly, it became integrated into commerce. On this point, Pulzer quotes this telling extract from *Kreuuzzeitung* by F.F. Perrot: 'Bank, share and stock exchange privileges are, as things stand, Jew's privileges. They are therefore protected and pushed with all their might by the Jewish press, by Jewish scholars and Jewish deputies.'[61]

Many anti-Semitic political parties sprung up and many political figures adopted anti-Semitism as a quick route to popularity. Adolf Stoecker, Lutheran, chaplain to the emperor, anti-capitalist and politician in the Christian Social Workers' Party which he founded, was thwarted in his efforts to garner sufficient support from the workers. This changed when he signalled his passionate adoption of anti-Semitism in a speech made in 1879, 'What we demand from Modern Jewry'. He argued that capitalism and the pursuit of profit was a base activity unbefitting of the noble and Christian German spirit. He laid the blame for its establishment in Germany with the Jewish community and associated good business with German-ness and Christianity, calling for a 'return to a Germanic rule in law and business, a return to the Christian faith'. The solution lay in radical legislative control over the Jews.

'The social abuses that are caused by the Jewry must be eradicated by wise legislation. It will not be easy to oust Jewish capital. Only thorough going legislation can bring it about. The mortgage system in real estate should be abolished and property should be inalienable and unmortgageable, the credit system should be reorganized to protect businessmen against the arbitrary power of big capital. There must now be new stock and stock exchange relations, reintroduction of the denominational census so as to find out the disproportion between Jewish capital and Christian labour, limitation of appointments of Jewish judges in proportion to the size of the population, removal of Jewish teachers from our grammar schools, and in addition the strengthening of the Christian-Germanic spirit – are the means to put a stop to the encroachment of Jewry on Germanic life, this worse kind of usury. Either we

[61] F. Perrot, *Die Ara Birmark-Delbruck-Comphausen* (Berlin, 1876), 17, cited in P.G.J. Pulzer, *The Rise of Political Anti-Semitism in Germany and Austria* (Wiley and Sons, 1964).

succeed in this and Germany will rise again, or the cancer from which we suffer will spread further.'[62]

In the 1881 elections the Conservative Central Committee put forward four anti-Semitic candidates, including Stoecker, and gained nearly one-third of the votes.[63] Stoecker was successfully voted in at Seigan.

The success of the anti-Semites has been largely attributed to a pamphlet written by Heinrich Von Treitschke[64] and published in 1880 entitled, 'A Word About Our Jewry'. The pamphlet was published a few months after Stoecker's speech, lending him instant gravitas. Heinrich Von Treitschke was Professor of History at the University of Berlin and had been a Reichstag deputy in the 1870s, representing the National Liberal Party. His pamphlet gave anti-Semitism a mainstream credibility or, as Pulzer puts it, he 'housetrained' anti-Semitism. The foulest sentiments were associated with right-thinking German-ness, and by the end of 1880 it had been printed in three editions. In 'A Word About Our Jewry', Treitschke railed against the 'alien' non-assimilating Jews who had undermined and indeed insulted German culture with base commercialism. He recalled the violence of the Hep-Hep riots and sinisterly argued that the anti-Semitism of the 1880s was more rational, just and deep seated.

> 'Are these outbursts of a deep, long suppressed anger really only a momentary outburst, hollow and irrational as the Teutonic anti-Semitism of 1819? No, the instinct of the masses has in fact clearly recognized a great danger, a serious sore sport of the new German national life; the current expression "the German Jewish question" is more than an empty phrase.'[65]

In contrast to other European countries where, he argued, there is not a Jewish problem because the Jews there are less in number and more willing to assimilate, Germany is swamped by non-assimilating Jews. In his words, 'our country is invaded year after year by multitudes of assiduous pants-selling youths from the inexhaustible cradle of Poland'.[66] Furthermore, 'We Germans, however, have to deal with Jews of the Polish branch which bears the deep scars of centuries of Christian tyranny. According to experience they are incomparably more alien to the European and especially to the German national character.'[67]

---

[62] A. Stoecker, 'What we demand from Modern Jewry' (speech given at a Christian Social Workers' Party Rally, 19 September 1879), reproduced in P. Mendes-Flohr and J. Reinhorz, *The Jew in the Modern World: A Documentary History* (OUP, 2010), 342.

[63] P.G.J. Pulzer, *The Rise of Political Anti-Semitism in Germany and Austria* (Wiley and Sons, 1964), 93. Also, see more from C. Wawrzinek, *Die Entstehung der deutschen Antisemitenparteien, 1873–1890. With a Bibliography (Historische Sutdien)* (Unknown Binding, 1927) '...10% of all districts, the anti-Semites polled more than a tenth of the vote.'

[64] A thesis advanced by J. Hawes in *Englanders and Huns: How Five Decades of Enmity Led to the First World War* (Simon & Schuster Ltd, 2014).

[65] H. Von Treitschke, *A Word About Our Jewry* (Hebrew Union College, 1958), reproduced in P. Mendes-Flohr and J. Reinhorz, *The Jew in the Modern World: A Documentary History* (OUP, 2010), 343.

[66] Ibid.

[67] Ibid.

Like Stoecker, Treitschke associated capitalist development with the Jews. They were responsible for the social dislocation of industrialisation; they were responsible for the financial deprivation following the 1873 crash. The guilt the Jews bore was not just for their usual failure to assimilate but for ruining German life in the process:

> 'But it cannot be denied that the Jews have contributed their part to the promoting of business with its dishonesty and bold cupidity, that they share heavily in the guilt for the contemptible materialism of our age which regards every kind of work as business and threatens to suffocate the old simple pride and joy the German felt in his work.'[68]

Such a view by such an eminent German citizen was highly inflammatory. And there was yet another element to the toxic cocktail of this new form of anti-Semitism. The association of capitalism and the crash with the Jews enabled anti-Semitism to be merged and nourished by the anti-Englishness in 19th century Germany. Treitschke was a renowned Anglophobe and his tirades against the English's base commercialism melded seamlessly with his anti-Semitism. The Jews were the Trojan horse for the 'Manchester philosophy'.[69] In *Englanders and Huns: How Five Decades of Enmity Led to the First World War*,[70] James Hawes argues that 'the base materialism which Treitschke accused the Jews of was exactly the same list of alleged sins which Treitschke and his followers had for several years been setting at the door of the Englanders. In fact, the idea that Jewishness and Englishness were somehow naturally related, perhaps even the same thing, had been bubbling under the murky surface of German nationalist thought for many years.'[71]

And of the significance of Treitschke's pamphlet, Hawes says:

> 'Sometimes, history moves in great, vague, slow-gathering shifts, but sometimes, the tectonic slip is extraordinarily sharp and clear. So let's be in no doubt. In November 1879, Germany's Jews found themselves suddenly accused, by a grand cultural guru, of being the sponsors of a wicked Modernity: they were accused of this in exactly the same terms which had for some years been flung against England, and by the very man who had been publicly leading that charge.
>
> Here, at last, we are getting to the root of the mystery which, for obvious reasons, has been endlessly debated by historians: *why was it Germany of all places which saw the birth of an entire and (in its own rank terms) cogent political programme centred on Anti-Semitism?*
>
> Germans, after all, did not invent modern, racial Anti-Semitism, nor did any of their nineteenth-century rulers publicly espouse it. Those black honours go to a

---

[68] Ibid, 344.
[69] Pulzer (n. 63), p. 140.
[70] J. Hawes, *Englanders and Huns: How Five Decades of Enmity Led to the First World War* (Simon & Schuster Ltd, 2014).
[71] Ibid, 194.

Frenchman and to Russia. The deadly, open pogroms of Tsarist Russia never happened in Germany, though physical abuse of Jews did occur in the wake of Stoecker's meetings; there was no parallel in Imperial Germany, ever, to the manic parliamentary and public outrages set off in France by the Dreyfus Case. But the great difference was that in Germany, the Anti-Semites had a real, proper *theory*.

Uniquely, German thinkers, from Hegel to Treitschke, had by 1879 developed a thorough-going, widely-disseminated, intellectually-backed system of thought aimed against a liberal "internal enemy." The theory was originally created to discredit any German who looked to Britain as a model.'[72]

Given the association of this new anti-Semitism with (English) commercialism, it would not be surprising if the boards of banks, with over a quarter of its board members Jewish men including those at the very top of the banking world,[73] decided to keep a low profile. Acting in an obviously self-interested way, ruthlessly pursuing the interests of banking and finance might be *de rigueur* for the American banks at this time, but for the German banks it might have fed the flames of anti-Semitism. If Jewish bankers had chosen to pursue a pro-bank approach through a proactive supervisory board, this would risk concretising anti-Semitic stereotypes of the money grabbing Jewish usurer, an amoral alien with no regard to the consequences of his actions.

Fear and Kobrak recognise the existence of anti-Semitism. Jewish bankers 'were well aware that strong bank intervention could elicit a populist, anti-Semitic reaction. The debate about "the power of banks" carried anti-Semitic undertones.'[74] However, they dismiss it as minor:

'the bottom line was that, while some German bankers were being given titles of nobility and elected to Parliament, their American counterparts were being hauled in front on U.S. congressional commissions to answer accusations that they were engaging in financial conspiracies against the public.'[75]

Anti-Semitism, they maintain, could be countered by cultural choices, so that 'Jewish bankers, in self-defence, cultivated the most refined, educated upper-class profiles in order to counteract the unholy association with base money'.[76] Perhaps they listened to Wagner as well.

However, anti-Semitism was not countered by cultural or religious assimilation. In 1933, Deutsche Bank removed Jewish members from the board of directors and the supervisory board. Banks were in turn used by party officials to press firms to remove Jewish directors and workers. Indeed, none of the Jews mentioned in this chapter escaped the murderous conclusion of German anti-Semitism. Eugen Guttmann's (noted by Hilferding above) elder son, Herbert, was ousted from his 16

---

[72] Ibid, 195–6.
[73] Famous banking dynasties like the Rothschilds, the Hirschs and the Seligmans originated in Germany.
[74] Fear and Kobrak (n. 46), 726.
[75] Ibid.
[76] Ibid.

directorships because of his Jewishness and died in poverty in England in 1942. Guttmann's youngest son, Fredrick, and his wife were murdered in concentration camps in 1944. Hilferding was tortured and murdered by the SS after being handed over by the Vichy regime in 1942.

So what the evidence thus far shows us is that German banks had considerable power over industrial companies. They had power from their role as creditors, shareholders and *de facto* regulators of the stock market. One of the key mechanisms through which they could exercise that power was through the supervisory board. Hilferding's work and the work of his contemporaries see no disjuncture between the power the banks possessed and their exercise of that power. However, scholarship over the last 10 years suggests that although the banks had considerable power, they did not exercise that power. Alternatively, if they did exercise power it was in a trustee-like manner. The supervisory boards did not seem to exercise their power to promote the interests of the banks. Their modest use of power in the boards is particularly striking when compared with the American banks, who had exercised (and abused) considerable power over American corporate capitalism. Why the German supervisory boards were more reticent than their American counterparts may have its roots in anti-Semitism. Contemporary research has uncovered a much deeper level of anti-Semitism in Germany than was acknowledged (at least publicly) before the First World War.[77] Jewish men were disproportionally represented in banking in Germany (as they were in America) and they were in the upper echelons of management. Whether Jewish bankers decided to take a more controlled and statesmanlike approach to their decision making in the supervisory boards in order to counter the prejudice that Jewishness was rampant commercialism and 'Manchesterism' would need to be further evidenced. Personal correspondence or articles in Jewish newspapers would provide some of that. Minutes from meetings in banks and in the supervisory boards themselves would likewise help to build a profile about what influenced decision making in the German supervisory board.

b. Women and the board

The board of directors in the UK has been peopled mainly by men. This is the case historically, it is the case now and it is the case globally. The result of having male dominated boards may be that boards have been shaped by male-orientated goals and male-orientated management skills. Thus the marked lack of representation of women in the top boards may not just evidence gender inequalities in society but may have produced a board of directors which is unbalanced and not as effective as it could be. This chapter is concerned with the question of whether women on the board make a difference to the functioning of the board and what mechanisms exist to promote gender diversity on the board.

---

[77] Hawes (n. 70).

Why are there so few women on the board of directors?

In Villiers' research on women in the board, she argues that because women are discriminated against in broader society, the shape of the board remains highly gendered and does not represent the best business minds.[78] This is the case despite the fact that public opinion is in favour of more women on the board. Villiers cites research from the Government Equalities Office which shows that 80 per cent of its survey participants think a balanced senior management team will be better at understanding their customers.[79] However, in assessing FTSE Female Reports from 2000–2009, she showed that 'women currently make up 12.2% of total directorships on FTSE 100 boards and women constitute only 14.7% of all new director appointments during 2009. In addition, women hold 7.6% of FTSE 250 board positions. Twenty-five FTSE 100 companies still have exclusively male boardrooms.'[80]

Villiers attributes the failure to have gender diversity on boards to a range of factors including stereotyping, lack of mentoring and networking for women and family responsibilities. Stereotyping gender characteristics has a tendency to separate men and women. Villiers argues that, 'Despite dramatic changes in these gender roles during the last generation, the reality is that perceptions about gender roles are slow to change.'[81] Men tend to merge their experience of women as wives or mothers with their experience of women in the workplace, making it hard to take women seriously. As women remain the principal carers of children even when working, this perception of women as not equal to their male counterparts is amplified. Villiers puts it like this:

> 'in the organizational setting leaders occupy roles defined in terms of hierarchy and the organizational leader is also bound by roles related to gender derived from consensual societal beliefs about the attributes of women and men. Similarly, expectation states theory implies that the lower status of women causes negatively biased evaluations to be made. More favourable traits are associated with men rather than with women. These stereotyped placements lead to organizational structures that perpetuate the inequalities arising from the biased evaluations.'[82]

Stereotyping underpins the 'subjective decision making processes' which tend to determine promotions. Whether you look like someone ready for promotion is frequently a gendered decision. Social fit is, Villiers argues, a major challenge to

---

[78] C. Villiers, 'Achieving Gender Balance in the Boardroom: Is it Time for Legislative Action in the UK?' (2010) 30(4) *Legal Studies* 533.

[79] Ibid, citing H. Coombs, E. Gray and D. Edmiston, *Representation of women and men in business and government – public attitudes and perceptions* (IPSOS MORI, March 2010).

[80] Villiers (n. 78), 535.

[81] Ibid, 537.

[82] Ibid, 538.

women's advancement in organisations and she cites research which shows that men tend to see other men as fitting their notion of managers.[83]

A lack of suitable mentors for women also hinders female progression. This is partly because mentors provide the kind of networking opportunities which men already enjoy. Villiers cites Schipani et al.'s assessment of the benefits of mentors and networks. A mentor 'can buffer an individual from overt and covert forms of discrimination, lend legitimacy to a person or position, provide guidance and training in the political orientation of the organisation and provide inside information on job-related functions'.[84] Similarly, networking 'helps an individual to increase visibility and get known, to enhance industry knowledge and improves a person's ability to offer innovative recommendations in the workplace'.[85] Paradoxically though, Schipani's research indicates that female-only networks 'appear to broaden the gap between the sexes rather than level the playing field'.[86] Only a gender-neutral network can be effective for women, argues Villiers.

This lack of network enhances the maleness of company culture. Villiers says that the company is a 'masculine and narcissistic organisation where the more valued features include achievement, heroism, assertiveness and material success … women are frequently judged negatively if they do not show these traits but they are also judged negatively when they do.'[87] The culture does not allow women's (arguably) innate tendency to cooperation and to relationship maintenance, to contribute to the organisation.[88] Other studies indicate that the dearth of mentoring available to women (and ethnic minorities) when they take on their first executive position results in their lower levels of additional appointments to other boards compared to male first-time executives.[89]

Finally, Villiers argues, women's tendency to cooperation and maintaining relationships extends to future relationships as they may hold back in their career in anticipation of a future family. When that does become a reality, it is women who will take off time and then return to a less demanding, more flexible job.[90] In other words, advancement is designed around a male model of advancement. Not only does this exclude most women, it requires that those women who do succeed have

[83] Ibid, citing M. Heilman, C. Block, R. Martell and M. Simon, 'Has anything changed? Current characterizations of men, women, and managers' (1989) 74 *Journal of Applied Psychology* 935.

[84] Villiers (n. 78), 540.

[85] Ibid, citing C. Schipani et al., 'Pathways for women to obtain positions of organizational leadership: the significance of mentoring and networking' (2009) 16 *Duke Journal of Gender Law and Policy* 89. See also K. Kram, *Mentoring at Work: Developmental Relationships in Organizational Life* (Scott Foresman, 1985), 100.

[86] Villiers (n. 78), 540.

[87] Ibid.

[88] Villiers cites Gilligan's research on this point. C. Gilligan, *In a Different Voice: Psychological Theory and Women's Development* (Harvard University Press, 1982).

[89] M. McDonald and J. Westphal, 'Access denied: Low mentoring of women and minority first time directors and its negative effects on Appointments to additional boards' (2013) 56 *Academy of Management Journal* 1169.

[90] Villiers (n. 78), 541.

to accept co-option into this male culture. In so doing, the very attributes which would make a board more diverse and creative are lost. When a women attempts to combine work with a family, she is also stymied by the long hours culture (which is still the norm in Western developed society, despite the existence of legislation). Attempts to provide more flexibility in the workplace are undermined by the long hours culture to the detriment of working mothers.

What is lost by the exclusion of women from the boardroom and how does that shape UK boardrooms?

The barriers to female entry into the boardroom, some of which are noted above, are clearly problematic from an equality perspective, but is it a problem from a governance perspective? Do women on the board make a difference to the functioning of the board? Some studies indicate that the prejudices which keep women out of the boardroom continue to dog women even when they have gained entry. For example, the announcement of a female executive appointment can result in an immediate drop in share value to the obvious detriment of the company. In Gregory et al.'s empirical study, they look at the levels of directors' own trade in shares and found that they reacted unfavourably to the announcement of a female executive. Their trading choices influence market trade because directors would be expected to have an informed sense of individual directors' competencies and therefore their choices provide a useful guide to investors. Gregory et al. also cite a paper by Dobbin and Jung which illustrates the gender prejudices of institutional investors: 'while an increase in board diversity has no effect on profits, it has a negative effect on stock price which they attribute to non-block institutional investors selling stock of firms that appoint women to their boards.'[91]

This response, however, might be a rational appraisal of how female executives are likely to fare in a male dominated world. The 'old boys' network which peoples the board of directors may not allow female executives access to inside information. Female executives may also find themselves excluded from the informal golf club-type networking locations for top business executives. Gregory et al. also look at the 'glass cliff' argument as a factor. The argument here is that women will often be appointed to ailing companies because of their competencies but the demise of the company is closely associated with new female executives. They fall off the glass cliff. The appointment of a female executive is a signal to the stock market that the company is ailing and so stock values will fall as a result. In both scenarios the preference of institutional shareholders for male executive appointments is not pure gender prejudice. However, the perverse result in the second scenario is

---

[91] A. Gregory, E. Jeanes, R. Tharyan and I. Tonks 'Does the Stock Market Gender Stereotype Corporate Boards? Evidence from the Market's Reaction to Directors' Trades' (2013) 24 *British Journal of Management* 174, 176, discussing F. Dobbin and J. Jung, 'Corporate board gender diversity and stock price performance: the competence gap or institutional investor bias?' (2013) 89 *North Carolina Law Review* 809.

that female executives are penalised by the market for possessing greater restorative skills than male executives.

However, Gregory et al.'s study found that the first justification for reacting negatively to a female appointment was unfounded as women were not 'informationally disadvantaged', at least in their UK sample.[92] They also found that although the glass cliff argument could be made, the directors' trades were more inclined to companies with female executives once they had been in position for a longer period. The initial announcement period had the worst effect on trading, but, 'in the long term, from three months up to a year after the trade, there was no substantive difference in the market reaction to male and female directors' trades'.[93] Sexual stereotyping is the initial reaction, but once a female executive is proven, the market treats female executives no differently than their male counterparts. The problem with this is that the ongoing commitment of policy makers and analysts to the short-termism inherent in the efficient market hypothesis (discussed in Chapter 3 in the Kay Review) may discourage them from seriously pursuing mechanisms to encourage more gender diversity in boards whose virtue is only evidenced in the longer term.

Other studies show that boards with more women are more responsive to social issues than boards with few or no women. Female executives seem to be more inclined to corporate social responsibility issues and to wider social approaches to management. In Jia and Zhang's study of the response of Chinese firms to disasters, they showed that women executives are more likely to respond empathically, viewing their responsibility as directors to be more holistic than just acting in the interests of shareholders.[94] In this study the researchers analysed 519 firms listed on the Chinese Stock Exchange before 2006 and made 1,038 observations in respect of firms' responses to two major natural disasters in China, the Wenchuan and Yushi earthquakes (May 2008 and April 2010 respectively). They concluded that where there was a 'critical mass' of women on the board (which they estimate as three women given a nine-person board), companies had a significantly more generous 'corporate philanthropic disaster response' than those companies without a critical mass of women. The difference in companies' response did not, however, occur when there was only a minority, or a token woman on the board. This study makes interesting claims about the importance of studying diversity in Chinese firms. First, in practical terms, China suffered two major disasters within a couple of years, and listed companies disclosed details of their response to the earthquakes, making the study very thorough. Also, there are significantly more women on the boards of Chinese firms compared with most other countries. Furthermore, in sociological terms, traditional Chinese culture emphasises gender differences; 'Confucianism,

---

[92] Gregory et al. (n. 91), 185.

[93] Ibid.

[94] M. Jia and Z. Zhang, 'Critical Mass of Women on BODs, Multiple Identities, and Corporate Philanthropic Disaster Response: Evidence from Privately Owned Chinese Firms', *Journal of Business Ethics* (2013) 118:303–317.

fundamentally affects women's social roles and defines the ethical differences between women and men.'[95] As a result, they argue, it is easier to distil the 'female response' than in countries where gender differences are minimised socially.

In Adam and Ferreira's study of US companies, they found a complicated set of outcomes resulting from the introduction of more diverse boards.[96] First, they found that women executives tended to show more commitment to monitoring, attending regular meetings, and were well appraised of the issues. Furthermore, the better attendance of women encouraged better attendance from male executives, improving monitoring by the board as a whole. On the other hand, where firms already had a good governance system, the introduction of female executives could lead to over-monitoring which, they argue, tends to lose value for the firm. However, other research noted by Villiers shows that the presence of women on the board not only improves board attendance, it inhibits staid ways of dealing with issues. Women tend to thwart 'groupthink' by both introducing fresh perspectives and encouraging self- and group evaluation.[97] Women simply 'seem to ask different questions than white male directors and bring different sets of experiences and concerns with them to the boardroom'.[98]

Yet another study based on the newly diverse board in Norway concluded that that there has been little change in company performance with the introduction of significant female representation aside from a tendency for companies to retain earnings or accumulate capital though debt.[99]

However, Villiers argues that there is a strong business case for including women. At the most fundamental level, the pool of talent available to companies is lost when only half of the qualified population is considered. Villiers also notes that as women tend to be the buyers in the market, either as individuals or within the family, including women on the board gives the company insights into its customer base. She also notes that women score higher than men in respect of a number of different skills including 'giving feedback, rewarding and motivating individuals and teams, and acting with integrity. Women also score higher than men on maintaining productivity, producing quality work, meeting project deadlines, generating new ideas, and moving projects forward.'[100]

The debate, however, is by no means one-sided. Board diversity is still a relatively new political aim and boards remain dominated by men. Big companies

---

[95] Ibid, p. 304.

[96] R. Adams and D. Ferreira, 'Women in the boardroom and their impact on governance and performance' (2009) 94 *Journal of Financial Economics* 291.

[97] Villiers (n. 78), 544, although she notes that the success of this depends of establishing a 'critical mass'. V.W. Kramer et al., *Critical Mass on Corporate Boards: Why Three or More Women Enhance Governance* (Wellesley Centers for Women, 2006).

[98] Villiers (n. 78), 544, citing D. Polden, 'Forty Years After Title VII: Creating an Atmosphere Conducive to Diversity in the Corporate Boardroom', Santa Clara University School of Law, Legal Studies Research Paper Series No. 06-08.

[99] H. Dale-Olsen, P. Schone and M. Verner, 'Diversity among Norwegian Boards of Directors: Does a Quota for Women Improve Firm Performance? (2013) 19(4) *Feminist Economics* 110.

[100] Villiers (n. 78), 544.

have a larger proportion of female executives than small companies, probably due to more stringent corporate governance procedures and sensitivity to reputational risks, but women are still very much the minority.[101] As such, the numbers – or 'critical mass' (generally understood to be around 30 per cent[102]) – are not there to make an accurate empirical study of the effect of female executives on corporate boards. Female executives are too few in number to make a significant impact and there is widespread use of token appointments of women.[103] This has led some scholars to maintain that arguments in favour of diversity are merely intuitive and emotional and not properly evidenced.[104]

What is evidenced is this. Women are better monitors and they tend to prefer a strong capital base. They respond to social crisis more readily and they are better at dealing with ailing companies. The perfect skill set for companies embroiled in a global crisis. Negative reactions by investors to female appointments tend to be short term, because in the long term female executives prove their worth. The factor which holds women back is simple gender prejudice.

Policy responses to the problem of gendered boards

Such gender imbalance in company boards became politically untenable, particularly after the financial crisis was attributed to managerial recklessness by numerous reports, the implication being that risky, reckless behaviour is more likely to be exhibited by men. The growing recognition of the need to address the exclusion of women was reflected in the UK Corporate Governance Code in 2010. One of the Code's 'Supporting Principles' (which reflect the values behind the specific stipulations of the Code) recognised this. The Supporting Principle states 'the search for board candidates should be conducted, and appointments made, on merit, against objective criteria and with due regard for the benefits of diversity on the board, including gender'.[105] This recognition is also reflected in other policy responses.

The Davis Report

In 2011 an extensive government-commissioned review[106] on board diversity headed by Lord Davis titled 'Women on Boards'[107] was launched. It came out strongly in favour of women on the board. The executive summary argued that the business case

---

[101] E. Chemi, 'For Women in the Boardroom, Bigger Companies Do Better', *Business Week*, 13 December 2013 <http://www.businessweek.com/articles/2013-12-13/for-women-in-the-boardroom-bigger-companies-do-better?campaign%5fid=ebsco>.

[102] J. Joecks, K. Pull and K. Vetter.

[103] J. Wolfers, 'Diagnosing discrimination: stock returns and CEO gender' (2006) 27 *Journal of the European Economic Association* 6132.

[104] S. Brammer, A Millington and S. Pavelin, 'Corporate Reputation and women on the board' (2009) 20 *British Journal of Management* 17.

[105] UK Corporate Governance Code 2010, Supporting Principle B.2.

[106] As part of the Coalition Government's Agreement to promote gender equality on the boards of listed companies.

[107] Department for Business, Innovation & Skills, *Women on Boards* (2011) <https://www.gov.uk/government/uploads/system/uploads/attachment_data/file/31480/11-745-women-on-boards.pdf>.

had been made: women made business better. It noted that although women performed better than men at all levels of education, this was not reflected in the boardroom. This indicated that companies were missing out on the best-educated candidates. Davis cited a range of scholarship on gender diversity and effective board activity. It concluded that a more heterogeneous board reduced 'groupthink' and 'a critical mass of 30% or more women at board level or in senior management produces the best financial results'.[108] Davis also cited research which shows that women encourage better corporate governance and better risk management.

The Davis Report cited statistics which showed the scale of female under-representation on the board, not just in the UK but globally. The Female FTSE Index Report produced by the Cranfield School of Management shows that in the FTSE 100 boards there has been a modest rise of women from 6.2 per cent in 1999 to 12.5 per cent in 2010. Tellingly, this is much lower in respect of executive directorship (2.02 per cent in 1999 and 5.3 per cent in 2010) but much higher in respect of non-executive directors (10.82 per cent in 1999 to 15.6 per cent in 2010). It seems that women are perceived as effective monitors but not inspired, value producing managers. Also it is much easier and quicker to recruit women to non-executive positions (so as to tick the diversity box) than promote women to real executive positions. The Cranfield Report also showed that 20 per cent of FTSE 100 companies had no female directors and over 52 per cent of FTSE 250 companies had no female board member. Globally, the picture is mixed but female under-representation is astoundingly high. In industrialised Europe, the average board had 9.6 per cent of women, in North America 11.4 per cent, and 6 per cent on average in emerging markets.[109] In the industrialised Asia-Pacific region, only 3.6 per cent of top companies had female board members.

Davis considered evidence which showed that determinedly proactive government intervention can quickly redress this. In other countries, 'The importance of improving the gender balance of corporate boards is increasingly recognised across the world. Some countries, including France and Italy, are considering significant action and some, including Norway, Spain and Australia, have made significant steps already.'[110] Significant action for some countries (Norway, Spain, Iceland and Finland) has been the introduction of quotas. In Norway, for example, the government gave companies three years to raise female board membership to 40 per cent. By July 2005 (the deadline) only 24 per cent had complied. Legislation was passed to give companies a final deadline of January 2008. If they failed to comply they could be fined or even dissolved. Full compliance was achieved by 2009.[111] However, Norway has a high proportion of state ownership. In 2010 the state owned 35 per cent of equities listed on the Oslo stock exchange. As such, failing

---

[108] Ibid, 8.
[109] Ibid, 25, Table 3.
[110] Ibid, 3.
[111] Ibid, 22. Quebec has, through legislation, also achieved full gender equality, equal male and female board members, ibid, 23.

to address the gender issue was increasingly untenable politically. State-owned companies reached 40 per cent by 2004 but other plcs had reached only 13 per cent by 2005. Mandating diversity was almost unavoidable.[112] It was, however, highly avoidable in the pro-market privatised UK, so, although using the law to achieve gender diversity was a proven success in other countries, it was rejected here.

To counter this, the Davis Report recommended that:

'1. All Chairmen of FTSE 350 companies should set out the percentage of women they aim to have on their boards in 2013 and 2015. FTSE 100 boards should aim for a minimum of 25% female representation by 2015 and we expect that many will achieve a higher figure. Chairmen should announce their aspirational goals within the next six months (by September 2011). Also we expect all Chief Executives to review the percentage of women they aim to have on their Executive Committees in 2013 and 2015.

2. Quoted companies should be required to disclose each year the proportion of women on the board, women in Senior Executive positions and female employees in the whole organisation.

3. The Financial Reporting Council should amend the UK Corporate Governance Code to require listed companies to establish a policy concerning boardroom diversity, including measurable objectives for implementing the policy, and disclose annually a summary of the policy and the progress made in achieving the objectives.

4. Companies should report on the matters in recommendations 1, 2 and 3 in their 2012 Corporate Governance Statement whether or not the underlying regulatory changes are in place. In addition, Chairmen will be encouraged to sign a charter supporting the recommendations.

5. In line with the UK Corporate Governance Code provision B2.4 "A separate section of the annual report should describe the work of the nomination committee, including the process it has used in relation to board appointments". Chairmen should disclose meaningful information about the company's appointment process and how it addresses diversity in the company's annual report including a description of the search and nominations process.

6. Investors play a critical role in engaging with company boards. Therefore investors should pay close attention to recommendations 1–5 when considering company reporting and appointments to the board.

7. We encourage companies periodically to advertise non-executive board positions to encourage greater diversity in applications.

8. Executive search firms should draw up a Voluntary Code of Conduct addressing gender diversity and best practice which covers the relevant search criteria and processes relating to FTSE 350 board level appointments.

9. In order to achieve these recommendations, recognition and development of two different populations of women who are well-qualified to be appointed to UK boards needs to be considered:

---

[112] Dale-Olsen et al. (n. 99).

- ▶ Executives from within the corporate sector, for whom there are many different training and mentoring opportunities; and
- ▶ Women from outside the corporate mainstream, including entrepreneurs, academics, civil servants and senior women with professional service backgrounds, for whom there are many fewer opportunities to take up corporate board positions.

A combination of entrepreneurs, existing providers and individuals needs to come together to consolidate and improve the provision of training and development for potential board members.

10. This steering board will meet every six months to consider progress against these measures and will report annually with an assessment of whether sufficient progress is being made.'[113]

Financial Reporting Council initiatives

In May 2011 the Financial Reporting Council issued a consultation on the Recommendations of the Davis Report.[114] It sought views on the measurable objectives companies could meet in respect of their gender policies but excluded the possibility of a quota system. However, the Financial Reporting Council did want to retain some notion of seeking a way of measuring progress on increasing women on the board. The resulting revised Code includes a gender-diversity Supporting Principle.[115] A separate section of the annual report should describe the work of the nomination committee. This section should include a description of the board's policy when making appointments which should ideally include 'due regard' for gender diversity.[116] The Code also includes a revised B.2.4 which requires the company to specifically report on its policy on gender diversity. The company should report on the activity of the appointment committee, and should describe how the committee has tried to achieve gender diversity and what measurable objectives it has set in place to implement the policy of increasing the number of women on the board. If any appointment is made without prior advertising (which would suggest appointing a known person) then the report should explain why this was done.

In respect of the board effectiveness review, the FRC introduced a new Principle (B.6) which requires the board to critically evaluate the diversity of talent on the board including that of gender diversity.[117] Chairmen are encouraged to be much more active in responding to such an evaluation and to address failures to be sufficiently diverse. Lack of diversity is to be understood as a weakness of a company board.

---

[113] Department for Business, Innovation & Skills, *Women on Boards* (n. 107), 4–5.

[114] Financial Reporting Council (FRC), *Feedback Statement: Gender Diversity on Boards* (October 2011) <https://www.frc.org.uk/FRC-Documents/FRC/Feedback-Statement-Gender-Diversity-on-Boards.aspx>.

[115] UK Corporate Governance Code 2012 <http://www.ecgi.org/codes/documents/cg_code_uk_sep2012_en.pdf>.

[116] UK Corporate Governance Code 2012 <http://www.frc.org.uk/Our-Work/Publications/Corporate-Governance/UK-Corporate-Governance-Code-September-2012.pdf >, Supporting Principle B.2.

[117] Ibid, B.6.

Davis 2013

The most recent report from Lord Davis has indicated a marked change in the composition of company boards:

> 'Women now account for 17.3% of FTSE 100 and 13.2% of FTSE 250 board directors (as at 1 March 2013), up from 12.5% and 7.8% respectively in February 2011. An increase of nearly 40%. In 2010, when I was asked to lead this inquiry, women made up just 10.5% of FTSE 100 board members and 6.7% of those in the FTSE 250. This means that since our work began in 2010 the percentage of female held board appointments has increased by nearly 50%.
>
> Crucially, women have secured 34% of all FTSE 100, and 36% of FTSE 250 board appointments since 1 March 2012, clearly showing that businesses are making real efforts to find and appoint capable women to their boards.
>
> Only 6 all-male boards remain in the FTSE 100, down from 21 in 2010, and for the second year running, all-male boards in the FTSE 250 continue to be in the minority at 26.8% (67), down from 52.4% in February 2011.'[118]

The recommendations of the 2013 Report included companies setting targets for more women on the board for 2013 and 2015 and for chairmen to announce these goals in the next six months. It also recommended that chief executives should review the percentage of women they aim to have on their executive committees in the same years. It also called upon the Financial Reporting Council to require listed companies to establish a policy on board diversity, through an amendment to the Corporate Governance Code. Shareholders are also called upon to play a more active role ensuring diversity, which includes considering diversity when looking at reappointments to a company board. It recommended that non-executive directors' positions should be advertised widely and that headhunting firms should have gender diversity policy in place when seeking to fill board level appointments.

CONCLUSION

That the particular social character of women would impact, and positively impact, on decision making in the board of directors is now largely (although not entirely) accepted. Policy makers, shareholders, academics and commentators largely agree that having significantly more women on the board of directors is a desirable goal which must be met. A male dominated board is no longer considered to be a gender neutral decision-making group and its gendered approach may have significant implications for the kinds of decisions that are made. The outstanding question, or debate, is as to how to get more women on the board.

---

[118] Department for Business, Innovation & Skills, Department for Culture, Media & Sport and Government Equalities Office, *Women on Boards 2013: Two Years On* (April 2013) <https://www.gov.uk/government/uploads/system/uploads/attachment_data/file/182602/bis-13-p135-women-on-boards-2013.pdf>.

Legal quotas are not an attractive option for a country wedded to market solutions to corporate governance issues and which has, since Cadbury, preferred persuading particular corporate behaviours rather than mandating them. On the other hand, there are clear obstacles to women reaching these positions because of their current socio-economic positioning. For example, women remain the primary child carers and this does not work well with the unrestricted hours that men, largely unencumbered by childcare responsibilities, are able to take on and which are considered the norm in that environment. As a result, progress in achieving the 30 per cent representation has been slow. Grant Thornton's 2012 Corporate Governance Review, differing from the Davis Report, noted the persistently low percentage of female executive directors: 5.1 per cent in 2012 (2011: 4.9 per cent) for FTSE 100 companies and a slight drop for Mid 250 companies in 2012 at 4.2% (2011: 4.3%). Female appointments are increasing but 'all-male boards endure. Eight FTSE 100 boards and 79 of Mid 250 companies have no women around the table.'[119] Reporting has risen. Seventy-eight per cent (2011: 28%) provide a basic outline, with 16% (2011: 6%) setting out detailed disclosures. However, despite this, Grant Thornton reported that only 23% of FTSE 100 companies and 7% of Mid 250 companies disclosed a target for women on the board.[120]

Grant Thornton's figures show that women remain highly under-represented on the board, notwithstanding that the academic performance of women up to graduate level outstrips that of men and notwithstanding the many studies which show the clear benefits of greater gender diversity on the board. Neither personal ability nor positive contributions to professional group decision making are objective obstacles to equal female participation on the board. The male-orientated corporate board seems to be, therefore, a product of broader social and gendered prejudices. Furthermore, these prejudices have been institutionalised into a structure which is not tolerant of flexible, family-friendly practices and which acts as a barrier to female entry. As such it delivers the decision making of successful men and not the broad spectrum of intellectual and social talent.

Reform of both company law and corporate governance are not simply a matter of changing the words of a statute or code. Laws have their users and the users may not respond to the laws in the way the reformers expect. This may result in new problems which will, in their turn, need some regulatory response. In respect of companies, it is the board of directors who make the decisions and who will have to respond to legislative and governance reform. To promote successful reform, we may have to stop looking at the board as a neutral structure through which instructions are filtered, or something that can be analysed purely as a decision-making group bringing together the benefits of group activity. Instead, how the board will interpret reform, understand it or submit to it might very much depend

---

[119] Grant Thornton, *Corporate Governance Review 2012: The Chemistry of Governance – A Catalyst for Change* (2012), 17 <http://www.grant-thornton.co.uk/Global/Publication_pdf/Corporate_Governance_Review_2012.pdf>.
[120] Ibid, 18.

on the nature of the people involved. It will also depend on broader structures which support their social position and networks which may reinforce inaction in respect of legal requirements for action.

In this chapter we have looked at circumstantial evidence which suggests that the huge power which German bankers possessed over industrial companies and which they could have exercised through the supervisory board was not in fact exercised. Instead, they acted with caution and with a view to promoting stability in the corporate economy rather than profit maximisation for the banks. The example may indicate that the nature of the actors influences the way in which the play is performed. Jewish bankers may well have acted to debunk anti-Semitic stereotypes about being soulless, unchristian usurers. In today's discussion around gender diversity on the board, similar issues arise. Women may be obliged to adopt a male culture in order to be accepted and to debunk gendered stereotypes. This might extinguish any benefit diversity might bring to corporate board decision making. It will also impede the purpose of reform in this area.

Further Reading

L. Dallas, 'The New Managerialism and Diversity on Corporate Boards of Directors' (2001–2002) 76 *Tulan Law Review* 1363.

J. Hawes, *Englanders and Huns: How Five Decades of Enmity Led to the First World War* (Simon & Schuster Ltd, 2014).

M. Jensen and J. Warner, 'The Distribution of Power Among Corporate Managers, Shareholders, and Directors' (January–March 1988) 20 *Journal of Financial Economics* 3.

R. Karmel, 'Should a Duty to the Corporation be imposed on Institutional Shareholders?' (2004) 60(1) *The Business Lawyer* 1.

J.E. Parkinson, *Corporate Power and Responsibility: Issues on the Theory of Company Law* (Oxford, 1993).

P.G.J. Pulzer, *The Rise of Political Anti-Semitism in Germany and Austria* (Wiley and Sons, 1964).

A. Stewart, *Gender, Law and Justice in a Global Market* (Cambridge University Press: Law in Context, 2011).

V. Warther, 'Board Effectiveness and Board Dissent: A Model of the Board's Relationship to Management and Shareholders' (1998) 4(1) *Journal of Corporate Finance* 53.

C. Villiers, (2011) 'Women on Boards: Report from the UK', *European Company Law*, vol. 8, pp. 94–99.

5

CAN HUMAN RIGHTS SHAPE THE MULTINATIONAL COMPANY?[1]

INTRODUCTION

Thus far we have considered how companies may be shaped by ideology, law, corporate governance and the board of directors (or supervisory board) which may itself be constituted by broader social norms. This chapter discusses the degree to which human rights initiatives and considerations may, or may not, shape the company.

The concern with the human rights impact of corporate activity is part of a broader discussion about the activities of companies in developed countries. Global business is constantly innovating organisational forms in order to enhance profitability. Those companies engaging in business in developing countries are likely to be outsourcing the productive part of their operation. They may do so by contracting out parts of their operation to companies or other business organisations in that developing country. Alternatively, they may do so through a corporate network where the parent company is incorporated in the developed country and production is undertaken by a subsidiary company or companies in a developing country. This legal arrangement has traditionally caused problems in terms of establishing parent company liability for torts committed by its subsidiaries.[2]

The destructive impact of many companies operating (in their variously innovating forms) in developing countries has been highlighted by court cases, the media, NGOs and a range of local and international activists. The most recent human rights initiatives to set some standards for corporate activity (measured at minimum by a requirement not to abuse human rights when engaging in business) can be seen as a response to their activism. However, as attractive as the notion of making companies attend to human rights is, and as morally right as it may seem, conceptualisation and implementation has proven very difficult. In this chapter I argue that human rights have not shaped companies to any significant

[1] I am grateful to James Harrison for his guidance on some of the issues raised in this chapter.
[2] See the list of readings in this area at the end of this chapter.

degree. Instead human rights themselves are bent to the shape of financial corporate goals. The demands put upon companies in respect of human rights are little more than paper responses, and in many ways, examined through this chapter, human rights initiatives have further enabled companies to act with impunity, particularly in the developing world.

This is in part because companies are politically conceived as private, despite the immense influence they have on political and economic activity. They are conceived as very distinct from individual states and their responsibilities are therefore deemed incomparable. Traditionally, it is individual states which owe a duty to observe internationally agreed and accepted human rights standards or norms. In terms of international legal instruments, human rights norms derive first from the Universal Declaration of Human Rights in 1948. Subsequently, international human rights norms have come to include economic, cultural, civil and political rights, and to deal with specific issues such as genocide, torture and, most recently, the rights of the child.[3] Individual states' observation of these norms is part of international law but companies' observation of these norms is not. The problem of company accountability for human rights abuses is a question that has become increasingly important as companies are the legal vehicle for the vast majority of business, nationally and internationally. Globally, the multinational company has become a crucial focus for human rights concerns, but none of the documents referred to above create any direct obligation on companies to observe human rights standards. The duty to observe human rights is primarily owed by individual states even when multinational companies are bigger than the economy of the state in which they operate.

Consequently, the United Nations has developed many human rights initiatives that attempt to create corporate responsibility to observe human rights standards. More recently, the Norms on the Responsibilities of Transnational Corporations and Other Business Enterprises (the Norms) were developed by the UN Sub-Commission for the Promotion and Protection of Human Rights from 1999–2003.[4] The UN Global Compact (the Compact) was launched in July 2000. Most recently, the UN special representative on the issue of human rights and transnational

---

[3] UN General Assembly, International Covenant on Economic, Social and Cultural Rights (1966) 993 United Nations Treaty Series 3 <http://www.ohchr.org/en/professionalinterest/pages/ccpr.aspx>; UN General Assembly, International Covenant on Civil and Political Rights (1966) 999 United Nations Treaty Series 171 <http://www.ohchr.org/en/professionalinterest/pages/ccpr.aspx>; UN General Assembly, Prevention and punishment of the crime of genocide (1948) A/RES/260 <http://www.hrweb.org/legal/genocide.html>; UN General Assembly, Convention Against Torture and Other Cruel, Inhuman or Degrading Treatment or Punishment (1984) 1465 United Nations Treaty Series 85 <http://treaties.un.org/Pages/ViewDetails.aspx?mtdsg_no=IV-9&chapter=4&lang=en>; UN General Assembly, Convention on the Rights of the Child (1989) 1577 United Nations Treaty Series 3 <http://www.ohchr.org/EN/ProfessionalInterest/Pages/CRC.aspx>.

[4] UN Sub-Commission on the Promotion and Protection of Human Rights, Economic, Social and Cultural Rights: Norms on the Responsibilities of Transnational Corporations and Other Business Enterprises with Regard to Human Rights (2003) E/CN.4/Sub.2/2003/12/Rev.2 <http://www.unhchr.ch/Huridocda/Huridoca.nsf/0/64155e7e8141b38cc1256d63002c55e8?Opendocument>.

corporations and other business enterprises, Professor John Ruggie, has produced a number of reviews of the current human rights framework, including how it relates to companies and how it can be implemented. In so doing, however, these initiatives have narrowed the responsibilities owed by companies to the people their activities detrimentally impact upon.

By way of a background to the UN special representative's work, this chapter will briefly assess the Norms and the Compact. The bulk of the chapter comprises a description and critical assessment of two key documents to have come from the UN special representative, Protect, Respect and Remedy: a Framework for Business and Human Rights (the Framework)[5] and Guiding Principles on Business and Human Rights: Implementing the United Nations 'Protect, Respect and Remedy' Framework (the Guiding Principles).[6]

1. BACKGROUND INITIATIVES TO RUGGIE'S FRAMEWORK AND GUIDING PRINCIPLES: THE NORMS AND THE COMPACT

The Norms drew on the existing body of human rights to utilise those considered most relevant for companies. The Norms also set out ways in which company adherence to these human rights would be monitored and incorporated into everyday business practice. The Norms include human rights standards on economic, cultural, social, civil, consumer rights and environmental standards. Perhaps the key innovation in the Norms was to make companies *directly* responsible for human rights obligations. Furthermore, in meeting human rights standards, the usual self-monitoring was to be supplemented by external monitoring. The Norms also recommended their incorporation into business contracts. Under the Norms, victims of the company's failure to observe human rights would be entitled to reparation.

Perhaps unsurprisingly, the Norms were immediately unpopular with business. The shift away from self-monitoring and the kind of voluntarism that had previously accompanied the governance of multinational companies made it both radical and alien to companies. Companies were accustomed to choosing their method of indicating observance of human rights and social issues. Enforcement, such as that promoted by the Norms, was all but non-existent. The business community and the government in both the US and the UK did not like the Norms' clarity and specificity on the responsibility of companies, nor did they like the independent monitoring or enforcement procedures. As Graham and Woods note, the US Council for International Business used 'evidence of on-going voluntary regulation to alleviate political pressure for coercive standards and convince governments on the UN Commission on Human Rights not to adopt the "Norms" document'.[7]

---

[5] <http://198.170.85.29/Ruggie-report-7-Apr-2008.pdf>.

[6] <http://www.ohchr.org/Documents/Issues/Business/A-HRC-17-31_AEV.pdf>.

[7] D. Graham and N. Woods, 'Making Global Corporate Self-Regulation Effective in Developing Countries' (2006) 34(5) *World Development Journal* 868.

The Draft Norms proceeded the Global Compact,[8] which had adopted a much looser set of requirements (although arguably a wider set of requirements) and the usual voluntarism in respect of its adoption. The Global Compact was therefore much more in line with business expectations then the Norms. The Global Compact is a set of principles which companies may choose to sign up to if they wish to signify their commitment to human rights. It is based on 10 principles which represent four main areas of social concern: human rights, labour, the environment and anti-corruption. The Global Compact requests companies to 'embrace, support and enact, within their sphere of influence, a set of core values in the areas of human rights, labour standards, the environment and anti-corruption'.[9]

Principle 1 states that 'Businesses should support and respect the protection of internationally proclaimed human rights'. It therefore encompasses the broad spread of internationally recognised human rights. Principle 2 requires companies to 'make sure that they are not complicit in human rights abuses', in order to extend this responsibility to acts done by states on their behalf, or done to enhance the attractiveness of these companies operating in that jurisdiction. This would seem to apply particularly to companies operating in developing countries with more aggressive governments. The next set of principles are more specific. So, Principle 3 asks businesses to uphold freedom of association and recognise collective bargaining, while Principles 4–6 seek to eliminate forced labour, child labour, and discrimination in employment. These principles reflect the approach of the International Labour Organization's Declaration on Fundamental Principles and Rights at Work.

Principles 7–9 are again less specific, asking businesses to support the precautionary principle in relation to environmental challenges, to generally promote environmental responsibility and commit to environmentally friendly technologies. The Compact notes its adherence to the Rio Declaration on Environment and Development in setting out these principles.[10] In respect of anti-corruption activities, the last Principle asks businesses to 'work against corruption in all its forms, including extortion and bribery'. In this, Principle 10 reflects the United Nations Convention against Corruption, but is really asking no more than the law already requires.

So, the Global Compact reflects a broad spread of agreed UN principles in the four areas identified above. In this respect it could be argued that the Global Compact is very ambitious in scope and highly inclusive. However, in terms of compliance, the Global Compact is much less ambitious. It expects companies to

---

[8] United Nations Global Compact <http://www.unglobalcompact.org/>.
[9] Ibid.
[10] Principle 7: Businesses should support a precautionary approach to environmental challenges; Principle 8: Businesses should undertake initiatives to promote greater environmental responsibility; and Principle 9: Businesses should encourage the development and diffusion of environmentally friendly technologies.

show some observance to the principles but there is no expectation that all the Principles need be adhered to in order for a company to be a signed-up member of the Global Compact. Seppala notes that companies more frequently adhere to the principles relating to labour, possibly, she argues, because they are more clearly defined.[11] The Global Compact is also non-binding. Corporations voluntarily sign up to these principles and there is no effective monitoring system. Companies must report on their enactment of the Compact or, if they do not report, face delisting. Thus there is a very minimal expectation of companies and compliance is left to the companies themselves. They are trusted to report truthfully and there are no formal checks on the accuracy of their statements, although NGOs and others may and do challenge companies' claims. However, despite the latitude given to companies under the Global Compact, a huge number of companies fail to comply with the communication of progress and a total of 4,173 companies have been delisted.[12]

The Global Compact has been vastly more popular with business than the Norms. Seppala notes that, unlike the Norms, business had been very involved in both the construction of the document and in its implementation, and 'in addition to business groups, involvement was also sought from individual CEOs to form a critical mass of companies that would provide leadership for the initiative'.[13] This involvement, plus the self-regulatory character of the Global Compact, has served to make it popular with business. 'Unlike the Norms, the Compact focuses on learning and progress over time rather than compliance with principles, which has made it easier for companies to get involved.'[14] For those same reasons, Seppala notes that human rights scholars and activists who want tighter controls over companies have been less enthusiastic about the Compact, arguing that 'companies receive the benefits of association with the UN without being forced to comply with a set of human rights standards'.[15] Furthermore, companies can design their own response to the principles, so that they can become what they, the companies, want them to be. This of course suggests the question: does the Compact have any value at all? It also makes it something of a curiosity that so many companies have failed to maintain their listed status.

Ongoing concerns by civil society groups with the human rights abuses of companies prompted further action from the UN in the form of work directed by the UN special representative Professor John Ruggie. Adopting the Norms was not a viable course of action. Indeed, Ruggie's commission emerged as a result of the

---

[11] N. Seppala, 'Business and the International Human Right Regime: A Comparison of UN Initiatives' (2009) 87 *Journal of Business Ethics* 401.

[12] <http://www.unglobalcompact.org/COP/analyzing_progress/expelled_participants.html>. Ninety-nine companies were delisted in the first six months of 2013; K. Coco, 'UN Global Compact Expels 99 Companies in First Half of 2013' United Nations, 2013 <http://www.unglobalcompact.org/news/339-07-01-2013>.

[13] Seppala (n. 11), 408.

[14] Ibid.

[15] Ibid.

unpopularity of the Norms with both business and with nation states, particularly America and the UK. The Office of the High Commissioner for Human Rights examined and reported on the Norms and, as a result of this report, the Human Rights Commission requested the appointment of a special representative to look at the role of companies in respect to human rights. Professor John Ruggie, a Harvard academic, was duly appointed. Ruggie was also involved in the Global Compact, and to some degree the Ruggie Reports are a synthesis of the Norms and the Compact.

The 2006 Interim Report of the Special Representative criticised the Norms for 'cherry picking' human rights.[16] In contrast, as noted above, the Compact might be said to have encompassed all internationally agreed human rights. Ruggie also criticised the Norms for the level of responsibility placed on companies. The Report argued that the Norms seemed to require companies to bear the same duty to protect against human rights abuses as that owed by individual states and in some respects to owe a higher and more expansive duty than states. Rightly or wrongly, Ruggie was keen to distinguish the *duty* owed by states for human rights abuses and the *responsibility* owed by companies for human rights. Duties, at least in this context, require higher levels of commitment than responsibilities.

The Ruggie Report of 2008 (the Framework)[17] accordingly set out a framework for addressing states' duty to protect human rights as distinct from non-state actors' (including companies') responsibility for human rights. Its 'protect, respect and remedy' framework sets out what states need to do to ensure that they meet their duty to protect against human rights abuses and what corporations need to do to ensure that they respect human rights. The Framework was followed up by a number of interim Reports which culminated into the 2011 Report, Guiding Principles on Business and Human Rights: Implementing the United Nations 'Protect, Respect and Remedy' Framework (the Guiding Principles).[18] The Guiding Principles address how to move from the conceptual framework of responsibilities to practical implementation. The Framework and Guiding Principles have achieved wide appeal. They have been endorsed or employed by 'Governments, business enterprises and associations, civil society and workers' organizations, national human rights institutions, and investors'.[19] Furthermore, its principles have been utilised in the documentation and policies of multilateral institutions such as the International Organization for Standardization and the Organization for Economic Cooperation and Development. Its approach to assessing compliance through due

---

[16] <http://www.reports-and-materials.org/Ruggie-statement-to-UN-Human-Rights-Council-25-Sep-2006.pdf>.

[17] J. Ruggie, Protect, Respect and Remedy: a Framework for Business and Human Rights <http://198.170.85.29/Ruggie-report-7-Apr-2008.pdf>.

[18] J. Ruggie, Report of the Special Representative of the Secretary-General on the issue of human rights and transnational corporations and other business enterprises: Guiding Principles on Business and Human Rights: Implementing the United Nations 'Protect, Respect and Remedy' Framework (2011) <http://www.ohchr.org/Documents/Issues/Business/A-HRC-17-31_AEV.pdf>>.

[19] Ibid, 4.

diligence is being reproduced in many different contexts and jurisdictions as noted later in the chapter. The remainder of this chapter will critically assess both the Framework and the Guiding Principles.

2. A CRITICAL ASSESSMENT OF PROTECT, RESPECT AND REMEDY: A FRAMEWORK FOR BUSINESS AND HUMAN RIGHTS (THE FRAMEWORK) (RUGGIE, 2008)

The Framework assumed that companies would like more guidance from government on the basis that the less governments do, the more they increase reputational and other risks to business. It assumed therefore that any future arrangements could go further than the Global Compact in providing guidance and boundaries for corporate activity. To that end the Framework was concerned to create a new structure for considering and clarifying existing human rights and how they applied to individual states and transnational corporations within the international legal system.[20] The Framework was ordered around three key areas:

(a) the state's *duty* to protect against human rights abuses, including those caused by non-state actors;
(b) the company's *'responsibility'* to respect human rights;
(c) the need for victims' access to *remedies*.

The Framework rests on three pillars. The first is the state duty to protect against human rights abuses by third parties, including business enterprises, through appropriate policies, regulation and adjudication. The second is the corporate responsibility to respect human rights, which means that business enterprises should act with due diligence to avoid infringing on the rights of others and to address adverse impacts with which they are involved. The third is the need for greater access by victims to effective remedy, both judicial and non-judicial. Each pillar is an essential component in an interrelated and dynamic system of preventative and remedial measures: the state duty to protect because it lies at the very core of the international human rights regime; the corporate responsibility to respect because it is the basic expectation society has of business in relation to human rights; and access to remedy because even the most concerted efforts cannot prevent all abuse.[21]

a. The state's *duty* to protect against human rights abuses, including those caused by non-state actors

This duty involves ensuring that all entities within their jurisdiction (including companies) comply with internationally accepted human rights norms. To meet

[20] R. McCorquodale, 'Corporate Social Responsibility and International Human Rights Law' (2009) 87 *Journal of Business Ethics* 385.
[21] Ruggie (n. 18), 4, para. 6.

this duty states must take all appropriate steps to prevent abuses and to locate and punish abuses. They must have appropriate law and regulations and effective enforcement agencies.

Implementation of this is really a continuation of the problems of global regulatory races to the bottom. Multinational corporations are in part attracted to developing countries because of their lax regulation, particularly in respect to labour. Many UK multinational corporations, for example, profited from exploiting the oppressed black labour available in South Africa under the apartheid regime.[22] Though an extreme example, many developing countries are keen to attract investment and so are loath to impose standards upon companies that might discourage investment. Furthermore, in developed countries like the UK whose economy is in part reliant on the provision of regulation for companies, imposing higher standards on companies incorporated in the UK is not an attractive prospect.

McCorquodale argues that the Framework, as it applies to a state's duty, limits the scope of already existing human rights norms. For example, he argues that states already have a duty to protect against human rights abuses by companies either because they have ratified the relevant treaty or because they are bound by customary international law. That being so, a state is bound to ensure that corporations also observe those obligations. A 'state's duty to protect against human rights abuses, including those caused by non-state actors'[23] underlines the state's responsibility and duty for ensuring that not only does *it* observe human rights but that it ensures that *companies* operating under its jurisdiction observe human rights. It creates an active duty to ensure that companies observe human rights where inaction or passive acquiescence will be a breach of that duty. So, McCorquodale argues, although corporations do not have a direct obligation to observe human rights, the states' obligation to protect against human rights abuses extends to those caused by corporations. The state can be in breach of those obligations by failing to stop a corporation violating human rights. This, he argues, applies even where the government is less economically powerful than the corporation, such as the Australian company BHP which 'had such a strong influence over the government of Papua New Guinea and its foreign currency income, that the government passed laws (understood to have been largely drafted by BHP itself) to protect BHP from legal challenge over its activities there, even though those activities had a profound negative impact on its own citizens'.[24]

McCorquodale also argues that the Framework drew the scope of a state's responsibility for companies' activities too tightly by not sufficiently considering 'whether a state's obligation to protect human rights extends to the extra-territorial activities

---

[22] Cases heard as a result of abuses of employees in South Africa include *Adams v Cape Industries* [1990] Ch 433.

[23] McCorquodale (n. 20).

[24] Ibid, 387.

of both the state and non-state actors'.[25] He argues that the Framework fails to consider the already existing circumstances in international law where a state's duty to protect human rights extends outside of its jurisdiction. The International Law Commission, in its Articles on the Responsibility of States for Internationally Wrongful Acts (ILC, 2001) which apply generally to international law, extends a state's duty outside of its jurisdiction, he argues. McCorquodale cites Duffy[26] on four situations where the state will be responsible for the acts of corporations if they breach an international obligation:

▸ A state may incur international responsibility where a company was empowered by law to exercise elements of governmental activity, which corresponds to ILC, 2001, Article 5. McCorquodale gives the example of private companies contracted by states to provide services, such as providing intelligence in occupied Iraq and services in Abu Ghraib. Indeed, he notes the 'increasing use of corporations by states in their extraterritorial military activities'.[27]

▸ A state may incur international responsibility where the company 'was acting under the instructions or direction or control of the state'. McCorquodale gives the example of an Australian corporation, AWB Ltd, which was previously a government agency but retained its original function of marketing and exporting Australian wheat. As a supplier of wheat to the Iraqi Oil-for-Food programme (set up to reduce the severely damaging effects on ordinary Iraqis of the long-term sanctions against Iraq), AWB bribed Iraqi officials to sell Australian wheat, contrary to UN resolutions and with clear impacts on the Iraqis' right to food.[28] Andrew Lindberg, director of AWB, has since been fined for his part in the scandal.[29]

▸ A state may incur international responsibility where the state 'adopts or acknowledges'[30] the acts of the company as its own, which is recognised in ILC, 2001, Article 11. McCorquodale notes that states are very active in supporting the activities of their own corporations which are operating in other countries. This can take the form of financing or, perhaps more importantly, entering into bilateral investment treaties, which may *inter alia* require a host country to pay compensation to a company if it takes action to secure human rights, in such a way which reduces value for the investing company. These 'stabilisation clauses' in investment treaties are discussed in more detail below.

▸ A state may incur international responsibility where it is 'complicit in the activity of the non-state actor or fails to exercise due diligence to prevent the effects

---

[25] Ibid.

[26] H. Duffy, 'Towards Global Responsibilty for Human Rights Protection: A Sketch of International Developments' (2006) 15 *Interights Bulletin* 104.

[27] McCorquodale (n. 20), 388.

[28] Ibid and 'Australia probes Iraq "kickbacks"', *BBC News* (London, 16 January 2006) <http://news.bbc.co.uk/1/hi/world/asia-pacific/4615908.stm>.

[29] A. Haddad, 'Iraq Accepted Bribes for UN Food Deal', *Nuqudy* (9 September 2012) <http://english.nuqudy.com/Gulf/Iraq_Accepted_Bribe-2758>.

[30] McCorquodale (n. 20), 388.

of the actions of non-state actors'.[31] This, argues McCorquodale, is being addressed through a more fluid approach to liability in groups of companies. So, formally, in terms of jurisdiction, he argues that 'the state has an obligation to act in such a way that it has effective laws and practices that protect actions and omissions by state agents and by non-state actors that violate human rights. What this requires is that a state must regulate and control corporations that are incorporated or active in that state (corporate national), in such a way that the corporations do not violate human rights.'[32] Problematically, the state only has jurisdiction over its own nationals, and multinational companies have subsidiaries incorporated near the outsourced production. However, to address this, some courts have made parent companies liable. The European Union is moving toward a 'centre of main interests' test, which focuses on the parent company's strategic and managerial importance.[33] Thus, the responsibility of a state may go beyond its jurisdiction under certain circumstances.

Thus in terms of conceptualising the scope of duties and responsibilities, the Framework may be backtracking on progress made to conceive of a nation's responsibility for corporations in such a way that reflects the global reach of companies. In setting out the obligations of a state and the separate obligations of the company, it may be containing responsibilities within national boundaries.

b. The company's *'responsibility'* to respect human rights

The Framework first makes the point that virtually all aspects of corporate activity can potentially impact on human rights:

> 'There are few if any internationally recognized rights business cannot impact – or be perceived to impact – in some manner. Therefore, companies should consider all such rights. It may be useful for operational guidance purposes to map which rights companies have tended to affect most often in particular sectors or situations. It is also helpful for companies to understand how human rights relate to their management functions – for example, human resources, security of assets and personnel, supply chains, and community engagement. Both means of developing guidance should be pursued, but neither limits the rights companies should take into account.'[34]

The Framework set out a table drawn from over 300 reports of 'alleged corporate-related human rights abuses'[35] which indicates some of the astonishing extent of the problem. Companies have negatively impacted on freedom of association,

---

[31] Ibid, 389.

[32] Ibid, 390.

[33] J. Armour and W.G. Ringe, 'European Company Law 1999–2010: Renaissance and Crisis' (2011) 48 *Common Market Law Review* 125.

[34] J. Ruggie, Report of the Special Representative of the Secretary-General on the issue of human rights and transnational corporations and other business enterprises: Protect, Respect and Remedy: a Framework for Business and Human Rights (2008), para. 52.

[35] Ibid, para. 53.

the right to organise and participate in collective bargaining, the right to non-discrimination, the abolition of slave and forced labour (including child labour), the right to just remuneration and a safe working environment. It has negatively impacted on gender-specific rights such as equal pay and equality at work. It has impacted on rights to a family life and leisure and rest. In respect of non-labour rights, business has negatively impacted on the right to an adequate standard of living, a right to education, the right to marry and have children, the right to have political opinions, religious freedom, freedom of expression, the right to life, liberty and security, freedom from torture and cruelty, a fair trial and freedom of movement, among many others. If just one of these abuses occurs in the course of business, business as usual is surely not an option.

The question for the Framework was, given that the activities of companies can 'impact' on the exercise of human rights, what obligations should, in consequence, be imposed on companies? Ruggie explicitly did not want companies simply to owe the same duties as owed by individual states to uphold human rights. Companies' obligations should be distinct and less onerous than those of the state. Ruggie settled on the notion of the *responsibility to respect* human rights.

The company's responsibility to respect essentially means, 'simply to do no harm'.[36] The standard is not to be defined by the courts; in most cases it will be considered by 'the courts of public opinion' which give a 'company's social licence to operate'.[37] Central to this responsibility was that any failure to respect must be addressed at source: 'a company cannot compensate for human rights harm by performing good deeds elsewhere'.[38] The Report also explained that to do no harm would often require companies to act positively. Ruggie used the example of a workplace anti-discrimination policy which would require the company to act by, for example, introducing 'specific recruitment and training programmes'.[39]

To ensure that companies know if they are respecting human rights, they must apply due diligence, the key to discharging this responsibility. Due diligence 'describes the steps a company must take to become aware of, prevent and address adverse human rights impacts. Comparable processes are typically already embedded in companies because in many countries they are legally required to have information and control systems in place to assess and manage financial and related risks.'[40] The scope of due diligence would have regard to the context and nature of their activities and of their relationships with state and non-state actors.

After consultation, Ruggie concluded that the positive action required by a corporation to exercise due diligence in respect of human rights would involve four specified elements:[41]

---

[36] Ibid, para. 24.
[37] Ibid, para. 54.
[38] Ibid, para. 55.
[39] Ibid, para. 55.
[40] Ibid, para. 56.
[41] Ibid, paras 60–63.

- having a human rights policy;
- assessing the human rights impact of company activity;
- institutionalising those values and findings;
- tracking and reporting activities.

In part because of companies' familiarity with due diligence processes, Ruggie considered this a useful mechanism for them to assess their compliance with this responsibility. However, in the corporate context, due diligence is utilised to assess potential harms or risks to the company, threats, that is, to profit maximisation. It is not utilised to consider the interests of those outside of mainstream corporate governance goals and indeed whose interests may conflict with meeting those goals. A due diligence database was created by De Shutter et al. which sets out over 100 examples of due diligence being utilised by over 20 countries.[42] The authors found that states utilised different methods to ensure human rights due diligence. Disclosure was widely used, for example Taylor argues that most states required companies to report on non-financial matters including the environment, labour issues and human rights that may impact on the companies' financial position.[43] In some EU states, advertising to consumers must be based on real evidence which advertisers are required to make available.[44] States also use 'conditionality', that is by engaging in due diligence companies may gain certain benefits from the state. Taylor uses the example of the requirement by a number of EU Member States of environmental and human rights due diligence as a condition for export credit or export insurance.[45] Due diligence may also be required to enable companies to comply with the law. For example, due diligence is required by most EU Member States to comply with environmental legislation. Environmental Impact Assessments in which companies must assess, prevent, mitigate and report on their impact on the environment are usually requirements for licences.[46]

While there is a great deal of variation in the examples set out in this database, the defensive nature of due diligence when applied by companies is very striking. Due diligence is used to create an a priori defence to potential claims including those of human rights abuses. For example, section 174 of the Companies Act 2006 requires directors to meet objective and subjective standards of care in respect of their duty to the company. There is no specific requirement to have a written policy which sets out commitments to corporate social responsibility or human rights; however, an absence of such a policy, which reflects a due diligence approach, would almost certainly constitute a breach of a duty of care.

---

[42] O. De Shutter et al. <http://hrdd.accountabilityroundtable.org/sites/default/files/Human%20Rights%20Due%20Diligence%20-Examples-.pdf>.

[43] M. Taylor, 'Due Diligence: A compliance standard for responsible European business' (forthcoming in *European Company Law*, Special Edition, 2014).

[44] The EU Directive on Unfair Commercial Practices (2005/29/EEC), cited by De Shutter et al. (n. 42), p. 40.

[45] Taylor (n. 43)

[46] Ibid and De Shutter et al. (n. 42), p. 20.

Furthermore, 'a written policy statement and a compliance program would be in the best interests of the company, because otherwise the company could be exposed to such harms as a fine or loss of business or reputation. This could amount to a breach of the duty of care by the directors, or at least those directors charged with responsibility for that area of the company's operations that have been ignored.'[47] The United States Alien Tort Claims Act 1789 (280 U.S.C. § 1350) enabled foreign plaintiffs to sue non-United States companies for harm suffered abroad. Since the 1980s this had provided a forum for remedying breaches of human rights by multinational companies. The negative publicity for companies of an Alien Tort Claims Act lawsuit had prompted many companies to adopt stringent written policies relating to human rights commitments. These policies involved a human rights impact assessment and measures to reduce that impact and further measures to ensure compliance. Liability under this head is less of a problem for companies since the decision in *Kiobel v Royal Dutch Petroleum Co.*, where the US Supreme Court held that the Alien Tort Claims Act did not apply extra-territorially.[48] However, it is an illustration of how due diligence processes provide a shield against civil actions and a way for companies to self-promote as responsible business citizens.[49]

c. The need for victims' access to *remedies*

Access to remedies is conceived to cover a multitude of state-based and non-state-based remedies. Remedies might take the form of state enforcement of claims against companies. The Framework expects the state to take positive steps to ease the process whereby victims of human rights abuses might access redress:

> 'Expectations for states to take concrete steps to adjudicate corporate-related human rights harm are expanding. Treaty bodies increasingly recommend that states investigate and punish human rights abuses by corporations and provide access to redress for such abuse when it affects persons within their jurisdiction. Redress could include compensation, restitution, guarantees of non-repetition, changes in relevant law and public apologies.'[50]

The Framework also addresses judicial mechanisms which, through doctrines such as separate corporate personality, have traditionally inhibited victims' redress against asset-wealthy parent companies, where it is subsidiaries that have injured or committed human rights abuses.[51] The Framework notes that there has been some movement within states on this issue, citing the United States Alien Tort Claims Act. This point looks substantially less robust since the decision in *Kiobel v Royal Dutch Petroleum Co.* noted above. The Framework also notes that

---

[47] De Shutter et al. (n. 42), p. 111.
[48] 133 S. Ct. 1659 (2013).
[49] De Shutter et al. (n. 42), p. 123.
[50] Ruggie (n. 34), para. 83.
[51] *Adams v Cape Industries* [1990] Ch 433.

courts are now less likely to dismiss a case on the basis that there is a more appropriate forum.[52]

Non-judicial grievance mechanisms are also considered to be useful on condition that they meet certain criteria. These include the need to be legitimate, with 'sufficiently independent governance structures', accessible, predictable, equitable, rights-compatible (that is they reflect internationally recognised rights) and transparent. The Framework also notes that internal corporate governance procedures may be used, if not too partisan. It also notes that there are a number of non-judicial state-based forums which are competent to hear issues. However, what the Framework seems to overlook is that access to remedies against human rights abuses is already a human right enshrined in the law in many jurisdictions.[53]

3. A CRITICAL ASSESSMENT OF GUIDING PRINCIPLES ON BUSINESS AND HUMAN RIGHTS: IMPLEMENTING THE UNITED NATIONS 'PROTECT, RESPECT AND REMEDY' FRAMEWORK (THE GUIDING PRINCIPLES) (RUGGIE, 2011)

After extensive consultation with human rights representatives, business groups and civil society groups, the 2011 Report, Guiding Principles on Business and Human Rights: Implementing the United Nations 'Protect, Respect and Remedy' Framework was published.[54] The Guiding Principles aim to set out ways in which the Framework can be put into action. The Guiding Principles do not intend to specify exact activity and indicate that it is beginning a process of change. They intend to establish 'a common global platform for action, on which cumulative progress can be built, step-by-step, without foreclosing any other promising longer-term developments'.[55]

The Guiding Principles further note that the intention is to draw out the implication of already existing human rights principles and to operate as a mechanism to bring existing principles into a single regime for action:

'The Guiding Principles' normative contribution lies not in the creation of new international law obligations but in elaborating the implications of existing standards and practices for States and businesses; integrating them within a single, logically coherent and comprehensive template; and identifying where the current regime falls short and how it should be improved.'[56]

The Guiding Principles are set within the existing recognition of:

---

[52] *Lubbe and Others v Cape plc* [2000] 1 WLR 1545.
[53] See, for example, the Human Rights Act 1998, Sch. 1, Article 6.
[54] J. Ruggie, Report of the Special Representative of the Secretary-General on the issue of human rights and transnational corporations and other business enterprises: Guiding Principles on Business and Human Rights: Implementing the United Nations 'Protect, Respect and Remedy' Framework (2011).
[55] Ibid, para. 13.
[56] Ibid, para. 14.

'(a) States' existing obligations to respect, protect and fulfil human rights and fundamental freedoms;

(b) The role of business enterprises as specialized organs of society performing specialized functions, required to comply with all applicable laws and to respect human rights;

(c) The need for rights and obligations to be matched to appropriate and effective remedies when breached.'

Furthermore the Guiding Principles apply to 'all States and to all business enterprises, both transnational and others, regardless of their size, sector, location, ownership and structure'.[57]

The first 'foundational' principle states that:

'States must protect against human rights abuse within their territory and/or jurisdiction by third parties, including business enterprises. This requires taking appropriate steps to prevent, investigate, punish and redress such abuse through effective policies, legislation, regulations and adjudication.'[58]

States are not responsible for human rights abuses but are responsible for failing to respond appropriately to knowable breaches of human rights. They may be responsible if the company can be attributed to them. Accordingly, they have a greater duty to protect against human rights abuses in companies which are owned or controlled by the state or companies which substantially benefit the state.[59]

The second principle states that:

'States should set out clearly the expectation that all business enterprises domiciled in their territory and/or jurisdiction respect human rights throughout their operations.'[60]

The commentary recommends nothing specific here and merely notes that international law does not require this, but that some human rights treaty bodies recommend that parent company home states take steps to ensure that their subsidiaries in foreign jurisdictions do not abuse human rights. It notes the OECD recommendations and that group reports are often required from parent companies of multinational corporations. The commentary notes that it may be in a state's interest to set out these expectations as it may affect its global reputation. The 'should' in this principle rests on states aligning their own self-interest with setting out 'expectations'. The alignment seems akin to the business case for corporate social responsibility (noted in Chapter 6) which makes human rights not a

---

[57] Ibid, Annex, p. 6. Also set out in more detail in Principle 14. The responsibility of business enterprises to respect human rights applies to all enterprises regardless of their size, sector, operational context, ownership and structure. Nevertheless, the scale and complexity of the means through which enterprises meet that responsibility may vary according to these factors and with the severity of the enterprise's adverse human rights impacts.

[58] Ibid, Principle 1, p. 6.

[59] Ibid, p. 4.

[60] Ibid, Principle 2, p. 7.

desirable end in itself but something that may be desirable if it enhances a particular state's reputation. That will, of course, depend on the kind of reputation a state wants to nurture.

The concept of 'expectations' has no legal implications (it can hardly be thought that states currently do not expect companies to behave) and gives little in the way of direction for companies.

Principle 3 sets out the need to underpin law-making with polices which meet a state's duty to protect. In respect of companies this includes ensuring that the laws which are applicable to them do not restrict their ability to respect human rights. It also includes a state's duty to provide guidance to business on how to respect and to encourage companies to disclose (where appropriate) how they address their human rights impacts. This support of business to ensure they respect human rights is particularly acute where those businesses are operating in conflict-affected areas where human rights abuses are much more likely.[61] This principle envisages the home state taking a lead role in the way multinational companies' subsidiaries operate in conflict-ridden host countries because a host country's state may not be in a position to do so. Home countries' states should give advice at an early stage, particularly in respect of sexual and gender-based violence. States should warn businesses of any heightened risks in host countries and review whether their policies address those instances of heightened risk.

In ensuring that states meet their human rights obligations, they should 'maintain adequate policy space ... when pursuing business related policy objectives with other States or business enterprises, for instance through investment treaties'.[62] There are a current estimated 2,800 bilateral investment treaty agreements which set standards for the treatment of investors of one country investing in the territory of another. As such this is a key issue in global corporate capitalism.[63] Failure by states to adhere to the terms of the agreement will allow companies to sue them for compensation. This makes bilateral investment treaties an extremely effective tool for investors as internal investment arbitration may award millions of dollars against a state for breaches of the agreement. However, these breaches are frequently the result of states trying to meet their human rights obligations. For example, one report estimated that the total potential value of claims against Argentina for breaches of investment agreements arising from the

---

[61] Ibid, p. 7.
[62] Ibid, p. 9.
[63] UNCTAD, World Investment Report 2011 Non-Equity Modes of International Production and Development (United Nations: New York and Geneva, 2011), 100. Also see UNCTAD, Investment Policy Monitors, available at http://www.unctad.org. Despite the most-favoured-nation principles (principles embodied in the World Trade Organization) which attempt to make tariff and trade practices equal or 'non-discriminatory', most nations negotiate their trade around a range of customised trade and investment agreements with different countries. Bilaterals (investment treaties and trade agreements between two countries) are attractive because they can cover areas not covered by the World Trade Organization's most-favoured-nation regime, such as government procurement, competition policy, and labour and environmental matters. R. Folsom, 'Bilateral Free Trade Agreements: A Critical Assessment and WTO Regulatory Reform Proposal' (2008) San Diego Legal Studies Paper No. 08-070.

2001–2002 crisis could reach up to $80 billion.[64] Argentina froze water prices charged by the private operators, who had a trade agreement which allowed them to set the tariff, in order to meet its human rights obligations to its citizens. Often, as in many of Argentina's breached treaties, these breaches are the result of the state attempting to address social problems or uphold human rights obligations.

Investment treaties are attractive to both investor nations and investee nations. Investor nation governments are supportive of their nations' corporations and will enter into bilateral investment treaties to help them.[65] Investee nations will seek investment to raise production and levels of technical advancement. However, these agreements frequently put states in a position where they cannot attend to both their human rights obligations *and* meet the terms of the agreement. This conflict can become particularly acute when circumstances change. For example, typically, the terms of the agreement will attempt to uphold investors' 'legitimate expectations'. So if a company expected to charge certain prices to the host country for certain services and is not able to do so, then that expectation will have been breached. However, there may be clear human rights obligations which require host states to change those prices, thwarting the company's expectation. For example, a state must uphold the human right to water under a resolution adopted by the UN General Assembly.[66] However, in the case of Argentina, noted above, the dispute was arbitrated, with the Argentinian state arguing the defence of necessity, but the court ruled in favour of the investors. Their expectation to be able to increase tariffs was legitimate and was thwarted by state action.

Investment and trade agreements usually provide for compensation for the investor in the event of expropriation, including *indirect* expropriation. This can be particularly problematic for host countries as indirect expropriation may cover a number of situations which the state cannot avoid, if it is to uphold human rights. This sort of provision, often in the form of 'stabilisation clauses', will require the state to pay compensation to corporations for changes, such as increases in labour rights, which will reduce the amount of profit they will make, thus reducing the value of their investment. Where a municipal authority in Mexico sought to uphold the right to health by refusing to give a permit for a hazardous waste facility, when permission had been given by the national government, it was held to be an indirect expropriation.[67]

Because of the overwhelming economic power which these agreements give to investor corporations at the expense of human rights, the Framework (2008) recommended that stabilisation clauses which restrict a state's ability to protect

---

[64] W. Burke-White, 'The Argentine Financial Crisis: State Liability Under BITs and the Legitimacy of the ICSID System' (2008) U of Penn, Inst for Law & Econ Research Paper No. 08-01, 5 <http://ssrn.com/abstract=1088837>.

[65] McCorquodale (n. 20), at 389, says 'This sort of active support can lead to the state being internationally responsible for the consequences of a corporation's activities.'

[66] UN General Assembly, Resolution adopted by the General Assembly: The Human Right to Water and Sanitation (2010) (A/RES/64/292).

[67] *Metalclad Corporation v United Mexican States* (ICSID Case No. Arb/AF/97/1), Award, August 30, 2000.

human rights should be removed from investment and trade agreements. However, despite the weight of political power that resides in bilateral treaties of this kind, the Guiding Principles only recommend that they should be carefully drafted so that any protections for investors against future changes in law do not interfere with the state's bona fide efforts to implement laws, regulations or policies in order to meet its human rights obligations. This falls far short of removing them completely but merely advises more careful drafting so there is space to accommodate for change. The wiggle room that the Guiding Principles suggest is unlikely to be negotiable by states desperate for outside investors. This puts them in the position of either breaching human rights or breaching bilateral treaties. The latter is usually a lot more expensive.

The nature and scope of the corporate responsibility to respect human rights and how companies should meet this responsibility is set out in Principles 11–24. Principle 11 states that: 'Business enterprises should respect human rights. This means that they should avoid infringing on the human rights of others and should address adverse human rights impacts with which they are involved.' The commentary explains that this responsibility is universally applicable, 'a global standard of expected conduct'. It exists notwithstanding the human rights abuses of the host state. 'It exists independently of States' abilities and/or willingness to fulfil their own human rights obligations, and does not diminish those obligations. And it exists over and above compliance with national laws and regulations protecting human rights.'[68] As well as being a standard bearer for human rights, companies must alternatively ensure that they do not undermine a state's ability to uphold human rights, specifically by undermining their legal system. 'Business enterprises should not undermine States' abilities to meet their own human rights obligations, including by actions that might weaken the integrity of judicial processes.' The latter requirement is useful and justifiable. Large multinational corporations are in a position to undermine the host countries' legal system though their economic and political power. The former requirement is, however, more problematic because it undermines state independence. Ruggie recommends that multinational corporations create their own micro-world of legal behaviour which may conflict with the host countries'. It is justified because they are adhering to 'the global standard'; however, as I will argue later, that so-called universal standard is whatever individual companies say it is through the medium of their human rights due diligence reports. As such it may well undermine the host countries' judicial system.

Another problem with the rights recognised by the Guiding Principles is that they are so expansive and include so many other human rights documents that untangling the actual responsibilities becomes very complicated. The nature of company responsibility to respect is defined as 'internationally recognized human rights – understood, at a minimum, as those expressed in the International Bill of

---

[68] Ruggie (n. 54), Principle 11, commentary.

Human Rights[69] and the principles concerning fundamental rights set out in the International Labour Organization's Declaration on Fundamental Principles and Rights at Work[70].[71] The commentary states that this responsibility may be extended in respect of special groups. For example, United Nations instruments have elaborated further on the rights of indigenous peoples; women; national or ethnic, religious and linguistic minorities; children; persons with disabilities; and migrant workers and their families. Moreover, in situations of armed conflict, enterprises should respect the standards of international humanitarian law. This formidable range of rights swamps rather than clarifies. Unlike the much-maligned Norms, there is little attempt to tease out what might be applicable to companies and those rights that they must adhere to. The Guiding Principles do not set out the kinds of human rights companies, as opposed to other actors, need to be cognisant of. Instead it directs companies to existing standards already required of states without guidance as to which standard would be applicable. As Deva states, 'this process of transplantation would neither be easy nor free from conceptual problems'.[72] He uses the example of a state's duty to recognise the right of people to 'the highest attainable standard of physical and mental health' under Article 12 of the International Covenant on Economic, Social and Cultural Rights to demonstrate how difficult it would be for a company to adopt that standard.

Principle 13 requires businesses to avoid adverse human rights impacts in their own activity (whether that includes their subsidiaries is not specified). Furthermore it requires that companies should 'seek to prevent or mitigate adverse human rights impacts that are directly linked to their operations, products or services by their business relationships, even if they have not contributed to those impacts'.[73] This would seem to be a very expansive duty, one with the potential to extend human rights considerations all along the value chain of multinational corporations and to enjoin them to enforce responsibility for human rights. However, the commentary limits this and is more precise about how this would be undertaken. Under Principle 19, mitigating adverse human rights impacts along the value chain is limited to those identified in their own impact assessments. They will act on those in the ways set out in Principle 19. There is no outside independent arbiter to deal with disputes throughout the value chain.

In Principle 15 the process by which companies may meet their responsibility to respect human rights is set out in brief, and is expanded in Principles 16–24. Principle 15 says that companies should have:

---

[69] Consisting of the Universal Declaration of Human Rights and the main instruments through which it has been codified: the International Covenant on Civil and Political Rights and the International Covenant on Economic, Social and Cultural Rights.

[70] Including eight ILO core conventions as set out in the Declaration on Fundamental Principles and Rights at Work.

[71] Ruggie (n. 54), Principle 12.

[72] S. Deva 'Guiding Principles on Business and Human Rights: Implications for Companies', *European Company Law*, vol. 9, issue 2, 101 at 103.

[73] Ruggie (n. 54), Principle 13.

'(a) A policy commitment to meet their responsibility to respect human rights;
(b) A human rights due-diligence process to identify, prevent, mitigate and account for how they address their impacts on human rights;
(c) Processes to enable the remediation of any adverse human rights impacts they cause or to which they contribute.'

It is on operationalising the Framework that the Guiding Principles become most problematic. In short, what is to be regarded as respecting human rights is a matter for the company, determined by its own self-analysis through the mechanism of human rights due diligence assessments. The start of this process is setting out a policy statement on human rights. Principle 16 states that to enable the embedding of respect, companies should have a statement of policy which is approved by senior management and informed by experts drawn from outside of the company. The statement should set out the human rights expectations of the business enterprise from all those involved with the business, specifically 'business partners and other parties directly linked to its operations, products or services'.[74] The statement should be publicly available and communicated to those within the organisation and those with whom the business deals. The statement should be embedded in the structure of the organisation and reflected in its operations.

Constructing the policy statement is therefore a largely internal process which the commentary explains will reflect the nature of a particular organisation and involve incentive schemes for management. And, while the statement should be publicly available and expressly communicated to business associates, investors and, where there are significant risks, to stakeholders, the latter will not be part of the process of embedding the responsibility to respect human rights. No dialogue with stakeholders is envisaged here.

In determining whether these polices are being followed and are effective, the Guiding Principles state that companies should use human rights due diligence. This will assist companies in identifying, preventing and mitigating negative human rights impacts. The process should involve assessing human rights impacts, acting on the findings, tracking the effects of the response and communicating how the impacts have been addressed. Guiding Principle 17 states that human rights due diligence:

'(a) Should cover adverse human rights impacts that the business enterprise may cause or contribute to through its own activities, or which may be directly linked to its operations, products or services by its business relationships;
(b) Will vary in complexity with the size of the business enterprise, the risk of severe human rights impacts, and the nature and context of its operations;
(c) Should be ongoing, recognizing that the human rights risks may change over time as the business enterprise's operations and operating context evolve.'

---

[74] Ibid, Principle 16.

Why should companies do this? Again the argument is instrumental. Companies should do this to protect themselves from legal action. The clear benefit of the impact assessment is that: 'Conducting appropriate human rights due diligence should help business enterprises address the risk of legal claims against them by showing that they took every reasonable step to avoid involvement with an alleged human rights abuse.'[75]

A number of commentators have pointed out the many flaws in this process. Harrison argues that human rights due diligence needs to be subject to stronger requirements in respect of 'transparency, external participation and verification; and independent monitoring and review'.[76] He argues that as the human rights due diligence provisions contain many of the procedural elements of existing human rights impact assessments, it is likely that companies will adopt human rights impact assessments as a way of meeting their due diligence responsibilities.[77] Consequently, he argues, the existing debate and concerns about human rights impact assessments become relevant and may assist in informing an effective way for human rights due diligence to meet human rights obligations. In particular, he argues, the self-regulatory elements of human rights impact assessments are reflected in human rights due diligence. Accordingly, he argues, the importance given to due diligence further underlines the intention to make self-regulation central to corporations' responsibility for human rights.

Harrison further notes that Principles 18–21 fairly well reflect existing practice in respect of compiling self-regulatory human rights impact assessments, in respect of consultation (Principle 18), action (Principle 19), monitoring the effectiveness of that action (Principle 20) and transparency in communicating to relevant persons how businesses are addressing human rights impacts (Principle 21). The Guiding Principles do not add any more to the mix in respect of participation, transparency and monitoring than is already offered by human rights impact assessments. A more detailed examination of these points is set out below.

a. Participation

In undertaking human rights due diligence, the process begins with an assessment of the human rights impact of the company's activity. In so doing, Principle 18 refers to the need for corporations to consult 'internal and/or independent external human rights expertise' and 'potentially affected groups and other relevant stakeholders'.

In the commentary it is made clear that particularly vulnerable groups should be considered. For example, differences in needs (such as between men and women) should be considered. All assessments should be made regularly 'in response to or

---

[75] Ibid, Principle 17, commentary. It also notes that this will not be an absolute protection.

[76] J. Harrison, 'An Evaluation of the Institutionalisation of Corporate Human Rights Due Diligence' (2012) Warwick School of Law Research Paper No. 2012/18, 1.

[77] While Ruggie notes the self-regulatory character of human rights impact assessments, he does not equate human rights impact assessments with human rights due diligence.

anticipation of changes in the operating environment (e.g. rising social tensions); and periodically throughout the life of an activity or relationship'.[78] It notes that 'potentially affected stakeholders' should be consulted or 'reasonable alternatives such as consulting credible, independent expert resources, including human rights defenders and others from civil society' should be considered.[79]

Principle 18 does not make consultation with stakeholders and affected communities central to the assessment. Indeed, it leaves much to the discretion of the corporation. As Harrison argues, 'the extent of the engagement is still very much up to the company to determine and "meaningful consultation" is open to a broad spectrum of interpretations'.[80] In failing to make stakeholders central to the assessment process, their traditional and well-documented importance in bringing human rights abuses to public attention is overlooked. Once this largely self-assessment is done, it is then integrated into the company's structure and operations.[81] Effective integration is said to involve responding to the assessment in internal decision making, budget allocations and monitoring. If the company's activity has caused adverse human rights impacts, the company should take steps to redress them.

Companies are required to act in respect of the adverse human rights impacts of business partners or other businesses in the value chain. However, the level of action required will depend on the level of economic power or leverage that the company possesses. In the final analysis, if a business associate commits human right abuses but that business associate is essential to the company's business, the company is not obliged to terminate the relationship. Instead, 'it should be able to demonstrate its own ongoing efforts to mitigate the impact and be prepared to accept any consequences – reputational, financial or legal – of the continuing connection'.[82] This is really a reiteration of the status quo. If you sup with the devil in business, you may find yourself, as Nike did, unpopular with consumers. However, it is worth remembering that these reputational issues became important because of the role of NGOs and stakeholders in bringing abuses to the attention of the world. The Guiding Principles seem to sideline these actors and bring observance of human rights impacts in house. Companies' own activity in engaging in human rights due diligence may then act as a shield against legal action or reputational damage.

b. Monitoring

Principle 20 sets out how the effectiveness of companies' actions in redressing human rights impacts will be monitored. It states that such monitoring or tracking should:

[78] Ruggie (n. 54), Principle 18, commentary.
[79] Ibid.
[80] Harrison (n. 76), 13.
[81] Ruggie (n. 54), Principle 19.
[82] Ibid, Principle 19, commentary.

(a) Be based on appropriate qualitative and quantitative indicators;

(b) Draw on feedback from both internal and external sources, including affected stakeholders.[83]

The commentary emphasises the need to track the effectiveness of companies' responses to the most affected groups of human rights impacts and to incorporate that tracking into their usual auditing, reporting and internal grievance processes. However, Harrison argues that this tracking is too internal to the company and lacks the credible independent body which could provide effective and external monitoring. Similarly Deva argues that companies can improve significantly on the tracking requirements set out in the Guiding Principles, 'by providing sufficiently concrete – rather than general or vague – information to stakeholders frequently and in an easily assessable format. An independent verification of remedial measures taken by companies would further enhance the validity of reporting.'[84]

Furthermore Harrison, Melish and Meidinger (in different papers) point out that external monitoring would not only improve the activities of the individual companies but would assist in pooling information about good practice. Melish and Meidinger argue that effective monitoring is key to effective management; 'following the maxim that it is not possible to manage that which is not measured.'[85] When companies are able to look at the performance of other companies they can learn and improve. Effective monitoring requires both the company and the community to establish positive goals, indicators to assess whether those goals are being reached, and a timetable within which to meet them. Then company actors can see how they and other companies have met these benchmarks:

'By determining a baseline and establishing a set of benchmarks or targets to indicate the level of performance expected by a given time, performance monitoring provides a mechanism by which distinct social actors can assess other social actors' relative success in making improvement in performance measures, such as the enjoyment of human rights for particularly affected communities.'[86]

Harrison argues that open, external monitoring would help level the playing field in terms of how companies respond to action and monitoring, where at present there is a huge divergence in approach and commitment. For example, he notes that the human rights impact assessment of BP's Tangguh LNG Project is merely a brief summary of recommendations. Nestlé claims to have undertaken human rights impact assessments in Columbia, Nigeria, Angola and Sri Lanka, though no documents are publically available of these assessments to judge.[87] Thus, there is

---

[83] Ibid, Principle 20.

[84] Deva (n. 72), p. 107.

[85] T. Melish and E. Meidinger, 'Protect, Respect, Remedy and Participate: "New Governance" Lessons for the Ruggie Framework', in R. Mares, *Business and Human Rights at a Crossroads: The Legacy of John Ruggie* (Martinus Nijhoff Publishers, 2012), 321.

[86] Ibid.

[87] Ibid, 11–12.

no broader educational value in the human rights impact assessments they have undertaken. In contrast, Nomogaia's human rights impact assessments are undertaken by independent experts and contain 'rigorous consultation processes and the methodology for assessment and full reports are made fully available on the internet'.[88] These are more believable and provide valuable insights which may be utilised by other companies.

c. Transparency

The issue of transparency connects closely with that of tracking of companies' actual progress in assessing human rights impacts and acting on those findings. The Guiding Principles require effective tracking to be communicated successfully to all affected parties. Principle 21 states that business enterprises should be 'prepared to communicate'[89] externally how they address their human rights impacts. Communication should be clear and with sufficient detail to be able to evaluate the company's activity. The commentary to Principle 21 sets up two kinds of communication. For companies likely to have lower human rights impacts, 'in-person meetings, online dialogues, consultation with affected stakeholders' are suggested as sufficient. For companies likely to have a 'severe human rights impact',[90] formal reporting is recommended which 'should cover topics and indicators concerning how enterprises identify and address adverse impacts on human rights'.[91] It notes that external monitoring can be useful as sector-specific indicators, but does not require it.

However, Harrison argues that this external communication is not sufficient and in order to make human rights due diligence effective, full publication of a company's methodology and assessment processes are required. This level of transparency is required for two key reasons. First, transparency may allow assessors to understand the due diligence process and to learn from each other. Work on human rights impact assessments, he argues, indicates that learning from others has been key to their development. The UN Guiding Principles on human rights impact assessments of trade and investment agreements were, he says, 'developed as a result of extensive examination and refection on existing practices in the field'.[92] Secondly, 'transparency facilitates effective engagement by a range of important actors; civil society actors, academics, UN actors, state officials, even consumers'.[93] They 'cannot hope to become educated about a company's performance if they do not have access to information about how due diligence processes were performed and the results they gave rise to'.[94]

---

[88] Ibid, 15.
[89] Ruggie (n. 54), 20.
[90] Ibid.
[91] Ibid.
[92] Harrison (n. 76), 12.
[93] Ibid.
[94] Ibid, 13.

Similarly, Melish and Meidinger underline the importance of transparency as key to effective 'participation' in human right impacts. Without participation, compliance with the Guiding Principles is likely to be only a formal tick box exercise, and participation relies on transparency. Furthermore, they argue, a lack of participation might actually arrest the kinds of activism which have exposed human rights abuses in the past. Lack of participation will encourage the 'paper compliance' or 'greenwashing' which has in the past enabled companies to use 'formal policy uptake to avoid exposure by activists while failing to engage in the more difficult and expensive process of actual implementation'.[95] Indeed, sharing information with stakeholders and those affected by corporate activity, while at the same time encouraging no real engagement in change, has the effect of homogenising reporting practices, but not changing operational practices. They see transparency as key to countering these tendencies because that will enable 'effective competitor programmes and social monitoring'.[96]

For Melish and Meidinger, good monitoring, transparency and participation would enable all effective actors, particularly the civil actors to participate in an effective socialisation of the company. They argue that the 'protect, respect and remedy' framework requires an additional pillar, that of 'participate'. Participation requires proper tracking and effective transparency, so that the Ruggie Framework does not facilitate the exclusion of all actors involved in human rights or affected by abuses. This would stop the Framework and Guiding Principles creating nothing more than a new *self*-regulatory regime.

d. Remediation

The Guiding Principles envisage companies' construction of a written human rights policy and the utilisation of due diligence as being the main vehicle to ensure that companies respect human rights. However, if despite this companies 'identify that they have caused or contributed to adverse impacts', they must redress this through 'legitimate processes'.[97] The commentary then specifies different possible remediation. First, if the company is directly responsible, it can utilise internal grievance mechanisms or state-based non-judicial grievance mechanisms. The essential characteristics of these mechanisms are set out in Principle 31. They should be legitimate, accountable, fair and enabling of trust from the aggrieved stakeholders. They must be assessable to the users, predictable, with set norms and procedures; they should be equitable, enabling fair access to information by the concerned parties. They should be transparent, keeping the parties abreast of developments. The outcomes of the procedure should 'accord with internationally recognized rights'. When utilising internal grievance mechanisms, they additionally need to be 'based on engagement and dialogue: consulting the stakeholder

---

[95] Melish and Meidinger (n. 85), 311.
[96] Ibid.
[97] Ruggie (n. 54), Principle 22 (for both quotations).

groups for whose use they are intended on their design and performance, and focusing on dialogue as the means to address and resolve grievances'.[98] The commentary also recommends that when adjudication is needed, a legitimate, independent third party should be engaged. The company-level grievance mechanisms set out in Principle 28 are avowedly designed to address the grievance of stakeholders at an early stage and to halt its escalation.[99] While this may be desirable in many instances where action is required quickly, it may also operate as a way of shutting down controversy to quieten legitimate grievances and avoid examining all the issues.

If the human rights impact in question has legal implications, such as criminal culpability, then the company must use state-based judicial mechanisms. Where the human rights abuses have been caused by an organisation linked to the company, it is not required to give remediation but assist and take a role in doing so. As Deva notes, this 'hands-off' approach may not be feasible anymore, especially when companies are seen to benefit from the abuses of business partners. However, it is more likely that companies will be obligated only to the extent of that set out in Principle 19.

CONCLUSION

The UN Norms attempted to create a focus around particular human rights which were appropriate for business, but the Norms alienated business. Problematically, in an international context a high degree of consensus is required and that consensus is difficult where levels of development and political power differ so greatly. The Global Compact restricted itself to setting out best practice principles with no monitoring and only loose self-reporting. This was much more palatable for business because it did not require real change. The Ruggie Framework attempted to draw together the initiatives of many different groups and formulated a framework for human rights around the notion of protect, respect and remedy, which retained the state's primary duty to ensure human rights but clarified the company's responsibility to respect human rights. The Guiding Principles set out how this Framework could be implemented. Ruggie has been highly lauded, and even those that are critical of parts of the initiative consider it to be, overall, a good thing.

To be sure, Ruggie has put human rights and companies together in a way which must have some impact on public perception. The Framework and the Guiding Principles have mainstreamed the association of the two, which commends their approach somewhat. However, in the spirit of controversy and debate, I am going to argue that this initiative is, overall, socially regressive.

Why? I would argue that the value of human rights per se is debatable and the value of Ruggie human rights even more so. On the first point, in the UK we have a Human Rights Act 1998, which sets out a number of rights we can expect to be

---

[98] Ibid, Principle 31.
[99] Ibid, Principle 29.

met. However, these are expressed in loose general terms. It is the courts that enforce these rights and it is the judiciary that defines and therefore limits these rights. The need to interpret is in large part because of the generalist nature of the wording of the Act. What constitutes my right to privacy or freedom of expression is not determined by me, the user, or by any other person who wishes to utilise these rights. It is not an expression of a democratically agreed perception of that right. It is driven neither by collective will nor individual assertion. Instead, it is the business of the courts to decide on our levels of privacy and freedom, and they have a fairly free reign to set those limits given the general nature of the rights under the Act. This lack of precision in the language of rights is even more present in Ruggie human rights. Furthermore, it is companies themselves, not the courts, who interpret what they mean. Overall, Ruggie human rights achieve much less than pre-existing human rights. The wide scope for interpretation of these human rights is coupled with a self-interest in setting the appropriate standards.

One of the reasons why Ruggie makes human rights worse is because the Framework's formulation of a state's duty to protect against human rights abuses by third parties such as companies actually limits the scope of already existing human rights norms. As McCorquodale's work shows, states already have a duty to protect against human rights abuses by companies either because they have ratified the relevant treaty or because they are bound by customary international law. He also argued that the Framework limits the extra-territorial responsibilities that already existed in international law, and he cited four situations where the state will be responsible for the acts of corporations if they breach an international obligation. The fourth of those cited, where a state may incur international responsibility where it is complicit in the activity of the non-state actor or fails to exercise due diligence to prevent the effects of the actions of non-state actors, is increasingly understood to cover instances of home countries' subsidiaries acting outside the state's jurisdiction. The Framework and the Guiding Principles provide for a much lower level of responsibility by states for extra-territorial abuses. Secondly, the Framework highlights the well-known problem of bilateral investment treaties, upon which over half of world's trade is based, which routinely incorporate provisions which can make a state's observance of human rights actionable and very expensive. I noted the example of Argentina here. While holding up the possibility of addressing this problem, which in itself is a manifestation of the asymmetrical power between nations, the ultimate solution noted in the Guiding Principles was that host countries should draft the agreements more carefully. To dismiss this as a problem of sloppy drafting is to entirely overlook the difference in power as between nations entering into bilateral investment treaties. Developing countries seek investment and may have to enter into very onerous agreements in order to obtain it from wealthier developed countries. The onerous nature of these agreements from the perspective of the developing nation is not the result of poor drafting, but of their relative economic powerlessness. In foreclosing this issue as a responsibility of states to draft more carefully, those states that find themselves torn between human rights or breaching a bilateral investment treaty may well find even less sympathy in the courts given that the Guiding Principles have pronounced their solution and they have ignored it.

The Guiding Principles have also enabled companies to be their own law-maker, regardless of the jurisdiction in which they operate. As noted above, the commentary to Guiding Principle 11 states that in upholding 'a global standard of expected conduct', companies can apply standards which are different from those in the host country. The responsibility to comply with standards that the company self-produces through the process of due diligence exists 'over and above compliance with national laws and regulations protecting human rights'.[100] Multinational companies operating in developing countries carry with them not only their considerable economic power but also their own private, bespoke jurisdiction.

Finally, the Ruggie approach to companies has underlined the private character of multinational corporations, notwithstanding that their operations frequently dominate the host country. It has done so first by characterising the duty owed by states as being significantly different to that owed by companies (in which all companies big and small are conceptually lumped together). The latter owe only a responsibility to respect human rights. Secondly, the Ruggie approach has concep-tualised companies as private by instituting a process of monitoring human rights impacts which is largely self-regulatory. Companies undertake their own human rights impact assessment; they overview ongoing tracking and monitoring. And though the process mentions stakeholders and those whose rights have been abused with great frequency, their role is in fact very marginal. Those voices that have been so important in revealing human right abuses are sidelined under the Guiding Principles. Human rights due diligence has brought the process of assess-ment and monitoring 'in house'. The company's incentive to undertake these processes is presented as cost-effective because they may improve company repu-tation and may provide protection against legal claims. In many ways the human rights due diligence process mimics the principles-based approach of corporate governance, as the table below indicates. The ultimate aim of these processes is to protect and enhance shareholder value.

The issue of human rights only grazes the surface of the problems caused by multinational corporations. Companies based in developed countries but operat-ing or outsourcing in developing countries have engaged in numerous activities which are detrimental for the host state and for the local people. The worst excesses of their activities impact on the basic human rights of the people of that country, as we have noted. But perhaps even more deleterious than human rights abuses are instances of routine exploitation which are not addressed by human rights. After all it is the exploitation of labour which motivates business activity,

---

[100] Ibid, Principle 11, commentary. This position is somewhat contradicted by the later statement in the commentary that, 'Business enterprises should not undermine States' abilities to meet their own human rights obligations, including by actions that might weaken the integrity of judicial processes.'

Table 5.1 The Governance of Corporations: Comparing Human Rights Due Diligence with the Corporate Governance Code

Human Rights Due Diligence	Human rights policies based on (Ruggie) Principles	Human rights impact assessment	Response to limit impact and report	Incentivised by costs of legal actions and reputational damage
UK Corporate Governance Code	Corporate governance policies based on (Code) Principles	Risk assessments (financial) Impact on environment, labour	Response to limit negative impact and report	Incentivised by reputational damage through market assessment – equities and listings

not a heartfelt desire to abuse human rights; that is just a by-product of exploitation. Given this, ensuring that companies do not impact on human rights seems a fairly low-level ambition, a distraction from the main problem. Yet even this has not been achieved.

Further Reading

P. Blumberg, 'Asserting Human Rights Against Multinational Corporations Under United States Law: Conceptual and Procedural Problems' (2002) 50 *American Journal of Comparative Law* Supplement 493.

S. Deva, 'Human Rights Violations by Multinational Corporations and National Law: Where From Here?' (2003–2004) 19 *Connecticut Journal of International Law* 1.

J. Dine and A. Fagan (eds), *Human Rights and Capitalism* (Edward Elgar, 2006).

J. Dine, *Companies, International Trade and Human Rights* (Cambridge University Press, 2005).

G. Frynas and S. Pegg, *Transnational Corporations and Human Rights* (Palgrave Macmillan, 2003).

S. Gan, 'Human Rights and Corporations' (2012) 5(1) *Journal of International Business Ethics* 27.

J. Harrison, 'Human rights arguments in amicus curiae submissions: promoting social justice?', in P.M. Dupuy, F. Francioni and E.U. Petersmann (eds), *Human Rights in International Investment Law and Arbitration* (Oxford University Press, 2009), 396–421.

R. Mares, 'A Gap in the Corporate Responsibility to Respect Human Rights' (2010) 36 *Monash U.L. Rev.* 33.

P.T. Muchlinski, *Multinational Enterprises and the Law* (Oxford University Press, 2008).

J. Ruggie, 'Business and Human Rights: the Evolving International Agenda' (2007) 101(4) *American Journal of International Law* 819.

R. Welford, 'Globalization, Corporate Social Responsibility and Human Rights' (2002) 9(1) *Corporate Social Responsibility and Environmental Management* 1.

M. Winston, 'NGO Strategies for Promoting Corporate Social Responsibility' (2002) 16(1) *Ethics & International Affairs* 71.

O.F. Williams (2004) 'The UN Global Compact: The Challenge and the Promise', *Business Ethics Quarterly* 14(4), 278–86.

Liability of parent companies and extra-territorial accountability for torts

S. Abraham and C.M. Abraham, 'The Bhopal case and the development of environmental law in India' (1991) 40 *I.C.L.Q.* 334.

L. Bergkamp and W. Pak, 'Piercing the Corporate Veil: Shareholder Liability for Corporate Torts' (2001) 8 *Maastricht J. Eur. & Comp. L.* 167.

P. Blumberg, 'The Corporate Entity in an Era of Multinational Corporations' (1990) 15 *Del. J. Corp. L.* 283.

M. Dearborn, 'Enterprise Liability: Reviewing an Revitalising Liability for Corporate Groups' (2009) 97 *C.L.R.* 195.

H. Hansmann and R. Kraakman, 'Toward Unlimited Shareholder Liability for Corporate Torts' (1991) 100 *Y.L.J.* 1879.

R. Meeran, 'Tort Litigation against Multinational Corporations for Violation of Human Rights: An Overview of the Position Outside the United States' (2011) 2 *City U.H.K.L. Rev.*

6

CAN COMPANIES BE MORAL?
AND THE ROLE OF CORPORATE
SOCIAL RESPONSIBILITY

How moral can a company be when it is principally bound to please the market? That is the question addressed in this chapter. It begins by considering the importance of the freedom to act for all persons, including legal persons, when they are required to act morally. The chapter argues that the market fetters that freedom, but it also considers scholarship which maintains that being bound to the market does not prevent companies engaging in moral decision making. The chapter goes on to consider the historical shift between periods when political policy reduced the effect of the market on corporate decision making, and those (including the present) when the financial market has dominated. It then considers the sorts of frameworks that might act as a bulwark against market-based decision making and enable corporate morality. This draws on the discussion in the previous chapter and introduces the focus on corporate social responsibility. In discussing corporate social responsibility, this chapter considers how the market is often elicited as a driving force for this form of morality. It considers the problems with the claim that there are market-based reasons for pursuing corporate social responsibility and argues accordingly that corporate social responsibility has low social ambitions. Finally, it considers whether mandating morality is possible given the pressure of the market, and utilises the example of mandatory corporate social responsibility in India as a case study which demonstrates the obstacles to doing so.

1. IS MORAL DECISION MAKING DEPENDENT ON FREEDOM?

In Macpherson's *The Political Theory of Possessive Individualism*,[1] he describes and analyses the debate on male suffrage within the New Model Army in the Putney

---

[1] C.B. Macpherson, *The Political Theory of Possessive Individualism: Hobbes to Locke* (OUP, 1962).

Debates of 1647, after the first civil war. Participants disagreed over who should be entitled to vote.

Cromwell and Ireton argued for the continuity of the 'freehold franchise' which had been offered to men who held 'freehold land of a value of 40 shillings a year and freemen of trading corporations' since the time of Henry VI. [2] It excluded *inter alia* leaseholders and artisans and, at the time of the debate, included around 212,000 men.[3] The Levellers, on the other hand, opposed the freeholder franchise and proposed enfranchisement for all men bar servants, criminals and alms-takers. This would have extended the franchise to around 417,000 men.[4] However, as MacPherson makes clear, much of the opposing parties' position was grounded in the same reasoning. The franchise should only be exercised by those who had the freedom of thought and capacity to make an independent judgement. Cromwell drew the line at freedom derived from private property ownership; the Levellers drew the line at those whose position (as servants or alms-takers) meant that they depended upon the will of other men and should be afraid to displease (them):[5]

> 'In short, Cromwell and Ireton held that only freeholders and freemen of corporations, and possibly those whose property was of an almost indistinguishable sort, such as some of the copyholders by inheritance, had the property basis upon which they could live as free men without dependence. The Levellers thought that all men except servants and alms-takers were free men. For both Levellers and army leaders franchise was properly dependent on freedom, and freedom meant individual economic independence. But the two groups, with different class roots, had different views of the property basis of economic independence.'[6]

It probably goes without saying that nobody thought women were sufficiently free and independent of mind to be enfranchised, but, that aside, the point being made is that to exercise political and moral choice, one must have sufficient freedom from the will of others to be able to do so. Correlatively, if a company is to be moral or at least to make some morally informed decisions, it must be capable of doing so. That is, it must be free and capable of independent decision making. The question is how free are companies?

Current debates about corporate morality are largely concerned with corporate social responsibility. The human rights initiatives discussed in the previous chapter provide guidelines for controlling human rights impacts and redressing negative impacts. Actively making positive moral choices is seen as contained within corporate social responsibility. Corporate social responsibility is premised on the assumption that companies are free to make positive moral decisions, but are they?

---

[2] Ibid, 112.
[3] Ibid, 114.
[4] Ibid. In fact they held a variation of views but remained the most inclusive group.
[5] Part of the debate, ibid, 123, citing A. Woodhouse, *Puritanism and Liberty: Being the Army Debates (1647–9 from the Clarke Manuscripts with Supplementary Documents)*, 2nd edn (University of Chicago, 1938), 82–3.
[6] Ibid, 129.

Are they instead constrained to pursue shareholder value, not social values, by other quarters such as the equities market where the valuation of shares (and thus the measure of management competency) is based on the expected returns to shareholders.[7] Furthermore, is corporate social responsibility just a creature of the market itself? The desire not to have state mandates to ensure corporate actions, but instead to allow corporations to volunteer actions, is a market approach. The contradiction is that this market approach is precisely that which arrests effective corporate responsibility. Corporate social responsibility does not address the deleterious effects of the market; *it is* the market in action.

Historically, the re-emergence of market interpretations of the company and of corporate goals has contained the issue of corporate morality into the narrow and unambitious notion of corporate social responsibility. Corporate social responsibility relies on market behaviours (such as consumer choices) to resolve the problems it identifies and is premised on the assumption that companies are indeed free to make moral decisions. Indeed, because corporate social responsibility is the going beyond that which is legally mandated, socially responsible acts by the company must, by definition, be voluntary.

On the other hand there is an argument that pleasing the market, enhancing share prices, does not restrict corporate morality but is itself a moral position. Enhancing the wealth of shareholders enhances the overall wealth of society, and at some level all members of society will benefit: a utilitarian argument. However, the assumption that share price does indeed guide efficiency and wealth maximisation is rather dependent on share prices being a good indicator of value. The efficient market hypothesis regards it as the most effective indicator – as it represents the accumulated opinion of all self-maximising market players. However, many theorists have debunked the assumptions of the efficient market hypothesis, arguing for example that market players are not abstract rational actors but have different levels of knowledge and ability to use that knowledge (information asymmetry and bounded rationality). Their rationality is bounded. Those actors have different motivations for acting. For example, management might launch a takeover of a company, not because it has unrealised value which the market is being notified of by the takeover, but because they wish to increase the size of the business they manage so as to make it more takeover proof.

Pleasing the market (and by 'the market', we mean, of course, the view taken by investors, or more often those representing investors, on the value of company performance, based on publicly available information) means pleasing a lot of players with a lot of different incentives. Corporate management will need to make clear signals to them. Taking a strong moral position will rarely be the kind of signal the market will reward, and therefore a company bound to the market does not seem to have much opportunity for the voluntary, moral decision making that might be effective in achieving social good.

---

[7] If the claims of the efficient market hypothesis are correct, claims which are highly contestable, as discussed in the Kay Review (see Chapter 3).

2. HAS THERE EVER BEEN FREEDOM FROM THE MARKET?

The freedom from the market (if not the law) that must accompany moral deci-sion making seems only present (if at all) during the periods c. 1930–1970 in the US and c. 1945–1970 in the UK. In 1930s America a new set of ideas emerged around the corporation. Institutional economists worked on the assumption that the emergence of the large corporation, characterised by a (mainly) complete separation of ownership from control, meant that the market no longer dictated their activities and goals. As near oligopolies, they dictated the shape of produc-tion and distribution, dictated how the corporation was organised, and the econ-omy was shaped around these corporate decisions. Freed from the market, these organisations could chose to be moral. Many prominent scholars, during a period that was to last over 30 years, assumed that these large institutions could and would set the corporate compass in the direction of a morality which provided for the needs of society as whole. The debate between Merrick Dodd and Adolf Berle, noted in the Preface, puts Dodd firmly in this camp.[8] The final chapter of *The Modern Corporation and Private Property*, in particular, puts Berle too in this camp.[9] Berle and Means showed that massive share dispersal had led to the growth of corporations and the emergence of corporations that were controlled by manage-ment, because shareholders no longer held shares in sufficient quantities to be able to exercise their existing (but now inappropriate) legal powers. Unburdened by shareholder demands for high returns and strong share values (which act as a stand in for market demands), management had the freedom to make decisions which could be considered moral. Share dispersal presented a unique opportunity for management to make decisions on behalf of the corporation that would be in the interest of the 'community'. Berle argued that shareholders' passivity meant that shareholders lacked a moral claim to management's full attention. Their claims were limited to liquidity and *some* return on their investment. However, corporations, in their consideration of their moral obligation to those affected by corporate activity, would organise production and distribution is such a way as to meet those obligations. This might entail increasing wages and benefits for employees, investing in product development and addressing environmental issues.

Keynes also considered companies fit to be moral, once they had reached a certain size and level of share dispersal. Companies would then effectively cease to be private organisations operating in the interests of private property claims and would become public institutions operating for social welfare. The company would thereby become 'socialised'. In his 1929 treatise, *The End of Laissez-Faire*, Keynes stated:

---

[8] A.A. Berle, 'Corporate Powers as Powers in Trust' (1931) 44(7) *Harvard Law Review* 1049; E.M. Dodd, 'For Whom are Corporate Managers Trustees?' (1932) 45(7) *Harvard Law Review* 1142, 1163
[9] A.A. Berle and G.C. Means, *The Modern Corporation and Private Property* (Macmillan, 1932).

'A point arrives in the growth of a big institution ... at which the owners of the capital, i.e. the shareholders, are almost entirely dissociated from the management, with
the result that the direct personal interest of the latter in the making of great profit
becomes quite secondary. When this stage is reached, the general stability and reputation of the institution are more considered by the management than the maximum profit for the shareholders. The shareholders must be satisfied by
conventionally adequate dividends; but once this is secured, the direct interest of
the management often consists in avoiding criticism from the public and from the
customers of the concern. This is particularly if their great size or semi-monopolis-
tic position renders them conspicuous in the public eye and vulnerable to public
attack.'[10]

American economist Carl Kaysen, writing in the 1950s, noted the entrenchment
of shareholdings, that is, long-term shareholders that were neither actively
involved in governance nor interested in selling their shares. They were engaging
in neither 'voice' nor 'exit', as we would say today. He argued that such shareholders should be redefined as, essentially, bond holders, rather than owners.[11] This
stable arrangement with shareholders enabled a stable relationship with employees, who could expect reasonable wages and a job for life. This desirable moral
outcome led Kaysen to call corporations 'soulful'. They were humane and capable
of moral decision making.

Today, the size of a company does not seem to present the same opportunity
for corporate morality. Instead, size seems to make a company immune to
change, a vessel bound to a market-based course, unable to change direction.
When it springs a leak, the public pays because it is 'too big to fail'. Companies
are anthropomorphised as an immense (leaky) toddler flaying around, inevitably
facing injury after injury as it plays with its rough and even more immense
friend, the anthropomorphised market. The public, an indulgent parent, band-
ages the injuries and sends them off again. Apparently lacking any authority to
say 'stop playing that game', the public sighs and says, 'companies will be
companies'!

3. WHEN AND WHY DID THIS CHANGE?

The fundamental orientation of the company changed in the early 1980s and the
change was ideological. An ideological hegemony around New Right pro-market
thinking emerged in this period. The institutional economists' period was characterised by a political commitment to stability, growth and redistribution. These
policies restricted what finance could do, and enhanced what labour and management could do. When finance tried to enhance its position, it was hamstrung by

---

[10] J.M. Keynes, *The End of Laissez-Faire* (Hogarth Press, 1926), 42–3.
[11] C. Kaysen, 'The Social Significance of the Modern Corporation' (1957) 47 *American Economic Review*
311.

legislative restrictions. When the New Right rose to prominence in the 1980s, those restrictions were gradually lifted and finance was able to proliferate to seek increasing fluidity and to create more fictitious property forms and more exchanges.

At the same time, organised labour was subject to increasing control and the removal of long-standing rights to industrial action. There is an old 19th century formulation which might help elucidate the problem:

$$M \rightarrow C...P...C' \rightarrow M'$$

In this diagram which represents the process of capitalist production, M represents money invested in the process of production where it becomes capital invested in labour, raw materials, rents and so on. This is C. P represents the process of production from which capital investment produces material goods, or commodities. These commodities are represented as C'. These commodities are sold with the intention of expanding the original investment, money. In its simplest form, the original investment is made by the same person or persons who are involved in the actual production process (the C...P...C' part), probably in a managerial/oversight role. They may have borrowed all or some of the money invested, requiring them to surrender part of the profit (M') to the lender. All of the operations in the formula are, paradigmatically, performed *within the company*. The company owns M, and M' (before distribution), as well as operating C...P...C'.

When the economy develops into an economy dominated by large organisations (the economy described by the institutional economists), the process of production remains the same except that control is reoriented away from the providers of capital to those involved in the actual productive process. In large corporations in which Berle and Means declared there was a separation of ownership from control, investors or shareholders purchase a title to revenue but cannot influence events which affect the value of that title. They are still part of the M and M' process but they play no part in the C...P...C' process. That part is controlled by management. Most scholars in the period from 1930–1960 thought that managerial control would have positive social outcomes. The persons occupying the C...P...C' process exercised a great deal of power over the decision-making process in the company and were insulated, to a degree, from market pressure. Those occupying the M → M' part had little or no influence over decision making in the company. Furthermore, the fluidity of financial products was restricted by political policy. For example, financial derivatives were prohibited.

4. WHAT WERE THE CHARACTERISTICS OF THE STRONG C...P...C' PERIOD?

In both the United States (c. 1930–1970) and in the UK (c. 1945–1970), there was general political consensus in favour of an empowered labour force. Elsewhere, I have called this consensus a progressive period of corporate governance.[12] Indeed, there was something of an alliance between the two. In both countries, unions were encouraged to act on behalf of their members, assisted by protective legislation. They sought better wages and conditions and were increasingly successful in this endeavour. In this way, the value that was created in production was retrieved closer to the point of production by the producers. At the same time, management was largely trusted to deliver on the political agenda set by government: a social welfare agenda. In this, investors waited more or less passively for their returns at the M´ end. These returns, while still significant, were significantly less than at the beginning of the 20th century.

Freed from control by the investors, management could make moral decisions in the interests of non-shareholder constituents. Why would they do that? Because they were reflecting the prevailing political zeitgeist that the redistribution of wealth was obviously morally right and part of the political goals of the government. As Mark Roe observes in his work on social democratic countries, management decision making is influenced by a desire to reflect the prevailing political norms of the government. A failure to do so has, in the past he shows, brought intervention by governments, which overtly supported the political activity of the unions.

An example is provided by the attitude to hostile takeovers. These were very rare in social democratic continental Europe – the first in Germany, for instance, was Vodafone's takeover of Mannesmann in 1999. As Roe says:

> 'Hostile takeovers were notoriously harder in continental Europe than in the United States and Britain … they regularly foundered due to the political pressure one would expect in a social democracy, as workers campaigned to block the takeovers and politicians sided with employees and against capital owners.'[13]

The favouring of employees over shareholders is, argues Roe, the preferred choice for management who are more likely to be in contact with employees and to see them as fellow employees to whom they owe a greater allegiance than to shareholders. This latter point is highly contestable, but what is more verifiable is that block shareholding remained prevalent in large companies in social democratic Germany. This is likely to have been influenced, Roe argues, by shareholders' desire to retain some influence over corporate activities. In Germany, long-term stability was enhanced by continuity of ownership at the M → M´ stage coupled with social democratic politics influencing the C…P…C´ process. As a result, exchanges were at a minimum and the rewards of production were divided more equitably between employees, shareholders and reinvestment.

C.A.R. Crosland made similar points about the UK in *The Future of Socialism*.[14] His thesis was that the business class had been usurped by the state, and the state

---

[12] L.E. Talbot, *Progressive Corporate Governance for the 21st Century* (Routledge, 2012).

[13] M. Roe, 'Political preconditions to separating ownership from control' (2000) 53 *Stanford L. Rev.* 539, 558.

[14] In *The Future of Socialism* (Robinson Publishing, 2006), Anthony Crosland cites the plight of the Jarrow workers as a potent symbol of capital dominance and governmental compliance.

was concerned to serve people rather than business. The end of business supremacy arose because of three key developments in British society. The first development was that 'decisive sources and levers of economic power have been transferred from private business to other hands'.[15] Those other hands being public authorities, including nationalised industries. Within nationalised industries, 'economic decisions in the basic sector have passed out of the hands of the capitalist class into the hands of a new and largely autonomous class of public industrial managers'.[16] Furthermore, the norms generated by these public industrial managers impacted on the business norms of private industry. The government directly engineered production patterns. It pursued full employment taxed directly and indirectly to encourage the economy to grow in particular ways.[17]

The second development was the enhanced political power of the workforce. There were more jobs than workers, and trade unions actively pursued labour's interest against business interests. Part of the reason for business's subordination to its workforce resulted from the third development Crosland identified, that of the 'psychological revolution within industry and the altered role of profit'.[18] Technological development in production had elevated scientists and specialist to the boards, usurping the old style manager owners who were now dependent on the formers' expertise.[19]

The rise of large companies headed by a specialist and non-share-owning management meant that managers were no longer self-interestedly committed to profit maximisation. They did not look to shareholders for investment and instead used profits for upgrading rather than using those profits for dividends. Unlike today, this disregard of share value did not negatively impact on a manager's reputation. Indeed, it tended to enhance it, 'by gaining a reputation as a progressive employer, who introduces co-partnership or profit sharing schemes'.[20] Managerial goals included 'democratic leadership' and 'permissive management'.[21]

For Crosland, nationalisation, strong government and especially strong unions meant that companies were bound to act morally:

> 'In the basic industries, nationalization has wholly deprived the capitalist class of its power of decision. But it has been similarly deprived in much of the private sector. The growth of the managerial joint stock corporation has transferred the function of decision making to a largely non-owning class of salaried executives, who suffer singularly little interference from the nominal owners. Even this new business class finds its freedom of action limited to an extent which its capitalist predecessors never did – partly from the growth in the role of government but mainly by the

---

[15] Ibid, 7.
[16] Ibid, 11.
[17] Ibid, 7.
[18] Ibid, 14.
[19] Ibid, 15.
[20] Ibid, 17.
[21] Ibid, 19.

growth in the power of labour, stemming generally from the rise in trade union strength and specifically from the altered conditions of the labour market.'[22]

So when the state's political objective is to protect labour and enhance their benefits, what happens in the C…P…C' part becomes very stable. Overseen by unions, more benefits from this activity returns to labour, and the workforce is reasonably secure, often guaranteed a job for life. Alternatively, the German co-determination model ensures a direct relationship between labour representatives and management, to consciously create harmonious industrial relations as the principal governance aim of companies. The shareholders, who are part of this process, sitting on the supervisory board with labour representatives, are drawn to this goal, or were in the height of social democracy. This makes the M ➜ M' process stable with few exchanges.

5. WHAT HAPPENS IN THE STRONG M ➜ M' PERIOD?

a. Financialisation in the United States

From the early 1980s the shift to the New Right or neoliberalism was accompanied by a removal of union power and an enhancement of freedom for finance. The controls that had held finance in check were gradually removed, and new financial property forms emerged and were exchanged with increasing rapidly. 'Deregulation' set aside many of the controls which arrested the proliferation of property forms. Neoliberal politics intended to replace the troublesome productive economy with the seemingly more manageable finance economy. At the same time financial players sought to develop a market in financial property forms.

In Lawrence Mitchell's account of the rise of financialisation in the United States, he charts the rise of exchanges, how the financial players stoked up exchanges and the consequences of this. He begins with stockbrokers seeking better commission, an ambition which was thwarted by low share turnover and long-term ownership. From 1931 to 1949 turnover averaged at 32 per cent. During the 1940s, for the most part, it ranged from 12–19 per cent, dropping further in the early 1950s. In order to increase stockbroker commissions, more people needed to own shares and more people needed to sell them frequently. The New York Stock Exchange (NYSE) commissioned a report from the Brooking Institute on share ownership which found that only a tiny 4.2 per cent of the public actually owned shares at all. Armed with this evidence, the NYSE started a campaign called the 'Own Your Own Share of American Business' and later called upon the Federal Reserve to take measures to increase the available money for new investors to invest further.[23] By 1958 the number of people owning shares had doubled from the number in 1952. By 1965 it

---

[22] Ibid, 30.
[23] L.E. Mitchell, 'Financialism, A (Very) brief History' (2010) 43 *Creighton Law Review* 323.

had nearly trebled. Mitchell falls short of making a straightforward causative argument but simple notes that the correlation between the NYSE's campaign and the rapid growth of share ownership is 'undeniable'. In 2001, he notes that more than half of American families 'directly or indirectly owned corporate stock'.[24] More frequent exchanges followed from this and from the increasingly large presence of institutional shareholders noted below. In 1952, 46 per cent of individually purchased shares were long-term investments. As Mitchell says, 'the Exchanges concluded that 75 per cent of all transactions had been for investment purposes rather than speculation. But particularly notable is the fact that the vast majority of individual stock purchases were in pursuit of capital gains rather than income.'[25] Any increase in share price from 1945 to the 1960s came from retained earnings. But after this period, he argues, investors sold their stock on the basis of future earnings.

The pressure on managers to maintain share price was exacerbated by institutional shareholders.

Institutional shareholders joined the growing number of investing and trading shareholders as changes in controls over pension fund investments meant that by 1950 they could invest in stocks. The value of the stock they owned grew rapidly from $812 million in 1950 to $2.9 billion by 1957.[26] Furthermore, the mutual funds that had all but disappeared after the 1929 crash were reappearing, and by 1959 'they were adding $4.5 billion in a single year'.[27]

Mitchell further notes that the principle institutions of financialisation, the commercial and investment banks, were encouraged by both stock exchange policy and government legislation to develop into risk-taking institutions whose core business shifted from financing productive industry to being individual rent seekers. The process began, argues Mitchell, with the extension of limited liability to investment banking which enabled them to take greater risks. The public offering of shares in the investment bank Donaldson, Lufkin in 1970, argues Mitchell, transformed investment banks into entities that could borrow heavily, that could massively enhance profits and offer huge executive compensation.[28] 'Where once banks made their money underwriting securities, arranging deals, and providing financial advice to clients, they now moved in the direction of proprietary trading, that is, trading for their own profits, and the development of what are generally referred to as "new financial products".'[29]

The shift in funding for reinvestment and development of productive assets from profits to debt has created yet another series of exchanges. In America, Mitchell noted that from the turn of the 20th century until the 1960s, retained earnings averaged in the range of 50–60 per cent.[30] Since then, reinvestment has

---

[24] Ibid, 327.
[25] Ibid 333.
[26] Ibid 328.
[27] Ibid.
[28] Ibid, 329.
[29] Ibid.
[30] Ibid, 331.

been increasingly drawn from debts, so that more profit could be returned to shareholders. By 2002 retained earnings stood at only 3%, rising to 11% in 2007: 'almost all the rest of the money needed to finance production came from debt, increasingly shoved in off-balance sheets to conceal corporations' true reliance on borrowing.'[31]

B. Financialism in the United Kingdom

Deregulation has also led to a rise of transactions within the M → M´ process as the claims of shareholders have become the fragmented claims of a chain of claimants. First, the composition of shareholding has changed. Those who tended to own shares in the past do not own shares now. Private shareholding declined from the 1950s as government tax and political policies favoured financial institutions, especially pension funds and life insurance funds. Over the last few years, partly exacerbated by the fall in equity values as a result of the financial crisis, the proportion of pension and life insurance funds has dropped to around 20 per cent of total equity markets. Today foreign investors own over 40 per cent of equities – although this tends to disguise the role of transnational organisations which appear as foreign but where the beneficiaries and management are, in fact, national; the largest asset manager in the UK, BlackRock with £530 billion,[32] falls into this category.

The table below, reproduced from the Kay Review (discussed in Chapter 3), shows the change in ownership patterns of company shares from 1963–2010.

Table 6.1 Historical Trends in Beneficial Ownership (Percentage Held)[33]

	1963	1975	1981	1991	2001	2008	2010
Rest of the world	7	5.6	3.6	12.8	35.7	41.5	41.2
Insurance companies	10	15.9	20.5	20.8	20	13.4	8.6
Pension funds	6.4	16.8	26.7	31.3	16.1	12.8	5.1
Individuals	54	37.5	28.2	19.9	14.8	10.2	11.5
Other	22.6	24.2	21	15.2	13.4	22.1	33.6

As well as shareholders themselves becoming more heterogeneous, there is a change in the way the shares are owned – partly arising from the change in ownership. So, when private ownership was dominant, the wealthy families who held the majority of shares would hold them as a long-term proposition and would exercise the decisions relating to them. When, and if, they wished to sell those

---

[31] Ibid, 331.

[32] Department for Business, Innovation and Skills, The Kay Review of UK Equity Markets and Long-Term Decision Making – Final Report (2012), 31 <http://www.bis.gov.uk/assets/biscore/business-law/docs/k/12-917-kay-review-of-equity-markets-final-report.pdf>.

[33] Table from the Kay Review, ibid, p. 31.

shares to the public, they would do so through a stockbroker. Today's dominant institutional shareholders, as noted in Chapter 4, have a much more attenuated relationship with their shares and engage asset managers to vote and to make investment decisions. The shareowners, therefore, are not engaged in decision making and therefore any moral consideration which that might entail. Instead, decisions are made by those who need, above all, to show that their activity and expertise has generated good returns.

The Cass Business School survey of ownership in the FTSE 100 showed that 69 per cent of equities were held by charities, financials, government, hedge funds, investment funds, investment trusts, company holdings and unclassified funds.[34] Each of these will be involved in a chain of activity and require a portion of the value obtained from capital ownership. So, while in law we understand sharehold-ers to have their names on the register, vote at meetings, enjoy the dividend, be beneficial owners of the rights attached to the shares and exercise the right to sell, today these roles are likely to be exercised by different people or institutions. Under this kind of arrangement with institutions (I use pension funds only for clarity), the formula for the process of production looks more like this:

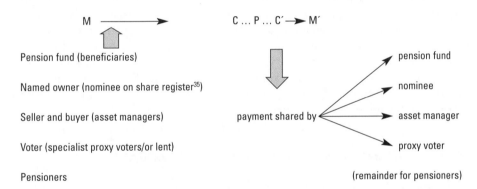

Figure 6.1 The network of investment and extraction of value

Each part of the chain must be paid for, including the costs of exchanges. This requires the C...P...C′ part to produce larger amounts of surplus and to make more of that surplus available to investors and their agents. Reducing the cost of labour and other expenditure, including research and development, becomes an inevitable part of the process if these intermediaries and shareholders are to be paid. The financial demands throughout the chain curtail the capacity of the

---

[34] Ibid, 32.

[35] This describes individual investors (owning around 11 per cent of total traded equities). They are less likely to be the named owners because 'with the introduction of electronic trading in the 1990s, retail investors were encouraged to hold shares in nominee accounts maintained by the principal banks and private client stockbrokers' (ibid, 29).

company to exercise moral decision making. Furthermore, the removal of control over exchange breeds yet more exchange. For example, as the Kay Review notes, 'each of these agents must employ its own compliance staff to monitor consistency with regulation, must use the services of its own auditors and lawyers and earn sufficient to remunerate the employees and reward its own investors.'[36]

The Kay Review attributes the growth of intermediaries, operating together with layers of monitoring intermediaries, to a loss of trust:

> 'a principal driver of the growth of intermediation has been the decline of trust and confidence in the investment chain. The role of custodian came into being because the asset manager could not be trusted to hold shares on behalf of the ultimate shareholder. Pension fund trustees have been required to supervise more closely the activities for which they are responsible.'[37]

However, this position is highly debateable. It could alternatively be argued that it is not the loss of trust but the loss of the kind of regulation which inhibited capitalism's tendency to exchange and to create new property forms in order to extract value. The self-regulation which becomes necessary for intermediaries, or the additional monitoring required for each part of the chain, is a necessary response to the liberty to engage in these chains at all. If there was no liberty to so act, there would be no need to monitor those actions.[38] The more intermediaries there are, the more monitoring will be required, and the more monitors there are, the more they too will need to be monitored. This cannot be magically solved by adding trust. Loss of trust is a necessary corollary of the increasing fragmentation of roles, property forms and the increase of exchange relations.

6. CAN FINANCIALISATION BE SAID TO BE MORAL?

It is possible to take a completely different approach to the morality of corporations. Freidman took the view that the correct moral position for companies was to make money for shareholders. A fairly orthodox view would be that by focusing on shareholder value, more wealth is created and this is beneficial for society as a whole. Accordingly, the shareholder value approach is morally superior to governance approaches which consider all those affected by companies' activities. Oliver Williamson has explicitly made the moral case for shareholder value, arguing that by creating internal governance structures which enable the pursuit of shareholder value, more wealth is created and efficiencies are enhanced.[39] As this is a desirable social outcome, it is morally defensible.

---

[36] Ibid, 30.

[37] Ibid.

[38] A theme in S. Picciotto, *Regulating Global Corporate Capitalism* (Cambridge University Press, 2011).

[39] O. Williamson, *The Economic Institutions of Capitalism* (The Free Press, 1985).

The more popular view on enhancing shareholder wealth is that it is better achieved through enabling market mechanisms, rather than the corporate governance mooted by Williamson. A vibrant market in shares will enable investors to know where best to invest, because share price reflects all the publicly known information about the value of the company. This view is known as the efficient market hypothesis. This theory, in its strong form, assumes the efficiency of market prices on the basis that all actors are rational self-maximisers. Thus share price reflects the views of many rational actors in the market, who are presumed to be equally able to act having equal abilities and knowledge. There are immediately obvious problems to this approach that would strongly suggest that share price does not represent an accumulation of the views of those best placed to make accurate assessments. First, there is a raft of evidence which suggests that market actors, being people, have all the flaws and prejudices of people. They do not always act rationally, or, alternatively, they will perceive rationality differently. There are many occasions in past and recent history when market actors have made decisions based on a feverish act of faith, or fervent hope for enormous wealth. The South Sea Bubble is probably the first example, and more recently share fever was seen around the dot.com companies in the 1990s. An excitement can build up around shares, where there is no rational reason for that excitement. It is purely speculative. Furthermore, as Schiller's work indicates, investors are often unwilling to except that the high returns on particular shares have come to an end and will continue to invest in the 'irrational expectation' that these shares will continue to deliver high returns.[40]

Market actors are subject to all sorts of cognitive biases which inhibit their ability to act as the finance economists' model think they should act. Williamson has argued that all actors' ability to act rationally is bounded by their own limitations. Actors also have different incentives to act and those may very well feed false information into the market. For example, engaging in takeover activity is said to enhance the market in corporate control. It certainly increases the value of the shares in the target company. However, there is much compelling scholarship which indicates that when management pursue a takeover, it is not, as the market in corporate control theory holds, because there is untapped value in the target company. Evidence suggests that it frequently gives management personal benefits by allowing them to create a large corporate empire which insulates the company (and them) from the threat of hostile takeovers. Furthermore, a larger empire means percentage payments from a larger whole. However, when a takeover is launched, the information given to the market is that the shares in the target company are undervalued. Management incentives deliver misleading information to the market.

Furthermore, as there are in fact many actors in the market representing the ultimate beneficiary (Figure 6.1), they will need to justify their own remuneration

---

40 R.J. Shiller, *Irrational Exuberance*, 2nd edn (Currency Doubleday, 2005).

by doing something. Inactivity does not justify reward, so these intermediaries must act. By acting they create movement in the market which is simply just reflecting the fact of their acting, not that there is any objective reason for acting. This 'doing-ism' is expressed well in the Kay Review:

> 'Corporate executives find that they can make a visible difference to the shape and perhaps performance of their companies by reorganisations, acquisitions and disposals; traders and market makers earn returns which are closely related to the volume of activity in the securities in which they deal; analysts are rewarded for the narratives they provide that generate buy or sell recommendations; investment bankers and advisers derive earnings from transactions; independent financial advisers have traditionally been rewarded by commissions and even after [current reforms] will recognise that their clients are more likely to be willing to pay for advice to do something than for advice to do nothing. Many people in the financial services industry who claim to be in the business of providing advice are in fact in the business of making sales.'[41]

The efficient market hypothesis also assumes parity in knowledge between the market actors. However, it is clear that there are information asymmetries which will skew any accurate reading. In the end, share price is the accumulation and average of what many different people with their own misaligned knowledge and perverse incentives, most of whom are not connected to, and have little knowledge of, the productive assets of the company, think about how well the productive assets will perform. The margin for error here is almost limitless!

But regardless of the merits of the efficient market hypothesis, it has been very influential in recent years. One outcome of this is that management remuneration is increasingly linked to the share price of the company (*as though* the efficient market hypothesis were proven). The result is, whether rational or not, managements are highly sensitive to movements in share values, and this affects their behaviour.

So when management make decisions on the company's behalf, they will do so with a view to getting a good review from all of the market actors, with all of their failings. Those signals must be clear. A trade dispute, especially one that ends with employees improving their pay and conditions, will be a negative signal and share prices will fall. From a neoliberal perspective, a loss to shareholder value, through a fall in price, has a negative social impact. The company is wrong, not just in practical terms, but also morally. However, this loss to shareholders is a net gain to employees. Depending on one's attitude to distributional issues, this may be a more moral outcome. If a UK company relocates to a developing country because environmental standards and labour laws are more lax, the company's shares are likely to rise. However, jobs are lost in the UK, unemployment rises, welfare needs increase and there is less money for wages in the economy. In the developing country, in the meantime, environmental damage is imported from the UK and labour is exploited. Is this a moral outcome?

---

[41] The Kay Review (n. 32), p. 35.

The claim that by enhancing shareholder value you enhance overall social welfare would seem to lack verification. While it is plausible to conclude that profit maximisation results in higher *total welfare* in the technical sense – that is, total value in the economy – this will probably not be the best outcome in human terms. This is because the total may be distributed in a way that does not optimise human happiness. Highly unequal distribution instils psychological discontent and practical dislocation from society.

7. CAN CORPORATE SOCIAL RESPONSIBILITY DELIVER CORPORATE MORALITY?

a. Corporate social responsibility and corporate standards

But even if the (socially imposed) constraints of the market prevent management operating on a fundamentally social useful, moral, basis, there remains the 'add-on' of corporate social responsibility. For corporate social responsibility to operate at all, there must be at least some freedom for the company to act in a morally motivated way. Corporate social responsibility advocates essentially view the challenge as one of persuading companies to go beyond their legal duties and to consider wider moral duties. Corporate social responsibility embraces a number of objectives a corporation might aspire to, but in the main it includes promoting human rights, protecting labour and pursing environmental goals. This is the so-called 'triple bottom line'. There is a debate about how much state intervention is required to ensure corporate social responsibility and whether soft law is sufficient, or whether the market itself will provide its own incentives to be moral.

Within the UK, the imperative to pursue responsible governance is constructed around certain interpretations of hard law, for example section 172 and section 417 of the Companies Act 2006, which require some account of corporate social responsibility-related activity. The corporate governance codes require listed companies to comply with certain corporate standards or explain why they have not. However, these are very weak guarantees of corporate responsibility especially when balanced against the raft of companies' legislation, listing rules, rules on takeovers and the orientation of the corporate governance Codes in favour of shareholders. In the global context, the massive imbalance between protections for shareholders and protections for non-shareholders is amplified.

Arguably the greatest social harms are caused by multinational enterprises. That harm is largely caused in developing countries that either do not have, or are unwilling to adopt, the kinds of regulation which would protect people and the environment. In this context a voluntary adoption of corporate social responsibility by corporations investing in developing countries would seem to be an affectation, a sticky plaster for a severed limb. Developing countries are often unwilling to adopt protective regulation because they want to encourage outside investment by having 'liberal' regimes, which enable multinational companies to freely exploit countries' resources in return for 'development'. In addition, they will often provide huge protection for outside investors through legally enforceable, (mainly) bilateral treaties:

> 'The protection of investors is entrenched in bilateral investment treaties (or Investment Promotion and Protection Agreements), through the 1965 Washington Convention which created the International Center for the Settlement of Investment Disputes, and through the World Trade Organization and the specific agreements on TRIPS, TRIMS.[42] In these instruments, we find states have bound themselves to treat investments fairly and equitably, to give them full security and protection, and to guarantee against unlawful expropriation. Investors have increasingly sought to use these provisions not just against government policies which aim to expropriate them, but equally against any government policies which affect their profitability.'[43]

Developing countries may also be reliant upon funding from the IMF or the World Bank which is made on condition of regulatory liberalisation, or low regulation of corporate activities. International law provides little protection. And, as the previous chapter showed, the international treaties covering human rights, labour rights and environmental rights, such as the Universal Declaration of Human Rights and the ILO's Declaration on Fundamental Principles and Rights at Work, do not directly apply to corporations. Instead they oblige governments to observe minimum standards in respect of these issues.

Historically, attempts to concretise corporate obligations to the countries in which they operate have met with massive resistance from multinational companies which prefer looser, more voluntary obligations. For example, as Muchlinski shows in his account of the origins of the OECD Guidelines for Multinational Enterprises, initiatives to enhance protection for developing countries were constantly subverted by developed countries' investors. In the 1970s, developing countries were seeking more protections from developed countries' multinational companies. In pursuance of these aims the UN set up a committee on multinational companies in order to create a binding code of conduct. In 1976, UNCTAD IV started to discuss codes of conduct in particular areas of business and competition, and the International Labour Organization drafted a set of 10 principles on multinational companies' activity. The growing strength of developing countries' perspective on multinational companies was compounded by a series of nationalisations in the 1960s and 1970s. 'To counter these developments the OECD ministers, urged on by the US government, decided to adopt their own policy on multi-national companies, which it was hoped would influence the UN's attempts at "codification" to move away from a highly regulatory position of "MNE control".'[44] The resulting OECD Guidelines

---

[42] TRIPS (Trade-Related Intellectual Property Rights); TRIMS (Trade-Related Investment Measures).

[43] D. Graham and N. Woods, 'Making Global Corporate Self-Regulation Effective in Developing Countries' (2006) 34(5) *World Development Journal* 868, pp. 868–83.

[44] P. Muchlinski, *Multinational Enterprises and the Law*, 2nd edn (OUP, 2007), 659.

(first adopted as an annex to the OECD Declaration on International Investment and Multinational Enterprises in 1975) were very much more voluntary and pro investors, rather than pro host country. Furthermore, notes Muchlinski, in the introduction to the Guidelines it was made clear that international minimum standards would prevail over a nation's power to control multinational companies' activities once their business had been admitted to the country.[45]

More recently, as noted in the previous chapter, the proposed adoption by the UN Commission on Human Rights of 'Norms on the Responsibilities of Transnational Corporations and Other Business Enterprises with regard to Human Rights' attempted to concretise moral corporate behaviour and met with corporate resistance. So, instead, voluntary international corporate responsibility initiatives have proliferated. Codes of best practice for multinational companies to voluntarily adopt have been created, and multinational companies have themselves adopted self-regulation and created their own codes of conduct in respect of labour rights, human rights and environmental issues.

One of the most utilised codes by multinational companies is the United Nation's Global Compact noted in the previous chapter.[46] The Global Compact sets out 10 principles, and corporations voluntarily sign up to them. It is popular amongst thousands of high-profile multinational companies, particularly European ones. The Global Compact has no defined and concrete obligations or effective monitoring system; companies must report on their enactment of the Compact or, if they do not report, face delisting. In governance terms, as a result of the weak human rights initiatives on the one hand and the strong investor protections on the other, there is a massive disequilibrium between protection for developing countries and protection for developed countries' investors. This is illustrated below.

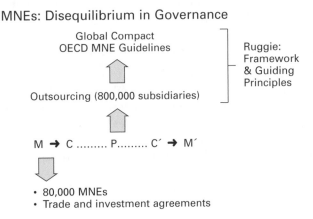

Figure 6.2 MNEs: Disequilibrium

[45] Ibid, 660.
[46] United Nations Global Compact <http://www.unglobalcompact.org/>.

b. Can corporate social responsibility institute moral behaviours despite its lack of enforceability and the governance bias in favour of investors in developing countries?

Many scholars argue that although international corporate law codes and other national codes are voluntary and unenforceable, companies will adopt their principles because in so doing they appease customers and attract investors. Indeed, the presence of these international standards is frequently understood to have a positive educative effect on the whole system of governance. For example, Graham and Woods argue that:

> 'Softer international conventions and commitments do not create robustly enforceable rights, yet ... there is a strong argument that they have other effects which contribute to the effectiveness of self-regulatory systems. International standards assist in mobilizing civil society within and across countries by creating standards and expectations that such standards might be upheld (Keck & Sikkink, 1998). This is captured in the UN Global Compact which seeks to encourage learning and best practice among participating companies who have all committed to existing international standards on human rights, environmental protection, and such like.'[47]

David Millon also favourably cites the soft law initiatives, the Global Compact, the International Labour Organization's Declaration on Fundamental Principles and Rights at Work and the Ruggie Reports. The value of these soft law mechanisms, he argues, is in supplying a set of standards which have 'the potential to shape corporate management's own sense of responsibility',[48] not least because their response comes under external scrutiny which may impact on investment. In other words, he argues, there is a market case for corporate social responsibility. Millon suggests that all these elements will encourage US companies to follow the more socially responsible path that he sees Europe and the UK pursuing.

c. So is there a market case for corporate social responsibility?

Many advocates of corporate social responsibility argue that there is a market case for corporate morality. Often they cite the popularity of corporate social responsibility with a large swathe of investors as many funds and fund managers market themselves as ethical, and will screen companies for their corporate social responsibility credentials before investing. To encourage the responsible investor, the United Nations (UN) set out its own initiative, the Principles for Responsible Investment (PRI).[49] PRI was launched in 2006 by the UN in conjunction with the UN Global Compact and the UN Environment Program Finance Initiative.[50] PRI is

---

[47] Graham and Woods (n. 43).

[48] P.M. Vasudev and S. Watson (eds), *Corporate Governance After the Financial Crisis* (Edward Elgar, 2012), 77.

[49] UN Principles for Responsible Investment, 'Principles for Responsible Investment Hit US$8 Trillion Mark on First Year Anniversary' <http://www.unpri.org/principles/>.

[50] An investor initiative in partnership with UNEP Finance Initiative.

a set of best practice guidelines for investors who wish to invest according to environmental, social and corporate governance issues.[51] Compliance with PRI is through self-reporting. This involves an annual PRI Reporting and Assessment survey in which members must undertake and show some progress in promoting environmental, social and corporate governance investment.[52] Members who consistently fail to show progress in their investment policies face possible delisting. The principles are self-avowedly 'voluntary and aspirational'.[53]

These kinds of public corporate social responsibility statements are clearly attractive to consumers as well as investors. Fairtrade is a popular brand with the ethical consumer and Starbucks PLC adopted all Fairtrade coffee in order to appease its customers and dissipate negative publicity about its operations. Nike and Ikea have both come out against the use of child labour and have taken many measures to ensure the proper treatment of workers. This was, of course, a response to negative publicity about its production and the negative response of its customers and to a certain degree its employees at the skilled end of production. In these cases there seems to be a market argument for corporate social responsibility activities.

Alternatively, advocates of corporate social responsibility initiatives argue that it improves risk management activities and thus avoids costly mistakes. Millon argues that a greater focus on risk management may reform corporate behaviours simply because fighting litigation for abuses of human rights or for causing environmental damage, in (usually) developing countries, is very expensive. He cites the Bhopal disaster in 1984, Unocal in Burma and Shell in Nigeria, arguing that the cost of litigation, settling claims and reputational damage are considerable incentives for companies to adopt better corporate standards. He recognises that litigation of this kind only really addresses the most egregious abuses of human rights. For example, Nike was famously obliged to reform in the 1990s after adverse publicity over its use of child labour. However, lower level abuses may be considered by management to be damaging to the company's reputation. Millon notes the importance of local communities, NGOs and the media whose activities influence management's adoption of corporate social responsibility.[54] NGOs like Amnesty International (which has extended its scrutiny of human rights abuses to include companies), Earthright and Greenpeace have provided the kinds of information on corporate activity which affect how the public view these corporations. NGOs' endorsement or criticism of corporations can have a significant impact on their reputation. However, Millon acknowledges that whether or not abuses will be addressed relies on management's own evaluation

---

[51] UN Principles for Responsible Investment (n. 51), 2. The Principles were established through a process involving 20 large institutional shareholders from 12 countries supported by a 70-person 'multi-stakeholder group of experts' coordinated by the UN.
[52] Ibid, 8.
[53] Ibid, 2.
[54] P.M. Vasudev and S. Watson (n. 48), 86.

of the corporation's self-interest, as management is the driving force behind expanded attention to human rights.'[55]

The market argument is clearly attractive to corporate social responsibility advocates who argue that the company can pursue wider social interests and appease consumers, and all without alienating market players like investors: the win, win perspective. However, the evidence that there is a market argument for corporate social responsibility is very sketchy. As Van Zile notes:

> 'While many studies show a link between profitability and socially responsible programs, these studies have been unable to prove that the correlation is caused by the implementation of corporate social responsibility – or that profitable firms are not simply more likely to engage in corporate social responsibility in the first place. Corporate social responsibility may make good business sense for some firms, namely, those that have marketed themselves as sustainable enterprises or large corporations with strong brands and fragile reputations, but not for most.'[56]

Van Zile cites Vogel's work[57] and concludes, 'there is little evidence that corporate social responsibility increases profits for most companies.' Indeed, 'Many of the most socially responsible firms from the 1970s, such as those in the "five percent club" for annual corporate social responsibility spending relative to profit, like Dayton-Hudson, Cummins Engine, and Control Data, have gone out of business or have been restructured.'

Other work has highlighted the problem of non-compatible data. Empirical studies differ on what is considered to be corporate social responsibility activity and also what they consider to be evidence of enhanced business performance; 'the sheer volume of variation makes comparison between case studies and surveys difficult, if not impossible'.[58] Bradshaw concludes that 'there is no consensus as to whether there exists a generalised positive relationship between CSR and CFP [corporate financial performance]'.[59] Similarly, Millon recognises that corporate social responsibility may only be effective in very limited cases and that only the worse abuses will be litigated, not the routine exploitation which accompanies multinational activity in developing countries. Furthermore, in appeasing public opinion, corporations will only do that which appeases and no more. They will not address social problems for their own sake.

---

[55] Ibid, 92.
[56] C. Van Zile, 'India's Mandatory Corporate Social Responsibility Proposal: Creative Capitalism Meets Creative Regulation in the Global Market' (2012) 13(2) *Asian-Pacific Law & Policy Journal* 274, 282.
[57] D. Vogel, *The Market for Virtue: The Potential and Limits of Corporate Social Responsibility* (Brookings Institute Press, 2005).
[58] C. Bradshaw, 'The environmental business case and unenlightened shareholder value' (2013) 33(1) *Legal Studies* 141, 145.
[59] Ibid, 144.

d. So if there is no market argument for corporate morality and insufficient international restraints, can nations mandate morality?

If companies are not free to make moral choices because of the market, if there is no real market argument for corporate social responsibility and if the international restraints to enhance corporate morality are ineffective, mandating corporate social responsibility may be a way of ensuring corporate morality.

The introduction of mandatory corporate social responsibility has been discussed in India for a number of years and legislation in this area has just been passed. The experience of India, therefore, is worth examining, particularly as it illustrates the problem of making corporations moral when market imperatives are strong, even when the political pressure to address corporate morality is itself also strong. Following independence, India pursued a socialist agenda, and though it has since embraced economic transformation on a market model, politicians remain politically pledged to economic equality, and voters remain wedded to this ideal and are expectant of its realisation. India's shift from a nationalised economy to the new 'liberal' economic programme of 1991 was premised on fulfilling those social goals and improving economic equality. Instead, the new economic programme has increased wealth inequalities. The massive increase in GDP has benefitted the minority in India, creating both the super-rich and failing to better the super-poor. At the same time, politicians do not want to return to nationalisation and do not want to thwart the (still) rapid growth of the economy. This is the political context in which the introduction of mandatory corporate social responsibility should be understood.[60]

In Van Zile's paper, written before the India Companies Act 2013 containing the CSR provisions was passed, she argues that mandatory corporate social responsibility should be seen as an attempt to deal with India's huge social problems and inequalities without resorting to high corporate tax. It is a half-way house between voluntary corporate social responsibility and more taxation. She argues that Indian politicians are keen to protect India's burgeoning economy and its on-going attractiveness to investors. As such, India seeks to adopt more 'market'-type regulation. For example, it wants to maintain corporate tax at the levels which are comparable to longstanding market economies like the US and the UK. At the same time, politicians have to respond to the electorate's demands for social justice and economic equality. Thus, Von Zile concludes, 'in proposing mandatory corporate social responsibility, the Indian government was likely attempting to bridge this

---

[60] It is indicative of the profound lack of corporate morality that Indian companies were not content with the concessions in the wording of the Bill. Throughout the discussion about mandatory corporate social responsibility, there has been an on-going demand from business for the two per cent corporate social responsibility requirement to be offset by a two per cent reduction in corporate tax. There were signs that the government was responding positively to this demand. 'Mandatory CSR: India Inc Asks For Tax Breaks in Return', *The Financial Express* (December 5, 2012) <http://www.financialexpress.com/news/mandatory-csr-india-inc-asks-for-tax-breaks-in-return/1040519>.

divide: to satisfy voters by forcing companies to promote social welfare, and to please companies by avoiding additional taxes while allowing them to benefit from the autonomy of choosing how and where they will support social goods.'[61]

So, although wealth inequality is very pronounced in India, it exists in a political system that promotes social and economic equality and is traditionally grounded in more left-wing aspirations. However, the government has been very cautious in its attempts to address its political commitments at the expense of capitalist development and investment; 'the liberal international market and a fear of competitive disadvantage has prevented India from raising corporate taxes considerably or increasing regulation. Given this context, mandatory corporate social responsibility can be read as a product of India's complex set of economic pressures and tensions.'[62]

The result of these complex pressures is that even though mandatory corporate social responsibility might help bridge the gap between political expectations and the market economy, the pressure from corporations is so great that both the mandatory and socially responsible nature of the proposed legislation have been watered down. The Act requires companies to 'make every endeavour' to see that the company spends at least 2 per cent of its annual profits (taken as an average over the previous three years) on corporate social responsibility activities. It applies to all companies incorporated in India with a substantial turnover and is expected to affect around 8,000 companies, raising a potential $2 billion for corporate social responsibility activities.[63] However, the Act falls a little short of mandating corporate social responsibility because although companies must ensure they spend 2 per cent of their average net profits, if they fail to spend that amount they must only disclose why they have not done so in their annual report. Furthermore, the Act does not provide any guidance on what would be considered an unacceptable reason for not spending that 2 per cent, which opens up all sorts of loopholes. Also, although the Act defines corporate social responsibility as that which promotes poverty reduction, education, health, environmental sustainability, gender equality, and vocational skills development, companies are free to interpret what that means and to invest within a broad spectrum of activities. This gives no real guarantee that any spending will deliver the social and economic equality which is sought and may well result in more self-serving spending. Alternatively, it could be argued that as corporate social responsibility-type activity is traditionally understood as being related to human rights, environment and labour, companies would be expected to spend on something which fell into these areas. However, there is still much scope for self-serving within these categories. Perhaps more problematic is that corporate social responsibility payments will be

---

[61] Van Zile (n. 56).

[62] Ibid.

[63] C. Ghuliani, 'India Companies Act 2013: Five Key Points About India's "CSR Mandate"' (*Eco-Business*, 28 November 2013) <http://www.eco-business.com/opinion/india-companies-act-2013-five-key-points-about-indias-csr-mandate/>.

spread amongst a wide selection of agencies which represent the issues noted in the Act. As one report notes, with an estimated 3.3 million NGOs in India, the money is likely to be dissipated in donations to agencies that do not have the skills or capacity to address the social problems that corporate social responsibility payments are designed to meet. The lack of due diligence required of companies making donations means that there is no incentive to seek out and fund credible organisations.[64]

CONCLUSION

The issues presented here indicate that if companies are indeed to link their activities to moral outcomes, they need to be much freer from the constraints of the market and the demands of market players. However, this in itself is not enough. Those exercising decisions on the company's behalf, the managers, need incentives to make moral decisions. Linking remuneration to performance (performance being some form of shareholder value maximisation), for example, undermines corporate morality. A long-standing neoliberal culture which links professional competency to the achievement of shareholder value maximisation needs to be redressed. Once those incentives are constrained, corporate decision making which enhances social wealth needs to be encouraged. Ultimately, it may only be the law that can create those clear moral guidelines that enable companies and companies' management to be *fit to be free*, as it did in the 'progressive' periods. Mandatory corporate social responsibility may help in providing some of that encouragement and guidance.

Further Reading

A. Carroll, 'Corporate Social Responsibility: Evolution of A Definitional Construct' (1999) 38(3) *Business & Society* 268.

A. Crane, 'Are You Ethical? Please Tick Yes or No: On Researching Ethics in Business Organizations' (1999) 20(3) *Journal of Business Ethics* 237.

T. Devinney, P. Auger, G. Eckhardt and T. Birtchnell, 'The Other Corporate Social Responsibility: Consumer Social Responsibility' (Fall 2006) 70(3) *Stanford Social Innovation Review* 299.

T. Donaldson, *Corporations and Morality* (Prentice Hall, College Div., 1982).

J. Frynas, 'The False Developmental Promise of Corporate Social Responsibility: Evidence from Multinational Oil Companies' (2005) 81(3) *International Affairs* 581.

W. Hoffman, 'What Is Necessary For Corporate Moral Excellence?' (1986) 5(3) *Journal of Business Ethics* 233.

J. L'Etang, 'Ethical Corporate Social Responsibility: A Framework for Managers' (1995) 14(2) *Journal of Business Ethics* 125.

---

[64] Ibid.

J. L'Etang, 'Public Relations and Corporate Social Responsibility: Some Issues Arising' (1994) 13(2) *Journal of Business Ethics* 111.

A. Lewis and C. Jurvale, 'Morals, Markets and Sustainable Investments: A Qualitative Study of "Champions"' (2010) 93(3) *Journal of Business Ethics* 483.

G. Lantos, 'The Boundaries of Strategic Corporate Social Responsibility' (2001) 18(7) *Journal of Consumer Marketing* 959.

G. Lantos, 'The Ethicality of Altruistic Corporate Social Responsibility' (2002) 19(3) *Journal of Consumer Marketing* 205.

L. Mitchell and T. Gabaldon, 'If I Only Had a Heart: Or, How Can We Identify Corporate Morality' (2001–2002) 76 *Tulane Law Review* 1645.

G. Moore, 'Corporate Moral Agency: Review and Implications' (1999) 21(4) *Journal of Business Ethics* 329.

H. Peterson and H. Vredenburg, 'Morals of Economics? Institutional Investor Preferences for Corporate Social Responsibility' (2009) 90(1) *Journal of Business Ethics* 1.

M. Schwartz and A. Carroll, 'Corporate Social Responsibility: A Three-Domain Approach' (2003) 13(4) *Business Ethics Quarterly* 503.

D. Vogel, *The Market for Virtue: The Potential and Limits of Corporate Social Responsibility* (Brookings Institute Press, 2005).

J. Wempe and M. Kaptein, *The Balanced Company: A Theory of Corporate Integrity* (Oxford University Press, 2002).

Y. Yoon, Z. Gürhan-Canil and N. Schwarz, 'The Effect of Corporate Social Responsibility (CSR) Activities on Companies with Bad Reputations' (2006) 16(4) *Journal of Consumer Psychology* 377.

7

WHAT THE COMPANY COULD BE

In this chapter I set out some ideas around what the company could be if corporate governance and company law were reformed. In the perspectives below, the company, if reconceived and reformed, is seen as an organisation which could operate in the interests of all those affected by its activities and who input into its activities. In so doing these perspectives reject the neoliberal premises of modern corporate governance. In the first section, the idea of shareholder primacy is rejected on the basis that it is socially regressive. The alternative model promoted is one which would enable the company to be sustainable and social. The second main perspective assessed rejects the law and economics model of the firm which has been utilised to understand all business forms, from small legal partnerships to large joint stock companies with dispersed share ownership. Instead, a model of the company is utilised which encompasses the notion of many stakeholders represented in many areas of law. The two perspectives adopted offer distinct views of how the company could be, but also contain many synergies. The first perspective promotes a labour-orientated corporate governance, as the goal which most effectively enables sustainability and progressive social outcomes. The second promotes the company as a resource owned in common, with many claimants. Both models seek sustainability and social progress.

1. TOWARDS A LABOUR-ORIENTATED CORPORATE GOVERNANCE

In *Progressive Corporate Governance*, I argue that the company has the potential to be a force for progress if it adopts a labour-orientated corporate governance. I argue that when companies adopt governance which focuses on the interests of shareholders, they produce regressive rather than progressive outcomes. A labour-orientated corporate governance does not necessarily involve direct labour representation in the corporate board (as would be found typically in European countries including ex-Comecon countries). Instead, it promotes decision making where the goal is the interests of labour because, in so doing, desirable social outcomes are achieved through corporate governance. This may or may not be achieved through direct labour representation.

In the UK we have never had a dual board which could give voice to the interests of labour within the company by giving labour a direct role in corporate decision making. Although labour representation on the board was frequently mooted from the late 1950s to the late 1970s, it was ultimately rejected. Then, it was those on the political right of the Labour Party who promoted it. Those on the left of the labour movement sought labour representation *outside* of the company, traditionally through the unions. They rejected the dual board as an attempt to co-opt labour into the company's governance, which would ultimately result in labour representing the interests of shareholders. From the left's perspective, labour's interests were not alignable with the company's and so they could not work together in mutual alliance. The interests of labour and shareholders were viewed as diametric opposites. Indeed, the balance of power between shareholders (represented by management) and labour could only be achieved by maintaining a strong outside 'countervailing power' (such as through the unions). This balance of power would ensure that one group could not overly exploit the other. The debate over labour representation was finally put to rest by the dawn of a new political era, Thatcher's New Right.

However, the tensions which underpin the earlier debate over labour representation on the board continue today – indeed in many ways contemporary globalisation has intensified them. Can board representation really promote labour's interest, or does it merely co-opt labour into the task of pursuing shareholders' interest? Are the interests of shareholders compatible with labour's interests? Should labour's interests continue to be subordinate to shareholders'?

I take the view that labour's interest is not compatible with shareholders' interest and that shareholders' interest is not compatible with enabling the company to be a force for progress. Labour-based governance can deliver sustainability, as labour's interest, I argue, tends to those outcomes which deliver progress and corporate sustainability. If empowered to achieve labour's interest, labour representatives on a board will not necessarily be co-opted into pursuing shareholders' interests. Labour's interest includes long-term development, good wages and concern with the environment in which the company operates (as labour is frequently located there). In contrast, shareholder-orientated governance will deliver only short-termism and has a regressive impact on society in a number of ways:

(a) It undercuts the consumer market.
(b) It drives increased liquidity which precipitates financial properties that are difficult to value.
(c) It lengthens the production chain without enhancing productive development.
(d) It drives down safety standards, working conditions and wages for labour.
(e) It deskills labour so that it cannot meet future challenges.

This list is not exhaustive but is illustrative of the difference between a labour-orientated governance and a shareholder-orientated governance, as in all of the above examples a labour-orientated governance would have the opposite goals and would tend to achieve the opposite outcomes. In what follows, I set out the claims in this list in more detail.

a. Shareholder-orientated governance undercuts the consumer market but labour-orientated governance enhances it

When company managers represent the interests of shareholders, they seek to increase the returns on their investment and thereby increase the value of the shares. This is partly achievable, in the short term, by reducing the cost of labour by, for example, reducing wages (through such mechanisms as having a flexible workforce) or by reducing the number of employees through redundancies. However, this approach to enhancing shareholder value has a regressive effect on society and on capitalism in the long term. This is because labour does not just produce commodities; it also consumes them. It constitutes a huge proportion of the buyers in the market in which commodities enter. Reducing wages or laying off labour means reduced consumption of general consumer goods. Less money chasing those commodities means reduced prices and falling profits. The money which is diverted from labour to a small wealthy elite is used to purchase prestige goods. This drives up their prices as well as the prices of unique items such as works of art.

Economic crises which reduce the buying power of labour may be redressed in a number of ways. For example:

a. Producers may sell to a different national market where labour has more income.
b. The state may intervene and extend cheap credit or reduce regulatory barriers to the extension of cheap credit.
c. Solution b. can be bolstered by the housing market (fuelled by low interest rates, 100% mortgages and deregulation).

Solution a. is dependent on a reasonably wealthy labour force, where shareholder primacy has not determined corporate governance because, although shareholder primacy economies can be highly productive, they are highly unequal in their distribution and so labour does not enjoy the benefits of productivity. Thus solution a. is dependent upon the gains made by labour in the other jurisdiction. The labour-orientated governance in these countries enables a consumer market for both their own national production and, in a global economy, the goods of those countries whose workforce has lower consumption power. However, eventually the shareholder primacy economies may undermine the labour governance economies as the goods produced by the well-paid consuming labour force are likely to be less competitive than those from an economy where wages are lower. Thus to protect the consumption power of the workforce, the state will have to subsidise consumption. It can do this more easily if it is possessed of valuable natural resources (such as Norway). If not, it will need to borrow, thus incurring a huge and unsustainable sovereign debt (as in the US or the UK). Alternatively, shareholders could accept lower returns on their shares.

Solution b. creates huge and unsustainable household debts which will eventually entirely disable households from purchasing anything more than essential goods. Solution c., which enhances solution b., involves the state engaging in activities which increase house prices. In the UK and the US, deregulation made mortgages easier to obtain and mortgages were extended to people with small or no deposits and whose income was uncertain. Mortgage lenders overcame their reluctance to lend to such people because they could sell the risk through mortgage-backed securities. Low interest rates also increased house prices, and this also supported increased household debt as householders possessed artificially enhanced house equity upon which credit was secured.

This strategy, however, in the current crisis, resulted in households that held mortgage and other debts which were unsustainable. In previous crises around the housing market there were huge numbers of home repossessions. This increases the shift of wealth to those that can survive and takes advantage of those who cannot; a shift facilitated by and partly paid for by the state. Repossessed homes, for example, can be bought up by the wealthier sections of society, for a fraction of their value, while the repossessed will require state-funded support in order to survive. In this crisis the state took action to reduce the number of repossessions, which has resulted in comparatively few house repossessions and a comparatively limited slump in the housing market. Each approach required massive public subsidy.

Thus solutions a.–c. are short-term solutions. None are sustainable, and indeed they create even greater problems to be dealt with in the future.

b. Shareholder-orientated governance seeks increased liquidity while labour-orientated governance seeks stability

Investors and labour act in different ways and pursue different goals. Investors seek liquidity in order to seek out the highest profits and to move away from poorly performing investments. Indeed the history of capitalist development is to a great degree the history of investment achieving increasing liquidity. In early capitalism there was very little liquidity. Capital investment was attached in law to the business assets. Investors were also entitled to the profits of production. This lack of fluidity in what Marx called the 'circuit of capital', where capital investment becomes attached and trapped by tangible assets, is, he argued, a source of anxiety for the investor. In the formula below (also examined in Chapter 6), M represents money, C represents that which money purchases (labour power and raw material, the means of production), P represents the production process, C´ represents the commodities produced and M´ the realised surplus value, or profit. Marx demonstrated how the circuit of capital is interrupted by property ownership of tangible assets. In this formulation Marx noted that 'the dots indicate that the circulation process is interrupted':[1]

---

[1] K. Marx, *Capital: A Critique of Political Economy Vol. 2* (Penguin Classics, 1992), 109.

'M – C … P … C′ – M′ (broken up into surplus enjoyed by the capitalist or returned to the finance capitalist and capital reinvested back into the production process) or M – C … P … C′ – M′ and so on.'

The experience of investors is that their money is bound up in a time-consuming process that that is not guaranteed to succeed. Indeed, the success of the process will not be fully known until the products are sold. This is undesirable and risky and would only be undertaken if the rewards were likely to be significantly greater than those of other capitalists involved in the process who retain flexibility, such as banks, lending for an agreed interest rate, or merchants, purchasing products at an agreed price. Historically, when investors were investing in a highly profitable enterprise, they were willing to accept that their investment was bound to the productive process and illiquid. However, when those returns dropped and the risk to the investment was greater, then investors began to seek great fluidity. The shift from high returns to lower returns in industrial capitalism in the UK came about in the last quarter of the 19th century. Then industrial capitalists began to use a legal form which would enable fluidity, the joint stock company with transferable shares.[2]

The facility for greater fluidity in investments in shares had already been provided by the middle of the 19th century. Parliament repealed the Bubble Act in 1825 which had forbidden the creation of freely transferable shares without a charter. Furthermore (as Williston noted as far back as 1888), the case of *Bligh v Brent*[3] held to the share becoming a claim to the surplus created by the chattels purchased by the money investment, not the chattels themselves. This, he noted, reversed all previous authorities which held the share to be a purchase of the company's equity where shareholders were co-owners in equity.[4] The Limited Liability Act 1855 enabled shareholders to be detached from company liability at the same time as they claimed company profits. Individually and together, the state and law have enabled and shaped the property form, the share, as an entitlement to profit divorced from the anxiety of being bound to the productive process and to the risk of losses. As noted earlier, the development of ownership without responsibility or risk led to Adolf Berle, and later to Peter Drucker declaring that shareholders should no longer be considered owners. Yet, we continue to bestow the power of ownership upon these irresponsible financial property holders, and shareholders' entitlement to vote has been protected throughout.

Similarly, both the state and the law have similarly allowed the proliferation of numerous other property forms designed to do the same thing – to give access to profits without loss of fluidity or risk of unlimited loss for the owner. This has created an inherent lack of sustainability in the economy as although no responsibility for loss is attached to the owners of these property forms, there is risk in

---

[2] L.E. Talbot, *Progressive Corporate Governance for the 21st Century* (Routledge, 2012), ch. 1.

[3] (1837) 2 Y & C 268, cited by Williston on this point.

[4] S. Williston, 'History of the Law of Business Corporations before 1800 – part II' (1888) 2 *Harvard Law Rev* 4. These points are discussed at length in Chapter 3.

the real economy upon which they are based. The loss must be borne somewhere and the difficulty in ascertaining where the loss is held makes the value of financial properties difficult to calculate. Historically, this leads to a loss of confidence in their values and to financial crises of ever-increasing seriousness. This is particularly true of the current crisis.

Capital undermines financial and productive stability in its search for greater returns. By becoming more liquid, the ownership of capital becomes a more passive activity, unattached to anything tangible for long and moved around by financial intermediaries, causing the problems noted (for example) in the Kay Review examined in Chapter 3. Labour, in contrast, seeks stability and continuity. The loss in production is directly borne by labour in redundancies or restructuring of work. Labour's activity and creativity directly impacts on the success of a business.

c. Shareholder-orientated governance lengthens the production chain while repressing development at the end of the chain

Lengthening the production chain and repressing development at the end of the chain are precisely contrary to labour's interest and thus contrary to governance that is labour orientated. In contrast, shareholder interest has driven profit maximisation activities which have lengthened the production chain along very particular lines. The low-tech end of production is outsourced to subsidiaries in developing countries, while the high-tech end is held by the companies based in developed countries which also possess (*inter alia*) the intellectual property rights and the marketing networks. An alternative (but similar) model is when the companies in developed economies just hold the intellectual property rights and outsource work to non-affiliated operations. So, as David Harvey frequently notes, Nike does not make anything. It simply contracts with other producers (over 600 contract factories situated mainly in Asia) to make the things it then trademarks and sells.[5] This latter (outsourcing) model of production severs all responsibility by the company to labour in the producing end of the production chain. The shareholder beneficiaries of large 'merchant' capitalists like Nike are geographically separate from the low-paid producer workforce which has included child labour, a practice which was only redressed following huge publicity and activism by civil society groups. In the former model, where production is held with a group or chain of subsidiaries, parent liability for subsidiary activities is generally limited by the corporate veil.

The division of labour in the production chain results in a number of outcomes which are highly deleterious for labour. First, the development of the productive capacity in the low-tech end is arrested. Secondly, the responsibility to labour becomes much more attenuated and their social welfare and basic safety is compromised. The first point may be illustrated through the example of Benetton's operations in the 1990s. The manufacture of Benetton's designs was subcontracted

---

[5] D. Harvey, *The Enigma of Capital* (Profile Books, 2011).

out to over 450 small producers who engaged in the labour-intensive part of the production process. The Benetton strategy involved a 'mix of high technology and high labour' with Benetton retaining ownership of the former and subcontracting the latter; 'by subcontracting the labour intensive operations it sheds the high cost elements to small family owned enterprises having lower cost structures. The cost benefits flow to Benetton.'[6]

Outsourcing also means that the producers in developing countries will have to compete for their business. The company that is outsourcing will not seek to make the producers' goods competitive by investing in the means of production. They will simply look to a producer that will provide the goods at a lower cost. This means that the western companies 'skip' the development that accompanied capitalist development in their own economies. This does not just impact on the development of production but also on the development of social relations which accompany industrial development. As Marx shows, industrial development has the eventual effect of freeing workers from the old hierarchical relationships. The model upon which Nike-like operations are developed maintains hierarchical relations: the workers are subject to the demands of either the 'lead' company, a middle man or the factory owner. Few skills are developed and workers are easily replaceable. Developing countries become entrenched at a low level of technical advancement, utilised only for cheap, low-skilled labour with no progress in social relations of production.[7] So although businesses using the subcontracting model do develop the overall means of production, globally development is highly uneven because most (though not all) development is located at the high-tech end which is geographically located in the West.

d. Shareholder-orientated governance drives down safety standards

There is no generalised impetus for development at the low-tech end in developing countries but plenty of incentives to cut costs, which ultimately impacts on safety. The state is frequently complicit in this and does not deliver the safety regulations and enforcements found in developed economies. Consequently, the lack of investment in the productive end, which includes safety measures, and the fierce competition has led to huge loss of human life. In April 2013, 1,127 people were killed in an unsafe garment factory in the Rana Plaza building in Dhaka. The building was quickly and haphazardly constructed with substandard material. It was then approved by corrupt officials and given a licence to operate. A report on the tragedy blamed the mayor for granting construction approval to an unsafe building, the building's owners for allowing the building to be used as it was, and the owners of

---

[6] P. Dapiran, 'Benetton – Global Logistics in Action' (1992) 22 *International Journal of Physical Distribution & Logistics* 6, 7.

[7] S.J. Lim and J. Phillips, 'Embedding CSR Values: The Global Footwear Industry's Evolving Governance Structure' (2008) 81 *Journal of Business Ethics* 143; D. Boje and F.R. Khan, 'Story-Branding by Empire Entrepreneurs: Nike Child Labour, and Pakistan's Soccer Ball Industry' (2009) 22 *Journal of Small Business & Entrepreneurship* 9.

the five garment factories in the building who compelled workers to return to work even after huge cracks appeared in the building and workers fled.[8] The report recommends the prosecution of these people who may receive life imprisonment.

Yet, although the prosecution of these people is undoubtedly right, this process of production is prompted and sustained by companies in developed countries pursing a fierce shareholder primacy governance. The companies which order these products (in this case clothing retail companies in the UK) force producers to compete for business, knowing that this will drive down safety standards. These companies made no investment into the development of the productive capacity or safety of these factories, yet they are deemed in law (at least) to be blameless. They are in law simply customers and the factories are not even their subsidiary companies. As the time of writing this at the beginning of June 2013, all these companies have been asked to do is to sign up to the Ethical Trading Initiative (ETI), a voluntary code requiring signed-up companies to ensure good labour practices from their suppliers. Justine Greening, Secretary of State for International Development, told the *Observer* that, 'The Department for International Development will work with companies to see how we can take the next step, whether it's signing up to ethical trading standards or going the extra mile in ensuring responsible business practices.'[9] The code is an industry-derived code and requires members to submit annual reports to the ETI board showing how they are dealing with labour conditions in the supply chains and how they have complied with the base principles noted below. The report must also show information on staff training and money spent on ethical trade strategies. There is no external monitor as such, but the ETI Secretariat conducts random validation 'to check that the company's management processes and systems for collecting data for its annual report are consistent and reliable'. This might sound effective but nobody seemed to notice that Primark, heavily reliant on clothing from the Rana Plaza, was already signed up.

A corporate governance which prioritised labour would, of course, prioritise safety. No-one exercising a labour-based governance would order employees back into a dangerous building. However, what a labour-based governance would also seek to do (unlike shareholder primacy governance) is prioritise the development of production and the development of labour skills. This would enhance the sustainability of the company by enabling it to remain competitive. It also enriches the labour experience as it enhances self-actualisation and creativity. A modern trained labour force also means that employees remain marketable and therefore they can continue to demand decent pay and remain active consumers.

[8] J. Yardley, 'Report on Deadly Factory Collapse in Bangladesh Finds Widespread Blame', *The New York Times* (New York, 22 May 2013) <http://mobile.nytimes.com/2013/05/23/world/asia/report-on-bangladesh-building-collapse-finds-widespread-blame.html>.

[9] D. Boffey, 'Topshop Among Clothing Stores Told to Help Improve Foreign Factories', *The Guardian* (London, 1 June 2013) <http://www.guardian.co.uk/fashion/2013/jun/01/minister-fashion-stores-improve-factory-conditions>. All companies who buy from the 500 clothing factories in Bangladesh are being urged by the government to sign up. The companies include Arcadia, Matalan, Aurora Fashions, Peacocks, Shop Direct, Hobbs, French Connection, Karen Millen and Austin Reed.

ETI Base Code[10]

1. Employment is freely chosen
   1.1 There is no forced, bonded or involuntary prison labour.
   1.2 Workers are not required to lodge "deposits" or their identity papers with their employer and are free to leave their employer after reasonable notice.
2. Freedom of association and the right to collective bargaining are respected
   2.1 Workers, without distinction, have the right to join or form trade unions of their own choosing and to bargain collectively.
   2.2 The employer adopts an open attitude towards the activities of trade unions and their organisational activities.
   2.3 Workers representatives are not discriminated against and have access to carry out their representative functions in the workplace.
   2.4 Where the right to freedom of association and collective bargaining is restricted under law, the employer facilitates, and does not hinder, the development of parallel means for independent and free association and bargaining.
3. Working conditions are safe and hygienic
   3.1 A safe and hygienic working environment shall be provided, bearing in mind the prevailing knowledge of the industry and of any specific hazards. Adequate steps shall be taken to prevent accidents and injury to health arising out of, associated with, or occurring in the course of work, by minimising, so far as is reasonably practicable, the causes of hazards inherent in the working environment.
   3.2 Workers shall receive regular and recorded health and safety training, and such training shall be repeated for new or reassigned workers.
   3.3 Access to clean toilet facilities and to potable water, and, if appropriate, sanitary facilities for food storage shall be provided.
   3.4 Accommodation, where provided, shall be clean, safe, and meet the basic needs of the workers.
   3.5 The company observing the code shall assign responsibility for health and safety to a senior management representative.
4. Child labour shall not be used
   4.1 There shall be no new recruitment of child labour.
   4.2 Companies shall develop or participate in and contribute to policies and programmes which provide for the transition of any child found to be performing child labour to enable her or him to attend and remain in quality education until no longer a child; "child" and "child labour" being defined in the appendices.
   4.3 Children and young persons under 18 shall not be employed at night or in hazardous conditions.
   4.4 These policies and procedures shall conform to the provisions of the relevant ILO standards.

---

[10] Reproduced with permission of the Ethical Trade Initiative (ETI), a leading alliance of companies, trade unions and NGOs that promotes respect for workers' rights around the globe.

5. Living wages are paid

5.1 Wages and benefits paid for a standard working week meet, at a minimum, national legal standards or industry benchmark standards, whichever is higher. In any event wages should always be enough to meet basic needs and to provide some discretionary income.

5.2 All workers shall be provided with written and understandable Information about their employment conditions in respect to wages before they enter employment and about the particulars of their wages for the pay period concerned each time that they are paid.

5.3 Deductions from wages as a disciplinary measure shall not be permitted nor shall any deductions from wages not provided for by national law be permitted without the expressed permission of the worker concerned. All disciplinary measures should be recorded.

6. Working hours are not excessive

6.1 Working hours comply with national laws and benchmark industry standards, whichever affords greater protection.

6.2 In any event, workers shall not on a regular basis be required to work in excess of 48 hours per week and shall be provided with at least one day off for every 7 day period on average. Overtime shall be voluntary, shall not exceed 12 hours per week, shall not be demanded on a regular basis and shall always be compensated at a premium rate.

7. No discrimination is practised

7.1 There is no discrimination in hiring, compensation, access to training, promotion, termination or retirement based on race, caste, national origin, religion, age, disability, gender, marital status, sexual orientation, union membership or political affiliation.

8. Regular employment is provided

8.1 To every extent possible work performed must be on the basis of recognised employment relationship established through national law and practice.

8.2 Obligations to employees under labour or social security laws and regulations arising from the regular employment relationship shall not be avoided through the use of labour-only contracting, subcontracting,or home-working arrangements, or through apprenticeship schemes where there is no real intent to impart skills or provide regular employment, nor shall any such obligations be avoided through the excessive use of fixed-term contracts of employment.

9. No harsh or inhumane treatment is allowed

9.1 Physical abuse or discipline, the threat of physical abuse, sexual or other harassment and verbal abuse or other forms of intimidation shall be prohibited. The provisions of this code constitute minimum and not maximum standards, and this code should not be used to prevent companies from exceeding these standards. Companies applying this code are expected to comply with national and other applicable law and, where the provisions of law and this Base Code address the same subject, to apply that provision which affords the greater protection.

e. Shareholder-orientated governance deskills labour so that it cannot meet future challenges

There are historical lessons which show that the failure of management to pursue labour-based governance by continuing to train employees has resulted in productive stagnation and loss of competitiveness. Lazonic and O'Sullivan argue that, in the United States, a corporate management, which had become too divorced from the shop floor, failed to address the reskilling of its workforce, resulting in the competitive failure of corporations as productive industries and forcing them to become financialised organisations. This resulted in a shift in corporate strategy from 'retain and reinvest' to 'downsize and distribute'.[11]

This divorce, they argue, arose because of the conglomeration movement which began in the 1960s, which meant that by the 1970s the American corporation had become too large and unwieldy to operate effectively: 'the over-extension of the corporate enterprises into too many different lines of business had helped to foster the strategic segmentation of top managers from their organisations.'[12] Management could not respond to the changes required at the shop-floor level and 'the central offices of these corporations were too far from the actual processes that developed and utilised productive resources to make informed investment decisions about how corporate resources and returns should be allocated to enable strategies based on "retain and reinvest" to succeed.'[13] One of the investment decisions they should have made, but did not, was to train the workforce. So, when stagflation hit in the 1970s, management were too removed from the business to 'understand what type of innovative strategies they should pursue and the capabilities of their organisations to implement these strategies'.[14] Thus, the poorly skilled shop-floor workforce 'proved to be the Achilles heel of US corporations'.[15]

In contrast, corporate America's greatest competitor, Japan, had the opposite strategy. Japanese companies invested in developing the skill of its shop-floor workers. Furthermore, Japanese managers were extremely good at communicating throughout the organisational structure, notwithstanding the companies' size:

> 'Japanese skill bases integrated the capabilities of people with a broader array of functional specialties and a deeper array of hierarchical responsibilities into processes of organisational learning. In particular, the hierarchical integration of Japanese skill bases extended from managerial organisation to shop-floor production workers and subsidiary firms that served as suppliers and distributors.'[16]

---

[11] W. Lazonic and M. O'Sullivan, 'Maximising Shareholder Value: A New Ideology for Corporate Governance' (2000) 29(1) *Economy and Society* 13, 17.

[12] Ibid, 26.

[13] Ibid, 15.

[14] Ibid, 26–7.

[15] Ibid 30.

[16] Ibid 15.

As a result they made rapid progress in the electronic goods and car industries – key areas for American capitalism.[17]

Harry Braverman's work on labour in the American corporation[18] illustrates a darker motive behind management failure to development workforce skills. He argues that it was part of management's strategy to retain personal power and to reduce the workforce's bargaining power, by enhancing knowledge and skills at the upper echelons of corporate hierarchy (executives managers) while diminishing knowledge and skill at the shop-floor level. A disempowered workforce would be unable to challenge the all-powerful executives. Indeed, even investors would bow to the self-created superiority of management.

What is also interesting about the life of the increasingly deskilled shop-floor worker was that their downgraded work activity was not reflected in their wages. They did not feel the economic effects of this during periods of prosperity and they enjoyed good wages. Retain and reinvest meant that the overall wealth was distributed more widely. Strong unions in both the UK and the US ensured that management were kept to their metal in terms of distributing corporate wealth to the workforce, even though the products made in these countries were uncompetitive, particularly in the outdated (but subsidised) car industry. However, the combination of stagflation and the oil crisis meant that this state of affairs could no longer continue. Management would have to reskill its workforce or do something else. As noted above, they were too divorced from the productive process to understand the required innovations so they chose another direction, one which was, in any case, being promoted in the universities and in political policies. Management aligned themselves with outside financial interests and pursued shareholder value strategies. Management policy became that of reorganising and downsizing the workforce and of returning increasingly large proportions of corporate profit in dividends to shareholders.[19]

This drift to shareholder value was also promoted by the growing importance of institutional investors from the 1970s. Institutional investors had been insignificant in companies before then because they were restricted from investing more than very small amounts in company equities. These restrictions began to be removed in the 1970s as a number of different issues were triggered from within the economy and because of outside pressures. Among these, note Lazonick and Sullivan, the oil crisis in the 1970s and the resulting rise in oil price coupled with the general inflationary economy meant that pension and life insurance funds could not generate enough income for their beneficiaries. In contrast, mutual funds, which were not regulated (although they then constituted a small proportion of the economy), could invest in a wide range of securities. To redress this imbalance the US government passed the Employee Retirement Income Security Act (1974) – which was

---

[17] Japan has of course since suffered other problems in its economy; however, this does not detract from Lazonic's central argument about approaches to labour skills.

[18] Discussed in Chapter 1.

[19] Lazonic and Sullivan (n. 11).

further amended to allow pension funds to invest in many risky securities. In the 1970s, banks too found it difficult to compete with the unregulated money-market funds, so legislation was passed to deregulate interest rates payable on deposits and loans. One of the effects of this was to make it difficult for saving and loans institutions whose assets were long-term, low-yield mortgages to compete for private investors. In response to this the government passed the Garn-St. Germain Act of 1982 which permitted saving and loans institutions to hold junk bonds, while still having depositor accounts guaranteed by the government.

Lazonick and O'Sullivan also showed that these developments meant that saving and loans institutions joined the hostile takeover movement of the 1980s. This movement was largely facilitated by use of the junk bond.[20] Famously, Michael Milken, as an employee of Wall Street investment bank, Drexel, Burnham and Lambert, induced financial institutions to buy and sell junk bonds. He first targeted mutual funds, but after the Garn-St. Germain Act Milken was able to target pension funds and insurance companies. Milken persuaded these institutional investors to sell their shareholdings in a target company to a bidder company and to purchase junk bonds instead, in order to affect a mutually profitable takeover. Thus emerged a powerful market for corporate control, where the market rather than management structures controlled corporate decision making. The most successful managers in this context were those who played to the market by shedding labour and selling off valuable physical assets in order to meet the costs of the takeovers and to increase the value of the company's stock. The measure of their success was enhanced market capitalisation.

The stock market crash of 1987 and various legal decisions on takeovers brought an end to the hostile takeover fever of the 1980s. However, as Lazonick and Sullivan note, 'shareholder value strategies continued' and the old 'retain and reinvest' management strategies were replaced by 'downsize and distribute'.[21] Thus when share prices were rising, the blue-collar workforce was substantially deteriorating; 'the "boom" years of the mid-1980s saw hundreds of major plant closures. Between 1983 and 1987, 4.6 million workers lost their jobs, of which 40 per cent were from the manufacturing sector ... even as the economy moved into recovery from 1991, the job-loss rate rose to ever higher levels',[22] and 'in the boom year of 1998 the number of announced staff cuts by major US corporations was greater than for any other year in the 1990s'.[23] Across the board, workers experienced a lack of job security and worked longer hours for less pay.

---

[20] One that rating agencies deemed below 'investment grade'.

[21] Lazonic and Sullivan (n. 11), 17.

[22] Ibid.

[23] Ibid, 20. Lazonick also attributes part of the explanation behind the new shareholder value orientation to long-standing practices in managerial culture. Since the 1950s top managers began receiving stock options as part of their pay, long before the agency costs debate. The tendency to have high pay-out ratios compared with European counties may have been a result of these pay deals. However, the tendency to pursue this goal exclusively was held in check by regulation and the overriding belief in 'retain and reinvest', strategies that characterised management goals up to the 1970s.

This shift in corporate strategy has also, argue Lazonick and O'Sullivan, impacted on the American education systems. The new emphasis on financial investment and engineering meant that corporations sought the employment of the most highly skilled and educated individuals. These were drawn from the elite institutions which drew talent from all over the world. The education of the broader population was less of a priority. 'The skills base bias of US corporate investment and the availability of a well-educated international labour supply have meant, moreover, that corporate America has had little interest in upgrading the quality of education available to most Americans.'[24] One of the current outcomes of this choice is that the education system in America is experiencing a downward mobility with only one-fifth of America's young adults reaching a higher level of educational attainment than their parents.[25] At the same time America boasts most of the finest (and most expensive) universities in the world.

Thus, where the skills of corporate management were shifting away from innovating with a large, skilled workforce to engaging in financial strategies to enhance shareholder value, the skills required of management changed too. This was a development anticipated by Veblen at the turn of the 20th century.[26] Its significance is that it presents a clear challenge to the development of labour-based governance, as management do not possess the skills required to facilitate such governance and furthermore have a huge self-interest in rejecting it.

Lazonick and Sullivan's work and Braverman's work provide a different slant to the explanation for the emergence of shareholder-orientated governance which is pertinent in the UK as well as the US. They show that management disengaged from the productive process and the development of labour's skills, either because of the demands of managing larger companies (as in Lazonick's explanation) or because of a self-protecting strategy to ensure their elite position (as in Braverman's explanation). This disengagement meant that labour's skills were increasingly outdated and unmarketable so that their diminished market power was at odds with their political power, expressed through collective action. At the same time the state was responding to a shift in the global economy by reducing the restrictions on institutional investors, thus enhancing their power as investors. Shifting to shareholder primacy, through downsizing the workforce and distributing more corporate profit and capital to shareholders, was a logical step to take. Readjusting labour's political power to align it with its market power was another role taken by the state, and with some alacrity in the UK, as noted in Chapter 6. Focusing on financial solutions to profit creation reflected and continues to reflect management skills. They are no longer fit for the task of managing actual production.

This explanation effectively challenges the neoliberal justification for the shift in corporate goals in the last 40 years. Neoliberalism argues that job losses, downsizing

---

[24] Ibid, 30.
[25] S. Coughlan, 'Downward Mobility Haunts US Education' *BBC News* (London, 3 December 2012) <http://www.bbc.co.uk/news/business-20154358>.
[26] T. Veblen, *The Theory of Business Enterprise* (Cosimo Classic, 2005, first published 1903).

and asset stripping occurs because it enhances value and puts capital where capital can be most effective. In so doing it encourages the kinds of innovation classically referenced with the example of Silicon Valley. However, as Lazonick shows, Silicon Valley did not result from shareholder value strategies but reaped the success of massive state funding over many decades: 'the prosperity of Silicon Valley in the 1990s owes more to the post war "military industrial complex", in which "retain and reinvest" corporations such as IBM, Hewlett Packard, Motorola and Xerox were central, rather than it does to a resurgence of entrepreneurialism.'[27]

If the shareholder governance strategies had yielded long-term success by dint of the efficiencies it claims for itself then the argument for a labour-orientated governance would not be as strong, or at least the principle argument for it would be around the more equal distribution of wealth. However, the 'success', as it seemed to be when Lazonick wrote this article, was in part built on the 'retain and invest' strategies of the past which enabled asset-rich companies to redistribute those assets to shareholders. The massive public subsidies noted above also enabled success in the private sectors. The other part was pure 'bubble', as the gains were not gains at all, but financial engineering now gone wrong and in need of replacement. The success of shareholder primacy, as the financial crisis has revealed, was illusory. It effect was to redistributed societies' wealth to a privileged few.

By replacing shareholder primacy governance with labour-orientated governance, sustainability and social progress would be achieved because it would:

(a) maintain a strong consumer base;
(b) reduce liquidity and clarify values;
(c) reskill labour, enhance labour creativity and self-actualisation;
(d) reduce pressure on profit maximisation and thereby:
  (i)   develop productive capacity throughout the production chain,
  (ii) increase safety,
  (iii) distribute more wealth at the point of production in wages and reinvestment.

f. Enforcement of labour-based governance

The question remains as to how to institute a labour-based governance. Enforcement by the state would seem to be the obvious choice. However, many states have been instrumental in the oppression of the labour force in the interest of investors. This is particularly vivid in many developing countries, such as Nigeria.[28] More generally, the race to the bottom in terms of regulation is thriving

---

[27] Lazonic and Sullivan (n. 11), 30.

[28] The Nigerian state has consistently abrogated labour rights and human rights in order to support the activities of Shell. Particularly notorious was the brutal suppression in the first half of the 1990s of the Ogoni people living in the Niger Delta. This culminated in the torture and execution of nine key Ogoni activists in 1995, including Ken Saro-Wiwa. In *Kiobel v Royal Dutch Petroleum (Shell)* the US Supreme Court ruled that the Alien Tort Claims Act could not be used against Shell in respect of its involvement in these human rights abuses.

as countries compete for investment. As a result of these pressures on developing countries, many commentators are sceptical about the capacity of the state to institute regulation which would enhance the interest of labour, particularly in the countries which most require it.

In contrast, private labour governance initiatives, derived from the activities of civil society groups, NGOs, transnational organisations and from industry itself, have been developing over the last 20 years. These are of differing quality. As noted in Chapter 5, the Global Compact, a UN initiative, is 'principle-based' (though reflecting the ILO standards on labour) and involves no monitoring. Similarly, the UN's Principles for Responsible Investment set out aspirations and involve no external monitoring.[29] 1,209 companies and investors have signed up to these initiatives.[30] The views on the effectiveness of this are mixed.[31]

Industry-derived initiatives are similarly modest in their requirements from signatory companies. The Ethical Trading Initiative, already noted above in this chapter, is an example of this. Others include the ISO 26000 to promote corporate social responsibility (CSR) in companies, published by the International Organization for Standardization (ISO). ISO 26000 requires no monitoring and provides no certification and only gives guidance on best CSR practice. In its words:

> 'ISO 26000:2010 provides guidance rather than requirements, **so it cannot be certified to unlike some other well-known ISO standards**. Instead, it helps clarify what social responsibility is, helps businesses and organizations translate principles into effective actions and shares best practices relating to social responsibility, globally. It is aimed at all types of organizations regardless of their activity, size or location.'[32]

There is a great deal of cross-fertilisation between industry and transnational organisations. The European Commission's new policy on corporate social responsibility, published in October 2011, enjoined European companies to affiliate to the 'OECD Guidelines for Multinational Enterprises, the 10 principles of the UN Global Compact, the UN Guiding Principles on Business and Human Rights, the ILO Tri-partite Declaration of Principles on Multinational Enterprises and Social Policy, [and] the ISO 26000 Guidance Standard on Social Responsibility'.[33]

---

[29] <http://www.unpri.org/> discussed in L.E. Talbot, *Progressive Corporate Governance for the 21st Century* (Routledge, 2013), pp. 179–80.

[30] United Nations Global Compact, 'Signatories to the Principles for Responsible Investment' <http://www.unpri.org/signatories/>.

[31] E.M. Zarbafi, *Responsible Investment and the Claim of Corporate Change: A Sensemaking Perspective on how Institutional Shareholders may Drive Corporate Social Responsibility* (Springer, 2011).

[32] International Organization for Standardization, ISO 26000 – Social Responsibility <http://www.iso.org/iso/home/standards/iso26000.htm>.

[33] 'The Commission defines corporate social responsibility as "the responsibility of enterprises for their impacts on society". To fully meet their social responsibility, enterprises "*should have in place a process to integrate social, environmental, ethical human rights and consumer concerns into their business operations and core strategy in close collaboration with their stakeholders*".' <http://ec.europa.eu/enterprise/policies/sustainable-business/corporate-social-responsibility/index_en.htm>.

ISO 26000 is designed to reflect existing established transnational norms, particularly those generated by the International Labour Organization (ILO), 'with whom ISO established a Memorandum of Understanding (MoU) to ensure consistency in ISO 26000 with ILO labour standards'.[34]

So the statements about ideal standards for labour exist and are reflected from one initiative to another. However, they are voluntarily adopted by companies, do not involve outside monitoring and in some cases, such as ISO 26000, do not even involved certification. Perhaps more significantly, they do not empower labour and give it any means to assert whatever codes or principles are adopted.

In contrast, some civil society-initiated codes have been favorably appraised by commentators. For example, the Social Accountability 8000 (SA8000), originally developed by Social Accountability International in 1998 to reduce sweatshop practice, is said to be 'regarded as one of the most stringent certification standards in the area of labour governance'.[35] In the current 2008 version, SA8000 states as its purpose to 'protect and empower all personnel within a company's scope of control and influence'.[36] This includes producers, suppliers, subcontractors and home workers. SA8000 requires detailed auditing to ensure that its very specific standards and requirements are met and are verifiable. Without this no company can be certified under SA8000. The aim of complying with SA8000 is that it enables companies to, first, take control of the treatment of labour and, secondly, to 'credibly demonstrate to interested parties that existing company policies, procedures, and practices conform to the requirements of this standard'.[37] SA8000 requires stakeholder engagement, through consultation and engagement with information relating to compliance, including monitoring. In addition the company must 'demonstrate its willingness to participate in dialogues with all interested stakeholders, including, but not limited to: workers, trade unions, suppliers, subcontractors, sub-suppliers, buyers, nongovernmental organisations, and local and national government officials, aimed at attaining sustainable compliance with this standard'.[38] All companies will be subject to announced or unannounced audits to certify compliance and they must keep appropriate records to show compliance.[39] Social Accountability International reports that SA8000 'is being used in over 3,000 factories, across 66 countries and 65 industrial sectors'.[40] However, even this 'good' example has been subject to substantial criticism. The Clean Clothes Campaign reported that SA8000 was failing to deliver because it was not easily enforcable and

[34] International Organization for Standardization, ISO 26000 – Social Responsibility <http://www.iso.org/iso/home/news_index/news_archive/news.htm?refid=Ref1490>.

[35] J. Donaghey, J. Reinecke, C. Niforou and B. Lawson, 'From Employment Relations to Consumption Relations: Balancing Labor Governance in Global Supply Chains' (Forthcoming, 2014) *Human Resource Management*.

[36] Social Accountability International, Social Accountability 8000 (2008) <http://www.sa-intl.org/_data/n_0001/resources/live/2008StdEnglishFinal.pdf>, 4.

[37] Ibid.

[38] Ibid, 10.

[39] Ibid.

[40] Ibid.

because of its failure to monitor the agencies qualified to certify a business as SA8000 compliant.[41]

Other scholarly research has indicated that effective labour governance is best achieved when there is a combination of consumer power driving governance and labour power. In Donaghey et al.'s forthcoming article, they accept that consumer power tends to affect the market's approach to labour, while labour power tends to directly affect collective agreement.[42] However, they argue, although these forms of power tend to affect different areas of governance, if they work in tandem they are a very effective way of improving labour standards. So, if a lead firm selling in the developed world becomes known as having exploitative labour standards further down the chain, and consumers choose to not buy its products, it will be under pressure to change those standards. If, at the same time, labour has some power, either because their skills are not easily substitutable, or they are an essential link in the production chain, or they are part of a broader collective agreement (or all three) then the conjunction of the production and consumption power is a highly effective mechanism to ensure labour standards. Indeed, argue Donaghey et al., each will bolster the other, so that a strong consumer-led campaign, often driven by NGOs, can have the effect of bolstering union activity. Labour-based campaigning can strengthen consumer power or it can have the effect of strengthening the relationship between international and local labour activists. A 'virtuous spiral' is created. They give the example of Fairtrade:

'In Fairtrade, the involvement of labour activists in the development of the Fairtrade standard has resulted in a strong focus on workers' rights. Yet in 2012, and together with trade union, labour rights activists, the workers themselves and especially the Workers' Rights Advisory Council, Fairtrade launched a workers' rights strategy to provide 170,000 workers employed on Fairtrade certified plantations with greater support to achieve freedom of association, a living wage, and decision power over Fairtrade premium monies. The strategy was aimed at a move from social compliance with standards to fostering the conditions that would equip workers with the tools and ability to negotiate their own wages and working terms.'[43]

However, it is difficult to reconcile the kinds of consumer choices made in the developed world with the needs of labour in developing world. With life experiences so different, it seems highly unlikely that labour in developing countries and consumers in developed countries will agree on the priorities, even in respect of the more obvious points of agreement, such as child labour. Locally, the issue of child labour will be complex and may form an important part of a family's economy. In contrast, for western consumers the issue is more likely to be a simple

---

[41] The Clean Clothes Campaign, 'Fatal Fashion: Analysis of recent factory fires in Pakistan and Bangladesh: a call to protect and respect garment workers' lives' <http://www.cleanclothes.org/resources/publications/fatal-fashion.pdf>, 24–7.

[42] Donaghey et al. (n. 35).

[43] Ibid, 29.

rejection on the grounds of child welfare. Indeed, the authors note scholarship which views consumer-led governance as a form of cultural imperialism where 'western consumer preferences become the yardstick for labour standards even if what is "desirable" for workers may differ substantially across cultural contexts'.[44]

Thus, much scholarship shows that parties who are far removed from the process of production, such as shareholders or consumers, are not well placed to decide on the best interests of labour, though their support may indeed strengthen labour's position. But, in order for a labour-orientated governance to meaningfully engage in labour's interest, the shaping of governance must, in part, reside with labour itself. Traditionally, this has been the province of labour unions and to be sure their role remains significant. However, as the experience of the UK and US car industry indicates, strong unions may forestall wage cuts and redundancies, but market pressures mean that unions cannot resist them indefinitely. The protection of outdated practices and skills can be undermined through the political and legal disempowerment of unions. This was the tactic adopted by the Thatcher government in the 1980s, and it successfully swept away large productive industries and replaced them with financial 'industries'. Thus in order to institute a labour-based governance, labour must be involved in making decisions about the productive process itself. Labour representatives who are close to the productive process must engage in what reskilling processes and restructuring is required to remain useful and competitive. Labour representation in the corporate decision-making process, through such mechanisms as the supervisory board, would enable this, thus enhancing the company's sustainability.

Labour representation is also required throughout the chain of production. And, where it branches out into other ways of accessing labour, such as through subcontracting, labour must remain part of the monitoring system. A successful monitoring system possesses many of the features of SA8000 (but is cognisant of SA8000's noted failures). This includes specific requirements rather than general principles, the involvement of stakeholders and an external monitoring system. The ambitions of all monitoring, though, should be raised above the limited aim of not breaching human rights and should aim to enable human flourishing.[45]

Initial ingredients of a labour-based governance

1. Empowered unions and dual board
   (a) redistribution at point of production
   (b) skilling labour
   (c) production over financialisation

---

[44] Ibid, 33. Aaron Dhir has also written a useful article reflecting on the different perceptions local people may have about the well-intentioned actions of company shareholders; A. Dhir, 'Shareholder Engagement in the Embedded Business Corporation: Investment Activism, Human Rights and TWAIL Discourse' (2009) Osgoode CLPE Research Paper No. 12/2009 <http://dx.doi.org/10.2139/ssrn.1416198>.
[45] See Chapter 6.

2. Government regulation
    (a) controlling financial property forms
    (b) protecting unions
    (c) requiring dual boards
    (d) company law reform
3. Civil society labour-based governance
    (a) enhancing monitoring
    (b) promoting high standards of human flourishing

2. THE CORPORATION AS COMMONS

Simon Deakin's article on the 'Corporation as Commons'[46] offers a model of the company based in legal norms as an alternative to the predominant neoliberal economic model. The legal model of the company, partly examined in Chapter 1, maintains, *inter alia*, that the company is an entity, that shareholders do not have property rights in the company assets or liability for company debts and that management is deferred to directors. For Deakin the separation of shareholders from asset ownership means that the company (being something that must be owned by someone) is communally owned by those that input into it, so 'there are multiple, overlapping and often conflicting property rights or property-type claims which the legal system is meant to adjust and reconcile'.[47] While company law itself is concerned primarily with property-type claims of shareholders, there are other claims against the company represented in other law, including employment law (representing employees' interests) and insolvency law (representing creditors' interests).

> 'Each of these areas of law has a dual function: specifying, on the one hand, the conditions under which various contributors of inputs (or as they are sometimes called, corporate "constituencies" or "stakeholders") can draw on the resources of the firm while, at the same time preserving and sustaining the firm's asset pool as a source of productive value. This is the sense in which the business enterprise is a "commons". It is the role of the legal system to maintain this commons where to do so generates a surplus for the parties immediately involved in the productive process and for society at large. The "corporation" and ancillary juridical concepts describing in legal terms the various features of the business firm together have the function of achieving this task.'[48]

So, given the law encompasses and represents many interests within the company, Deakin seeks to adopt an economic theory which reflects this. The economic theory of the commons encompasses the idea that certain properties (usually natural

---

[46] S. Deakin, 'The Corporation as Commons: Rethinking Property Rights, Governance and Sustainability in the Business Enterprise' (2011–2012) 37 *Queen's L.J.* 339.
[47] Ibid, 367.
[48] Ibid, 368.

resources) are held in common. The resource held in common is defined by scholars in this area as that possessing the following characteristics. The resource in question must be subject to collectively held rights of access (the ability to enter the resource), rights of withdrawal (the right to utilise and take away from that resource), rights of management (a right to regulate use and to improve the resource, inputting creatively) and rights to exclude others from certain usages of the resource, and finally, although this is least important, the right to alienate a commonly held right through sale or loan.[49]

The advantage of a resource held in common is that it is managed in a way that encourages sustainability. By encompassing a wide range of claimants, resources held in common can be preserved through a complex system of management. Deakin says this:

> 'The economic theory of the commons is in essence a theory about the conditions under which collective action to preserve and sustain resources of value to society becomes possible. The theory has had its main application to natural resources in the form of "common-pool resources" such as collectively managed irrigation, fishery and forest systems. The core insight gained from over two decades of intensive empirical work on the operation of these systems is that overexploitation of shared resources—the "tragedy of the commons"—can be overcome through forms of collective resource use and management. The conditions needed for the emergence of successful resource management regimes are complex, diverse and often highly localized.'[50]

The company, which holds both physical and non-physical resources, is held in common (according to the definition above) by a large group of stakeholders. However, like many natural resources, companies operating under a shareholder primacy governance can be said to have been plundered. They have suffered their own 'tragedy of the commons'. This has occurred precisely because management represented one set of interests, shareholders, and did not give voice or consideration to other claimants.

To successfully manage resources as commons, empirical research cited by Deakin has shown that prerequisites must be met. Eliner Ostrom's research[51] showed that despite the huge diversity of practice in utilising and managing common resources, there are general features which enable successful management. Two key elements are a 'substantive content of the relevant property rights' and the 'institutional conditions that are capable of generating those rights'.[52] The institutional conditions will have been developed over a long period and their existence is therefore testimony to their effectiveness. Ostrom set out eight principles of design which have been shown to deliver effective management, not just

---

[49] Table set out in ibid, 370.
[50] Ibid, 368.
[51] Ibid, 368, citing E. Ostrom, *Governing the Commons: The Evolution of Institutions for Collective Action* (Cambridge University Press, 1990).
[52] Ibid, 369.

for current users but for future generations, which Deakin reproduces in his article and which I reproduce again here.

Table 7.1 Design Principles for Common-pool Resources[53]

Design Principle	Description
Well-defined boundaries	Rules defining the boundaries of a resource system and the set of users with rights over it facilitate cooperation and rule enforcement
Proportionality between benefits and costs	Equivalence between inputs and returns enhances the legitimacy of rule systems and assists observance and enforcement
Collective choice arrangements	Where all or most users participate in rule formation, rules are more likely to fit local contexts and be adaptable to changing circumstances
Monitoring	Monitoring should be conducted by individuals or officials who are accountable to users
Graduated sanctions	Graduation of sanctions allows for infractions to be recognized while acknowledging the possibility of misunderstandings, mistakes and exceptional circumstances
Conflict-resolution mechanisms	Localized, low-cost dispute resolution mechanisms allow for conflicts in the interpretation and application of rules to be settled in such a way as to maintain trust
Minimal recognition of rights	Rights of local users to make their own rules should be recognized by higher-level entities
Nested enterprises	Where common-pool resources are part of a wider system, local units should be allowed to match rules to local conditions, within a wider framework of institutions designed to govern interdependencies among smaller units

Deakin argues that the commons model is a useful one for the modern business organisation because it encompasses and accommodates the varying rights of different stakeholders who make different inputs into the business. He further argues that the collectivism of the company is not necessarily undermined by the seemingly wide ability of stakeholders to exercise their right of alienation because complete alienation is not possible in the context of the company. So, although the joint stock company offers a high degree of alienability for the shareholder, the shareholder cannot claim back his original input. That is retained by the company together with other inputs. Similarly although employees may leave the company, they may not take with them any inputs, physical or intellectual or social (such as business contacts), that they have made while employed.

---

[53] E. Ostrom, *Governing the Commons: The Evolution of Institutions for Collective Action* (Cambridge University Press, 1990), 100–1. Reproduced with permission of Cambridge University Press.

Deakin argues that the theory of the commons should underpin future empirical work on the company because it would enable an understanding of 'the corporation itself as a collectively managed resource' which would 'aid understanding of the role the corporate form can play in generating the conditions for social and environmental sustainability'.[54] It would be study grounded in legal norms (rather than irrelevant economic models) where the emphasis was on corporate sustainability.

Finally, Deakin argues that utilising a commons model would have clear ideological advantages. It would enable a seismic shift away from concentrating on strategies that promote shareholders because it conceives of the company as a collective or public institution. Furthermore, because the model focuses on commonly held resources, it necessarily diminishes the importance of alienability and fluidity in the market, which as noted earlier in this chapter has a deleterious effect on progress and sustainability. In Deakin's words:

> 'Commons research stresses, as we have seen, the complexity and heterogeneity of property rights regimes, and the relatively subordinate role played by alienation rights, particularly in comparison to access and management rights. From this perspective, the emphasis on the importance of shareholders' alienation rights in current corporate governance theory and practice looks misplaced. Shareholders' alienation rights are at the core of the operation of the market for corporate control and the functioning of a liquid capital market in which claims on the corporation's assets are transparently priced and corporate performance is efficiently evaluated. The exclusion of other stakeholder groups, especially employees, from participation in managing the firm is frequently justified by reference to agency-cost considerations, or more simply, by appeals to the importance of shareholders' property rights.[55]

He concludes that the commons model would enable reform of company law which utilises stakeholder governance, strengthens the company's internal integrity and enables a capacity to resist market pressure. In this way the company would reflect local and national political and cultural choices.

Deakin's 'company as commons' perspective, while having certain similarities with stakeholding, has much more political integrity. First, it does not a make a market case for the commons but instead prioritises good management of company resources and the fair representation of stakeholders in managing and benefitting from those resources. It embraces the company as a joint endeavour where the company represents the contributions of large sections of society. Deakin maintains that 'the sustainability of the corporation depends on ensuring proportionality of benefits and costs with respect to the inputs made to corporate resources, and on the participation of the different stakeholder groups in the formulation of the rules governing the management and use of those resources'.[56]

---

[54] Deakin (n. 46), 376.
[55] Ibid, 377.
[56] Ibid, 380.

However, what the commons approach outlined here fails to do is to take account of the disparity in power between the stakeholders noted. Employees, though they input a great deal into the company, are the most vulnerable. Not only may their investment in the company be easily terminated without their consent, but their investment will be less transferable than that of, for example, shareholders. Their investment, their labour skills, will have been built around the company and may be very specific to that company. In contrast, shareholders will alienate their investment for money, the most transferable of all inputs. The company in commons perspective, not unlike the stakeholder approach, does not acknowledge the deep-seated conflict of interest between labour and capital and assumes that parties can negotiate in the best interest of the company as if what is in the best interest of the company is uncontroversial. This is not so. Neoliberal or law and economics theorists argue that what is in the best interest of the company is indistinguishable from what is in the interest of shareholders, the 'downsize and distribute' approach outlined by Lazonick above. However, this approach is not in the interests of labour. They fare better under the 'retain and reinvest' approach, and labour's interest is in job security, reskilling, good wages and safe working conditions. These goals are likely to be contrary to the interests of investors. The conflict between shareholders and labour is explicitly acknowledged in the labour-orientated governance. This approach attempts to redress the balance of power between labour and investors by siding with labour because the objective interests of labour are compatible with the goals of sustainability, productive progress and social equality.

Both company as commons and labour governance perspectives acknowledge that containing the alienability of shares is desirable and this would require radical reform. If investors were required to hold shares for the long term, they would have to consider and value a range of issues rather than just short-term profit maximisation. The issue of restricting alienability of all financial properties is certainly an area in need of further research.

Deakin's model is interesting and attractive. From one perspective it could be charged with conservatism, in that it (largely) does not seek reform but a reconceptualisation of what already exists. However, in embracing a communal ownership perspective where 'there are multiple, overlapping and often conflicting property rights or property-type claims which the legal system is meant to adjust and reconcile',[57] it has the potential to be the most radical model of what the company could be. It may provide a feasible model for a redistribution of power in the company; one that would both improve company governance and one that would properly reward labour. The labour governance model could then provide a mechanism for how that redistribution of power and reward could be achieved.

---

[57] Ibid, 367.

CONCLUSION

The purpose of debate in the area of company law and governance, as I see it, is to explore existing ideas in order to reach for something better. This will involve controversy and it will involve mistakes. It will involve teasing out details and it will involve seeking out the grand overviews, the new models and theories. Above all it involves a passion for argument and for change. The material with which to exercise these passions are all in the subject of company law and governance for the keen and clever student.

The two models I have set out here represent what I see as the two most radical current models. Others will no doubt disagree. Like the early 20th century progressives, these models are concerned with distributional issues, so that a critique of shareholder primacy is also a critique of how this model of governance distributes the wealth generated by companies (societies' productivity) unevenly and unfairly. Thus, whether these distributional issues are addressed through labour governance, where more wealth is returned as wages and labour development, or whether they are addressed through a commons approach, fair and social distribution is central to the alternative social model of the company. However, these alternative models are also concerned with production and the management of production. This takes a more complex approach than simple efficiency evidenced by share price. Good production and good management, toward achieving sustainability and social progress, may well involve less profit and *even* less productivity. A market argument for these alternative approaches is counterproductive. This is not the tune radicals should be dancing to. The starting point for the governance of companies must be that posed by the radical models. The company must represent the complexity of interests of those people involved in it, to the extent that they are involved.

Company law and governance airbrushes most company contributors out of the picture, whether it is company law's preoccupation with directors and shareholders or corporate governance's saturation in the agent/principal relationship between manager and investor. Radical models tend to do the opposite and show the whole social picture with the messy, possibly irreconcilable complications and conflicts between the many participants in the company.[58] As the earlier parts of this book have argued, it remains important not to depersonalise company participants. Company reform will entail a great deal of mediation through the board of directors, and the board is not a neutral organisation but a body of persons deeply lacking in social diversity. The book also argues that focusing on shareholders as the true claimants of the company is wrong, and further that requiring them to show themselves as the true claimants through involvement in governance is disastrous. Current research shows that the argument about a broader social

---

[58] For a snapshot of those involved and how they experience that involvement, see the EU public opinion survey: European Commission, 'Flash Eurobarometer Reports' <http://ec.europa.eu/public_opinion/archives/flash_arch_374_361_en.htm#363>.

purpose for the company is being won. However, the current preoccupation with shareholder involvement in governance tends to neutralise that advance. Thus the challenge for radicals today is to debunk this approach and to find the right way to execute social corporate governance and company law reform.

Further Reading

A.A. Berle and G.C. Means, *The Modern Corporation and Private Property* (Transaction Publishers, 1991).

K. Greenfield, *The Failure of Corporate Law: Fundamental Flaws and Progressive Possibilities* (University of Chicago Press, 2006).

L.E. Mitchell, *Progressive Corporate Law: New Perspectives on Law, Culture, and Society* (Westview Press, 1995).

S. Piciotto, *Regulating Global Corporate Capitalism* (Cambridge, 2011).

L. Stout, *The Shareholder Value Myth: How Putting Shareholders First Harms Investors, Corporations and the Public* (Berrerr Koehler, 2012).

L.E. Talbot, *Progressive Corporate Governance for the 21st Century* (Routledge, 2012).

L.E. Talbot, 'Why shareholders shouldn't vote: a Marxist-progressive critique of shareholder empowerment' (2013) 76(5) *Modern Law Review* 791–816.

INDEX